VOICES OF CORK

Vincent Power

BLACKWATER PRESS

Editor
Rosemary Dawson

Design & Layout
Paula Byrne

Cover Design
Bernard Mortell

ISBN
0 86121 936 8

© 1997 Vincent Power

Produced in Ireland by
Blackwater Press
c/o Folens Publishers
8 Broomhill Business Park,
Tallaght, Dublin 24.

Dedication

To my father and mother

CONTENTS

INTRODUCTION

CHA turns to Miah and says: 'C'mere, boy, I read in De Paper the other day that Cork is being described as the Paris of Ireland.' Miah replies, crossly, with a question: 'Is that so? And why aren't they calling Paris the Cork of France?' Strangers may think that Cork hardly rivals Paris, but the wise ones don't say so too loudly. Strong local pride means that most places, and things, tend to be compared either favourably or unfavourably with Cork. Someone once remarked that even the Turin Shroud would be compared to Cork. Outsiders joke that if a wall was built around the place, within a week the people would have declared an independent republic and be speaking their own language. Local chauvinism is one of the characteristics of the people. That's not a bad thing, though.

Cork pride – or what could loosely be described as the 'Paris' factor – is part of the driving force that makes the people hungry for success: whether playing for Cork in Croke Park; writing best-selling novels; representing the people in government; building an empire of shops from small beginnings on Patrick Street; creating the ingredients for a famous restaurant and cookery school; convincing a small rural community to achieve things beyond their wildest dreams, even bringing Europe to their doorstep; reporting history in the making from the frontline and bringing the news first to the people; or fighting in legal battlefields to keep cities and towns free of criminals. These are just some of the achievements of the men and women profiled and interviewed in this book. All share a common heritage, though a few may have set down new roots further afield. Their successes span the worlds of sport, business, politics, education, literature, law, media, entertainment and the arts. *Voices of Cork* is their story.

The charms of Cork have seduced well-known names in Ireland, and others from the rest of the world, some of whom wouldn't live anywhere else. They are familiar with the many voices of Cork: heard in the street cries of the *Echo* boys; in the melodic hum of conversation over pints at the Long Valley or Château; in the banter over the fish stalls of the English

Market; in the sporting post-mortems on the streets of Blackpool; in the whispered gossip on the bus to Bishopstown, and secrets shared over morning coffee in the cafés off Pana; in the play of children on a lazy Sunday afternoon along the leafy Marina; and in a rousing chorus of De Banks that can be heard anywhere, anytime.

These voices are part of the tapestry of life in Cork. They are just as important as the symbols of the place: *The Examiner* and *Evening Echo*; Murphy's Brewery; D'Opera House; the imposing facade of City Hall; the steps of Patrick's Hill; the history-steeped Imperial Hotel and moneyed South Mall; the bells of Shandon; the lanes of Blackpool and hills of Montenotte; Fr Mathew and his statue overlooking Pana; the bells of Shandon; the banks of the Lee; the bridges and alleys; the yacht clubs and golf clubs; the clash of the ash at The Park; the swans of the Lough; the Boys of Fair Hill; the Dixies showband and Arcadia dancehall; the hurlers, bowlers and soccer players; the horses and hounds; and, of course, tripe and drisheen.

The voices of diverse characters – both past and present – enrich this tapestry: Jack Lynch, Christy Ring, Cha and Miah, Billa O'Connell, Joe Mac, Katty Barry, Humphrey Moynihan, Klondyke, The Rancher, Bernie Murphy and a lot more besides.

There are remarkable people to be found in every city, town and village of Ireland. Cork isn't unique in that regard. Each has a story to tell. The world moves at such a lightning pace that there isn't time to listen. The best stories that everyone talks about and means to write down all too frequently melt away after closing time. This book isn't meant to be a platform for self-indulgence, parochial or otherwise, or a sentimental sojourn into the past as seen through rose-tinted spectacles. Rather, it is a platform for a varied group of people who share the same heritage, drawn from different generations, to tell their stories. It is an appropriate time for reflection as we prepare to enter the twenty-first century. There are tales of great achievement, but also heartbreak and disappointment. Judgements have no place on these pages.

My thanks go first and foremost to the people who participated in *Voices of Cork* and shared my enthusiasm for the project. My unenviable task was to limit the number of profiles; there are many other personalities who equally merited a place in this book. Thanks to the publisher, John O'Connor, who commissioned the book and to the editors, Anna O'Donovan and Rosemary Dawson, and all the team at Blackwater Press.

On a personal note, I want to acknowledge the encouragement of my wife, Mary, and our two children, Stella-Marie and Vance, who are the best in the world. There was support, too, from my colleagues in *The Examiner* and *Evening Echo*. For me, *Voices of Cork* has been an enjoyable adventure, a journey of discovery and, above all, a lot of fun. I'd like to share it with you.

Vincent Power,
Cork,
October 1997.

Cork to me is kith and kin,
politics and sporting wins,
happy days by West Cork's sea,
mighty talk and craic cois Laoi.

Taoiseach Bertie Ahern TD

I taught at Scoil Mhuire for a year in 1960-61, and I regarded Cork as an amazing city at the time. I think it's only now that I appreciate the wonderful sense of pride that Cork people have in their city and, of course, their great sense of fun.

Maeve Binchy, Writer

My home town, New York, was lovely in the old days, but it doesn't have the same flavour for me anymore. Hollywood has no attraction for me, apart from my friends in the movie business who live there. I've been living in Rathcormac for 20 years, while working around the world, and that's where my heart is now. I just wish I could have a longer life there.

Hurd Hatfield, Actor

Although I left Cork for England when I was very young, I still have my Cork passport. For me, it's the Venice of Ireland. I always joke that I left Cork in short pants and they sent me back in a frock.

Danny La Rue, Comedian/Actor

When I arrived in North Cork and discovered everybody is an actor here with a great theatrical sense of humour, I decided it was the place for me. People are always taking the piss out of each other and winding each other up which I find delightful. There are no planes, no mad development, and nobody hacking down trees. I'm surrounded by cows who seem to be more intelligent and make a lot more sense than the people I used to know in the movie business.

Oliver Reed, Actor

I spent many years in Cork and have many happy memories in the Opera House. Relatives of mine moved to Cork and they wouldn't go back to Dublin for all the tea in China. It always struck me that there is a continental ambience about the place: every time you turn a corner you get a different picture. I love it.

Maureen Potter, Actress

I love the Beara Peninsula. Where I live there are 2,000 sheep, 65 people and three pubs. The roads are so narrow it's difficult for a donkey cart to negotiate, and I hope it always stays that way.

Brian Dennehy, Actor

I've lived in West Cork for 24 years after leaving the groovy music scene in Los Angeles. I'd never live anywhere else. When touring now, I only go away for three weeks at most because I have to come back to regain my sanity. Jimi Hendrix would have felt right at home in West Cork. Rumour has it that he's living in Dunmanway with Elvis Presley.

Noel Redding, Musician

The spirit of Cork was once summed up for me by a woman in the street during the 1969 General Election. I asked her if she would be voting for Jack Lynch.
She said, 'Of course I am, boy. He has a handsome face and he's one of our own.' I thought that was a gem.

Henry Kelly, TV Presenter/Writer

A haven in a stormy sea
For wandering bands, the likes of me
You shelter all our family
We thank you all most gratefully
For all that I have strived and won
Between the arcing moon and the sun
I value this, my Celtic home
Wherever I may roam.

Donovan Leitch, Singer/Songwriter

Of all the beautiful places of Ireland, the Beara Peninsula for me is the most magical, mystical and mysterious.

Deirdre Purcell, Writer

It was the sea and sailing that first brought me to West Cork over 30 years ago. But it was the place and the people I fell in love with for the rest of my life, and I found a wife in Castletownshend.

Sir Peter Jay, Broadcaster/Writer

Anybody who knows West Cork and doesn't fall in love with it needs to have their heads examined.

Sir David Puttnam, Film Producer

TED CROSBIE

READ ALL ABOUT IT!

TED Crosbie didn't like the Iron Lady. The Irish newspaper publisher met Margaret Thatcher on two occasions. She growled, glared or grunted at him but did not indulge in conversation. The first encounter took place in 1980 at a lunch for Press Association (PA) members in London. The PA chairman made the introduction saying: 'This is Mr Crosbie, our Irish director.' The British Premier glared and dismissed him with a grunt. 'Well, we thought we'd like an Irish director on the board,' the chairman added, apologetically. 'Pshaw,' growled Mrs Thatcher, and walked away.

Later in the year, they came face to face again, this time at a retirement bash for the PA lobby correspondent in the House of Commons. The Premier had just concluded a successful 8 December summit at Dublin Castle with the then Taoiseach, Charles Haughey. The two political leaders had agreed to examine the totality of relationships between the UK and Ireland. However, Ted discovered that his relationship with the PM was still frozen solid. He had hoped the summit might make a useful talking point to break the ice. 'How did you enjoy your day in Dublin?' he asked, politely. She dismissed him once more, muttering under her breath. Denis Thatcher was grand; no problem at all. He collared the Corkman later and said: 'C'mon, we'll have a gin.' The pair went off for a drink together. Ted says of him: 'He was a most charming man, unlike his wife.'

Ted's great-grandfather, Thomas Crosbie, was a founder member of the PA in 1868, which he describes as the 'milk cow' of the newspaper industry in the UK and Ireland. Ted maintained those historic links on 4 December, 1979, when he was co-opted to the PA board. Seven months earlier, Margaret Thatcher had moved into 10 Downing Street.

'The interesting thing about my time on the PA is that I witnessed the early Thatcher years and I saw what she did,' he reflects. 'Basically, she changed the whole attitude of top management from being liberal to being very self-centred; very finance-centred. She brought out the most unattractive side of the Englishman, namely his greed. What she did was totally necessary in many cases, but it was the way that she did it and the triumphalist way that she did it that I found objectionable.' The Thatcher legacy was evident in Ireland too. 'To be perfectly honest, I think the woman has a lot to answer for over here,' he says. 'Since England started to become apparently more successful after Thatcher, with problems in the industry removed in a surgical fashion, a lot of people over here started aping her without quite the necessity to do so. It's much easier to be destructively unreasonable rather than to be constructively reasonable. What saved her bacon, of course, was the Falklands War.'

Ted had a ringside view of the upheaval in the British newspaper industry during the '80s, particularly the epic battles for circulation between the two biggest media players, the late Robert Maxwell and Rupert Murdoch. He met Maxwell at a PA lunch and recalls being introduced to 'this enormous man sitting alone in a corner brooding'. They shook hands and exchanged pleasantries. 'Nice to see you, Mr Crosbie,' said Maxwell. Ted remarked: 'I see you've made a great colour job of *The Mirror*.' Maxwell thanked him and the conversation petered out. 'I could see he was disinterested,' recalls Ted. 'To be honest, I didn't want him getting too interested in me, either. I discovered afterwards why he was so contemplative. Murdoch and himself were competing to buy *Today* which was on the market at the time. Murdoch bought it later and closed it.' The real agony of Robert Maxwell would only become clear after his death on 5 November, 1992, when his media empire came crashing down around his two sons and thousands of *Daily Mirror* pensioners. 'Maxwell was a crook, nothing more,' says Ted. 'Any fellow who'd raid the pension scheme deserves contempt. You can't do the kind of deals that he was doing and get away with it. Money doesn't grow on trees.'

Things were done differently in Cork. The introduction of new technology to *The Cork Examiner* and *Evening Echo* had always been bloodless, ever since the first big change from the traditional linotype 'hot metal' to the Web Offset process in 1976. This had given the company the most modern printing plant in Ireland. Similar exercises in London and New York led to all-out warfare between employers and unions. The Crosbies have had only one strike in the 125 years of their control of the paper; that was in the difficult year of 1921 but the paper appeared every day. This record is cherished. The good labour relations at Academy Street is no surprise to anyone in a city where the paper has always been seen as a benign regime. Yet, to achieve the landmark advances in technology and computerisation in 1976, 1986 and 1994 required considerable skills of negotiation on both sides. It wasn't all plain sailing. Ted steered the firm through the first two changes, first as production director and later as chief executive, and handled the delicate labour relations job until the 1994 change which was implemented by the new current management. Nobody could deny that he held the company together when his technological expertise was most needed.

The Crosbies and their papers, *The Examiner* and *Evening Echo*, are part of the fabric of Cork life. That's the way it's always been; and that's the way they hope to continue. *The Examiner* office is the soul of the city. No weekday would be complete in Cork without De Paper and D'Echo, as they are affectionately known. *The Cork Examiner*, now called *The Examiner* since 1996, has been around since 30 August, 1841. The Paper has seen the city through good times and bad; a friend and companion pursued in the strangest of times and strangest of places, from the docksite to the golf clubs. The Paper is, of course, a great institution. Other institutions which shaped the character of Cork are long gone: giants like Ford, Dunlop and Sunbeam.

'Echoooo...Evening Echoooo.' The catchcry is the daily music of Cork. It sounds a bit like a Chinese singsong to strangers; a tongue-twisting call into the afternoon air. The cry of the *Echo* boys is as much a symbol of Cork as tripe and drisheen, the Bells of Shandon, or the clash of the ash. And the *Echo* is as much part of Cork folklore as Katty Barry, Fr Matthew, The Park or the exploits of the Boys of Fair Hill. Echo boys –who never really grow old – have delivered the news for over 100 years. In the early years they plied their trade barefoot. Typically, the then Taoiseach Jack Lynch first learned of the death of Christy Ring from *Echo* boy Johnny Kelleher. The State car returned to Cork from Dublin on 2 March, 1979, and swept into the city along Penrose Quay where Lynch bought the *Echo* from Kelleher. 'Did you hear the sad news?' shouted Kelleher in the window. 'Ringy is dead.' Kelleher will never forget the Taoiseach's response: 'That can't be.' The *Echo* brought news of momentous events since the first edition hit the streets on 14 July, 1892, costing one halfpenny. Uniquely, there were two special *Echo* Sunday editions: first, in 1914 bringing news of the course of World War One, and second, on 3 September, 1939, to report the declaration of World War Two when thousands thronged Patrick Street to get the news. When President John F. Kennedy was assassinated on 22 November, 1963, Kelleher sold 1,000 *Echos* at the Coliseum corner. This *Echo* boy's fancy footwork, weaving deftly through flows of traffic at the bottom of Summerhill, brought him to national attention. Kelleher made the news himself: profiled on the pages of *The Sunday Express*, and then filmed selling papers at the

Coliseum corner by Frank Hall's *Newsbeat* TV programme. That clip has since become a gem of the RTÉ archives.

Arguably the most famous *Echo* boy was Michael 'Mickey' O'Mahony: a small, soft-capped figure who stood for the best part of 72 years selling newspapers at the junction of Shandon Street and Cathedral Road. He sold *Echos* in the gas-lit streets of yesteryear at a time when top hats and bowlers were the fashion. On his coffin was placed his hat and a copy of his beloved *Echo*. His vendor's badge went to his lifelong friend, Donal O'Mahony, who distributes the *Echo* today and whose late father, Johnny, managed the *Echo* boys before him.

Many *Echo* boys were better known by their nicknames: Robot, Whacker, Doc, Con Con and Wallo. This symbol of Cork was immortalised when a bronze *Echo* boy sculpture took up his permanent stand in Cook Street.

Ted was the fourth generation of Crosbies to manage the paper, along with his cousins, George and Donal. Two members of the fifth generation – Ted's son, Tom, and George's son, Alan, the present chief executive – are represented on the board of Examiner Publications (Cork) Ltd.

Ted describes himself as a chemist by training, a shovel engineer by vocation and a manager by desperation. Others have called him one of Cork's last remaining merchant princes. Above all, he is the quintessential newspaperman.

He knows every nut and bolt in the place. He is happiest in the machine room, at the very heart of the paper, observing the daily rituals as the presses roar into life, like some giant awakening from sleep. Ted was the dominant force of the paper for three decades, and still seen to be so by many of the employees. His influence was all pervasive; little escaped his attention. He led the advances in technology that required massive investment, in spite of the risks. In the words of a veteran printer, who often saw him appear in the machine room in the dead of night to solve a problem, 'Ted ploughed away on his own for a long time'. He is a practical man, who doesn't suffer fools gladly. He tells it like it is, whether to fellow board members, junior reporters or paper sellers. He is a wealthy man, but doesn't flaunt it. *The Sunday Times*, which is printed in Cork, rated the three Crosbie family trusts among their list of Ireland's Richest 75. Ted avoids ostentation, as does his own family, and leads a relatively modest lifestyle. A lifelong passion has been sailing, which he inherited from his father and remains one of his few indulgences.

Ted's bloodlines were clogged with newspaper ink. Thomas Edward Crosbie, known as Ted, was born into the familial dynasty on 30 April, 1931. Ted is the great-grandson of the first Thomas Crosbie who took over the newspaper in 1872 on the death of his partner, John Francis Maguire, its founder in 1841 and Nationalist MP in the British Parliament. Maguire had backed Daniel O'Connell in the campaign for Catholic Emancipation and, later, Repeal of the Union. He started *The Cork Examiner* to give the ordinary people of Munster a public voice. He laid down the policy in his first editorial: to report without fear or favour the proceedings of the region, to do everything possible for its advancement and to maintain a politically independent stance. It set the tone for subsequent generations.

The first Crosbie joined the paper as a reporter in 1842 at the age of 15, at a time when it had a modest weekly payroll of £21. In spite of limited formal schooling, he was a gifted journalist, a powerful prose writer with a sharp sense of humour and a captivating speechmaker. Maguire devoted more time to politics, and Crosbie immersed himself in journalism. In time, Crosbie became his partner and edited the newspaper; he campaigned for the development of Irish agriculture and industry and wrote the leading articles every day.

Such was his reputation as a journalist that *The London Times* once offered him the job of Leader Writer with a huge salary of £700 a year. However, the offer was withdrawn when they discovered he was a Catholic. Crosbie expanded the paper from a thrice-weekly afternoon publication to a morning daily and later added the *Evening Echo* and *Cork Weekly Examiner* to the fold.

Crosbie had strong competitive instincts as a newspaperman: in the days before trans-Atlantic cables he scooped the rest of Europe with news of the ending of the American Civil War by meeting incoming liners at Queenstown (later Cobh). He collected the American papers and sent the details to London before the liners arrived in Britain.

Crosbie was a founder member of the Press Association in June 1868. The Crosbies have maintained close connections with the PA through the generations. From small beginnings, the PA now transmits daily, via satellite and telecommunications links, about 1,500 stories and 100 pictures and graphics to national and regional print, broadcast and electronic media.

After 30 years in the business, Crosbie succeeded Maguire as sole proprietor upon his death in 1872, paying a pension to his widow and rearing his family. Thomas Crosbie remained Editor in Chief of *The Cork Examiner* until his death in 1899; his second son, George Crosbie BL, joined the paper during the mid-1880s and is properly credited with turning the 50-year-old Victorian daily into a modern business. George introduced modern printing methods in the mid-1890s: linotype machines and rotary presses. He launched the first half-penny evening paper in the south of Ireland in 1892. The price stayed at a half-penny for many years until it jumped by 100% to a penny. The majority of the masses who bought the *Echo* for a halfpenny in 1892 were earning 5, 10 or 20 shillings a week. On Christmas Eve, 1892, he made history by publishing, for a penny, the biggest paper ever printed in Ireland. That Christmas *Examiner* consisted of 112 columns. By all accounts, great-grandfather Thomas Crosbie was a genial proprietor, and a great friend of the journalists; he was twice elected President of the Irish Association of Journalists and, subsequently, President of the Institute of Journalists. Crosbie hosted a Christmas dinner for *The Cork Examiner* literary staff at his own house every year. He liked to tell the story of how one of his journalists tried champagne for the first time. The journalist called Crosbie's son, George, over and blurted out: 'Mister George, could you ever give me a drop of the real stuff? I can't stand these mineral waters.'

Thomas Crosbie died at his summer residence in Aghada on 30 June, 1899. He was succeeded by his son, Senator George Crosbie, who held the reins as chairman until his death in 1934. The Senator, who had qualified as a barrister, is credited with having encouraged a blend of local, national and international news. He pioneered a number of important developments: the installation of high-speed telegraph machines, the opening of a London office linked by wire with 95 Patrick Street, and the recruitment of special correspondents during World War I. His elder brother, James, served alongside him on the board. After the foundation of the Irish Free State, *The Cork Examiner* opened a Dublin office. In Cork, a new high-speed rotary printing machine was installed to enable faster and more reliable production. George Crosbie, an aspiring politician, suffered defeat at the polls on two occasions, but was elected to the Senate in 1932 as a nominee of the Cosgrave party. He championed the industrial development of the south and played a part in the advent of the Ford factory to Cork in 1916. He died on 26 November, 1934; his brother, James, died before him in 1931.

Now the leadership passed to Senator Crosbie's two sons: Thomas, the eldest, who went into the family firm after leaving school in 1914, and Commander George, who joined after two years' service in the British Navy during World War I. They were joined on the board by their cousin,

James Crosbie, a barrister, who succeeded his father. They represented the third generation of the family's ownership and direct control of *The Cork Examiner* and its publications. Thomas Crosbie succeeded his father as chairman of the company in 1934 and led the board of directors for over 30 years through the difficult '30s, the paper-starved war years of 1939-1945 and the post-war period.

Ted was the second eldest, the only son in a family of four, raised by Thomas and Gladys Crosbie who had met socially and married in the '20s. Gladys Whitaker, a Presbyterian, came from a family of butter merchants. It was one of the first inter-denominational marriages in Cork after independence.

'People tend to forget the extraordinary effect that the First World War had on Irish society,' says Ted. 'There was a huge tranche of people from all branches of society that went to Flanders and many were killed. My father, who had very bad sight, didn't go but 80% of his contemporaries went to France and a lot of them didn't come back. Those who stayed were the lucky ones: a lot of them had a conscience that they hadn't left their bones in Flanders along with their friends. After the war ended in 1918, a lot of people really didn't pay too much attention to the War of Independence until it got a bit lively with events like the burning of Cork and the looting of Patrick Street by the Black and Tans. There was a tremendous amount of gaiety after the First World War, a lot of dancing. They put down the local problems through sheer spirit.'

Ted and his three sisters – Mary, Ruth and Sally – grew up in Woodlands, Montenotte, overlooking the River Lee. Ted's grand-father, Senator George Crosbie, bought Woodlands from the Arnott family in 1916. Senator Crosbie consistently advocated a constitutional policy and adhered to the Anglo Irish Treaty of 1921. He suffered in the defence of opinions which he believed to be right in 1922. The machinery in *The Cork Examiner* was broken up by the Irregulars in August 1922. In March 1923, during the Civil War, the newspaper plant was wrecked and his home, containing a lifetime's collection of beautiful pictures, was destroyed. Throughout the War of Independence and the Civil War, the paper was attacked on three occasions, 'for writing the wrong thing at the right time or writing the right thing at the wrong time'.

The house was rebuilt in 1925. Within months of returning to Montenotte, Ted's grandmother, Eva, died. Senator Crosbie lived there with his son, Thomas, and daughter-in-law until he remarried in 1931.

Ted remembers playing in their big garden at Woodlands as a small child. A particularly vivid memory is of being thrown over the head of a donkey in the garden. Lucky to escape injury, he recalls the donkey 'putting his two legs on my chest and staring down at me'. The experience left an indelible impression. 'Ever since, I've never been comfortable with four-legged beasts!' Ted shared his father's lifelong love of yachting and the sea. He learned to row a punt at an early age, and to swim in the sea at Crosshaven.

It was a happy and loving home. Ted's mother, Gladys, was a 'superlative' housekeeper in a large house with staff decreasing as the years went by. She supported many causes in the city, and was particularly busy with Presbyterian and Church of Ireland charities. Ted and his sisters were brought up as Catholics, 'probably better than we would have been by a Catholic mother'. She had a 'great sense of duty'. Ted remembers his father, even late in life, turning to Gladys and asking: 'It's six years since Vatican Two, do you think I still have to have fish on a Friday?' Tom Crosbie was a good father, devoted to his children. Ted says he was always a voracious reader and, to this day, his father's collection amounts to nearly 7,000 books. Tom was good with his hands and liked to experiment with wood and metal. He made model yachts. Another memory is of a house filled with cigarette smoke. 'They talk of a passive smoking problem today, but everyone smoked in our house, including the staff, and I was like a pickled herring,' says Ted. 'Of course, it was the height of bad manners then to complain about smoking. Nobody regarded smoking as anything other than a social condition in the '30s and '40s. I didn't mind cigar smoke or pipes too much but I've always had a hatred of cigarette smoke.' Tom Crosbie smoked 60 cigarettes, half a box of small cigars and three pipes every day. And he lived to the age of 76. Ted recalls, too, as a small boy, watching the arrival of Cork's élite to parties at Woodlands. They had a great ballroom where several big dances were held. 'I can remember, about the age of six, sticking my head out the banisters and watching Cork's finest and best enjoying themselves.'

Ted was tutored by a governess until the age of eight when, in 1939, he started schooling at Christian Brothers College junior school where his father had also been a pupil before him. He had already been well tutored in English and Maths, although he had to start studying Irish from scratch. 'I was put into the lower infants, but they discovered that I could read and do sums and various other things,' he says. 'I was moved from junior to senior infants. They skipped first class, then put me into second class and I started eventually in third class.' The Brothers imposed strong discipline: there was no problem as long as pupils treated the teachers with respect and worked hard.

Of his male contemporaries in the Crosbie families, Ted was the only one who didn't go to boarding school. 'I never really felt the want of it either.' He was a reasonably bright student: always in the top third of the class at Christians secondary school. 'I was strong in English and Science,' he recalls. 'I was strong in Maths too until it came to Leaving Certificate Maths which I found a pain in the butt.' He liked sport, particularly rugby and sailing. He thinks rugby helped to clear up his bronchial problems as a teenager. 'After a year or two of playing rugby I got fit and quite used to being knocked around and I toughened up,' he says. 'I never really looked back after that.' He played on the junior and senior teams.

The Emergency – Ireland's euphemism for the Second World War – is remembered through images of home and school; of historic events in the war being conveyed by teachers and by his parents. Ted's uncle, George, a seaman, joined the Marine Service at its inception at the start of the war and became its first commanding officer in Cork. In February 1941, he received his commission as Lieutenant Commander in the Naval Service. He retired with the rank of commander. Ted's father was also in the Maritime Inscription, an ordinary seaman and 'a source of considerable difficulty for the poor commander, his younger brother, because he used to go down to the manoeuvres, having raided the till in *The Cork Examiner*, and create terrible disciplinary problems by taking the ratings to Cobh for drinks'. News of the war came via *The Cork Examiner*, the *Echo*, the BBC and *The London Illustrated News*. Radio Éireann's news coverage was poor. 'Occasionally you'd hear of something that happened down in the harbour,' he recalls, 'when survivors were being brought ashore.' He was in second year at Christians' secondary school during 1944 when the History teacher told the class: 'Lads, this is an historic day. The allies have landed in France.' He remembers listening to Winston Churchill's famous attack on Taoiseach Eamon de Valera over Irish neutrality on the BBC on 13 May, 1945, and also listening to de Valera's historic reply. The most powerful image, stamped forever in his consciousness, came from the war report of *The London Illustrated News*. They published three photographs of women being de-loused in a shower at Belsen concentration camp. 'These women were laughing in the shower, and in the background you could clearly see stacks of stick-like bodies. That left a big impression on me.' He remembers all the excitement about VE Day in May 1945 when the war in Europe ended. Later, on a beautiful summer's day in August, he learned from his father about the A-bomb being dropped on Hiroshima. Ted was aboard their yacht at Glandore.

His father went ashore to get *The Cork Examiner* and returned to give him the news: 'It's all over in Japan. The Americans dropped a superbomb'. Ted says he remembers that moment 'as if it was yesterday'.

Ted was encouraged to become familiar with the family business during his school years. At the age of 12, in 1943, he delighted in conversations with the fitters and watched how the presses and linotype machines worked.

Craftsmen, who had a powerful union but were always willing to answer questions, put clumps of lead type metal into steel frames to create the pages of the newspaper. It was a dirty and noisy business. The linos, full of speeding cogs, clattered away. Weighty cast metal plates were made for the presses which finally thundered into action to deliver the day's news. Ted spent his summer holidays in the office and, literally, learned the business from the ground up. The war played havoc with newspaper production. 'The fitters were having all kinds of problems because they couldn't get any replacements or spares and lubricants were unobtainable,' he says. 'The engineers had constant problems with the presses seizing up.'

Ted had access to the workshops and remembers in particular one outstanding fitter, Mick Hegarty, who came to *The Cork Examiner* from the tool room at Ford's in Dagenham. Hegarty was second engineer at the paper during a time 'when the real work in this place was keeping the linos going'. During the war, paper restrictions saw the size of the *Echo* reduced to a single sheet, priced one penny. Later, Hegarty taught him machining skills and elementary fitting. 'It's like riding a bicycle,' he says. 'You never forget it.' He doesn't think he got any special treatment being the chairman's son. His father had probably told Hegarty and the others 'not to let me lose any fingers in that bloody machinery'.

It was considered inevitable that Ted would join the family firm, particularly being the only son. While studying sufficiently hard to pass his school exams and gain entry to college, he watched other older family businesses go to the wall through neglect or inefficiency. 'A lot of what you might call the upper level of Cork's social activity revolved around golf courses and sport generally at that time,' he explains. 'Significantly, a lot more of it revolved around racecourses which was one of the reasons why some family businesses didn't last.' At Christians, his interest in chemistry led him towards a science degree at UCC. He had been doing home chemistry for some time and was 'fascinated' by the subject. Away from study, his passion for sailing was intense: he won an Irish championship in 1950. He was enthralled, too, by the development of modern engineering and model making. He managed to acquire a chassis, a 1929 Morris Minor, and built a car in the early '50s, which he christened Aluminium Alice. 'I spent many happy years with her and learned quite a bit about engines,' he says. 'I learned to use my hands, which stands to me today.'

Meantime, James Crosbie, who served as a Senator in 1938, 1943, 1944 and 1953-56, had earlier joined the company as a director in 1931 after the death of his father. He left *The Cork Examiner* after the war to work in Europe with UNRWA, a relief body, and he became involved in the foundation of the Council of Europe in 1949. He returned to *The Cork Examiner* board years later. Jim's son, Pat, had a short but glorious career as editorial director of *The Cork Examiner* from 1948. There were no bounds to his energy; he pioneered early editorial innovations. His premature death from melanoma in the summer of 1959 was a huge blow to the firm. For Ted, it was his first experience of close family death.

After graduating from UCC in 1952, Ted joined the firm full-time and left Cork to spend nine months studying cellulose chemistry and paper testing in Sweden with the big Stora paper mills, *The Cork Examiner's* major paper suppliers. 'Sweden was the first place where the big industrial environmental revolution started. When I returned there on my honeymoon eight years later the place was totally cleaned up; acid extraction of cellulose had stopped.' During his nine-month apprenticeship in 1953, he learned 'great respect for good scientific and engineering principles applied properly. I've always tried to apply them here.'

Although Ted started full-time in *The Cork Examiner* in May 1952, he had actually been on the books since 1949. He collected his 40th anniversary watch in 1989. He also spent some time working in the photo engraving department where the plates for the illustrations were made; this was a complex process which produced, from a photograph, a metal plate ready for reproduction. It was one of the first departments to be modernised. He concentrated on the technical aspects of the business. During the first couple of years he re-motored all the linos, and changed every motor including those on the presses. The fourth generation of Crosbies moved into management roles. Ted joined his cousin, George, son of Commander Crosbie, who had already been given responsibility for commercial matters, and cousin Pat Crosbie who headed up the editorial department. After Pat's death in 1959, he was succeeded by Jim Crosbie's other son, the late James Roger, 'a charming fellow who wasn't for the rough and tumble of newspaper work'. James Roger was succeeded by another of Commander George Crosbie's sons, Donal, who left the bar to join the family firm in the early '60s and he later became editorial director.

Ted was assigned immediately to the technical development of the paper, and made a director of the company. 'The fact that I was made a director so soon was probably most unfair on everyone else,' he says. 'I suppose nepotism had to come into it somewhere but, in fairness, I think it was done largely because of death duty arrangements.' All three were given places on the board although their fathers, Tom Crosbie and Commander George Crosbie, retained control for another 20 years. The firm was crying out for change. The after effects of the war were still apparent. 'We were still on small papers,' recalls Ted. '*The Cork Examiner* was 10 pages on four days a week; 12 pages one day a week; and if we were lucky 16 pages on a Saturday.' The machinery was poor.

Working practices in the case room were expensive and outdated. There was a substantial overdraft. The firm didn't spend money on new machinery until 1954. 'At that time, if you bought 300 tons of paper you paid for it before it left Sweden,' says Ted. 'There was no such thing as credit.' Ted's father was suffering ill health. 'Dad wasn't terribly well at the time,' he recalls. 'Two wars had taken their toll on him; he was a sensitive man and very tired. He took a lot on his shoulders. We didn't have the management structure of today. Management, with the exception of the bookkeepers, was a rather gentlemanly activity.' Ted learned a lot from his father, whom he respected greatly. 'Nobody has ever given him the credit for being the kind of administrative journalist that he was. He really knew what journalism was about. He had a great sense of what was right for the paper and what shouldn't go into the paper. I absorbed a lot of editorial principles from him.'

What made the Paper so unique were the kind of characters it attracted: people of wit, flamboyance and unpredictability who worked in all departments. Ted got an early piece of advice from Gussie Lynch, a towering figure who collected debts and 'used to go around town menacing the shops for advertising'. Gussie, who spent his life working in the paper, told him: 'Mr Ted, it doesn't really matter what you do as long as you're here. Be here, and be here regularly.' Gussie's kingdom was the front office, which overlooked Patrick Street. He was also the biro minder. He guarded the supply of biros as if his life depended on it. Commander Crosbie borrowed a pen from one of the office clerks one morning and returned it by lunchtime. 'If I can summon up enough courage in the afternoon,' the Commander told him, 'I might ask Gussie for a biro.'

The Reporters' Room had wonderful characters: the likes of Larry Lyons, Cathal Henry, George Cronin, Willie Spillane, Joe Russell, Crichton Healy, Walter McGrath, Sylvester O'Sullivan, John O'Sullivan and Tom Barker. Most had joined *The Cork Examiner* during the late '30s and 'came up the hard way during the war'. They were meticulous reporters and proficient shorthand writers in the days before tape recorders became commonplace. They covered news and sport with equal competence. Larry was one of a kind: a top-class reporter with a sharp news instinct who could sniff out a story quicker than anyone. He interviewed presidents and paupers and got most of the plum assignments. His annual 'beat' was the Cork Film Festival where he delighted in mixing with movie stars and directors. The tale of how he once encouraged Dawn Addams to take a milk bath, as a publicity stunt, became a talking point of the festival for years. Larry was the envy of the office because he got the job of interviewing the rich and famous on board the passenger liners that called to Cork Harbour. During the late '40s, he was sent to interview Rita Hayworth, the red-haired Hollywood sex goddess who had the world at her feet. She had been the pin up queen of the Second World War, and her picture even adorned an atomic bomb. Word leaked out that she was on board a Cunard liner off Cobh, in the company of her new husband, moslem prince Aly Khan. Larry had another scoop on his hands, but in his excitement he forgot to return to the office.

The Chief Reporter, Joe Russell, despatched a telegram to Cobh ordering him back to base. Larry replied with a brief message: 'If Aly Khan, Larry can.' Russell played with words too in his next telegram: 'Aly Khan, but Larry can't. Come home you bastard.'

Ted recalls a memorable occasion when an *Echo* boy resorted to exaggeration to sell a good story. It happened on a night of near tragedy in Cork Harbour. The 10,519 ton Greek liner, *Neptunia*, struck Daunt Rock on 4 November, 1957. She was carrying 31 passengers and 215 crew. The Greeks attempted to scuttle the ship, but a harbour tug took her in tow and beached her on the eastern bank. The passengers disembarked safely. The ship was later refloated and scrapped.

A team of reporters, some of them hidden behind bushes in pitch darkness, sent back a 'magnificent' story. The Crosbies decided to publish a special Saturday night *Echo*. 'In our enthusiasm, we put out about 2,000 *Echos*,' recalls Ted. 'They didn't sell very well.' As he left the office late,

Ted noticed an *Echo* boy on a street corner, still trying to sell out his bundle of papers. The boy wailed into the night: 'Horror tragedy in Cork Harbour ... Liner Neptunia sinks ... Hundreds of passengers drowned ... Captain shoots himself.'

A job in *The Cork Examiner* was considered quite a prize in Cork. It was a traditional company that paid good wages. It was a job for life. Sons followed fathers into *The Cork Examiner* office. The employers showed a paternal attitude to their employees. It was a family atmosphere in which those with personal problems were looked after, quietly and without any fuss. Sackings were almost unheard of. Loyalty was rewarded. Today, the great characters of the office are either retired or dead.

Ted buried himself in work during the '50s, and loved every minute of it. 'Up to the time I got married, I suppose I was in the office every day and three or four nights a week as well,' he recalls. 'I'd put in 12-14 hour days, no bother at all. After I got married I eased back to five days a week.' Ted was liked and respected by the staff; they knew he was good on production and, in many ways, ahead of his time.

Ted fell in love with Gretchen Kelleher from Hazelton, Western Road, Cork, during Easter 1959. They met at the Clongowes dance in the Metropole Hotel. Ted pinched her from a friend, 'and he never really forgave me'. Ted remembers her then as 'a great rock and roller'. They started dating and it soon became clear their relationship would become permanent. 'We made up our minds in September and we were married the following Easter. So I only knew her about a year. We had a marvellous life together.'

A fourth generation of Crosbies were being groomed to form a management triumvirate: Ted and his two cousins, George and Donal. Their fathers still retained overall control. Ted was made production director in 1962. 'It was just a title,' he says. 'It meant nothing. They didn't give me any money to do it. I had to beat every bob out of the board eventually.' In time, Donal assumed editorial responsibility and inspired many changes to improve the quality of the papers. He appointed new editors, encouraged the recruitment of younger reporters and set up the regional reporting staff. It was a newspaper era when the Foreman Printer wielded considerable influence. His word was final in many cases. When US President John F. Kennedy was assassinated in Dallas on 22 November, 1963, Donal, as editorial director, took a landmark decision to dump a paid advertisement from Page One. He got his way, but only after a battle with the Foreman. Two years previously, Page One news had arrived, clearing aside forever the adverts that had filled the entire page since 1841. *The Cork Examiner* and the *Irish Independent* agreed to make the changeover on the same day. 'I'm afraid that kind of cooperation wouldn't exist today,' says Ted. Circulation was rising gently; advertising growing rapidly.

Nothing was ever the same after the '70s. Ted, as technical director, hauled the newspaper from the traditional hot metal process, invented by Caxton, into the new age of high-tech Web Offset printing. The old process had familiar ingredients: lead, ink, sweat and sometimes tears. Web Offset heralded the end of the traditional craft of printing. Now paper print-outs from a Linotron 303 computer replaced the heavy galleys of lead. Small keyboards producing punched tape to feed the computer supplanted the Linotype machines. Page-sized sheets, on to which the printouts and picture bromides were pasted, ousted the heavy metal frames. Paper-thin alloy plates for the new Offset process replaced the weighty cast metal plates. The biggest advantages of the new system were clear reproduction and greater flexibility of layout.

Ted had been studying changes in the print industry since the early '60s, and was one of the first in Ireland to see that the days of hot metal were over.

One of the first visible indications of the changeover was the construction of a new Crabtree-Vickers printing press. Ted had laid down the specifications, and it was taking shape in the press room. 'We watched as the massive foundations were laid,' recalls the then *Examiner* editor, Tim Cramer. 'The foundations were capable of taking the enormous strain and vibration when the huge press was finally commissioned. Slowly, from these rose the bright blue frame of the machine, its rollers and webbs, its folders and electrical ancillaries.' The technical people were sent on training programmes to England. Cramer, accompanied by Donal Crosbie and then *Echo* editor Cathal Henry, saw the system in action in England. Finally, on Saturday, 8 May, 1976, the last hot metal *Echo* was sent to bed. The changeover would be made for *The Cork Examiner* on Monday, 10 May. The countdown was nearly over. Computer keyboards replaced the old linotypes; wooden cutting boards and paper page make-up sheets replaced the old steel stone. On Sunday night, Ted formally pressed the button on the new Crabtree-Vickers. Cramer recalls the moment: 'It began to rumble and then roar. We all held our breath as the blank sheet rolled swiftly through the huge machine. With a bang the inking system came into play and we could see that it was actually printing. As the first copies came off, clean as the proverbial whistle, a great cheer went up to herald the beginning of a whole new era.

The elegant new *Examiner* was about to hit the street, complete with fine reproduction and, above all, on time. The following day, I received a note from a reader which summed it all up: "The bridegroom you sent us this morning was beautifully attired".'

Inevitably, there were teething problems. 'It became a fierce bloody grind for about six months after that,' says Ted. 'You'd struggle with *The Cork Examiner* and then you'd say, "Christ, it's one o'clock, there's an *Echo* now". You'd be no sooner finished the *Echo* than you'd be struggling with *The Cork Examiner* again. For a fortnight it was very hard work. We had a whole bunch of staff to be trained on that press as well, and that was the biggest part of it. You couldn't really train them on the press without printing papers. It's a vicious circle: you can't print papers for the bin because it costs too much money. So you just take the waste and carry on. In fairness to the lads, they did very well.'

The relatively smooth changeover was the envy of Dublin newspapers, and further afield in England where similar efforts got bogged down in disputes.

The Crosbie formula had been to guarantee that no forced redundancies would follow the increase in productivity. The unions were on board anyway, realising that change was inevitable. Ted attributes the success to three factors. 'First, the way the technology was arranged, it was visible. Nothing was hidden. It could be seen and people could understand it. Second, we kept it very simple. It only became a little complicated afterwards. Third, we had people in management on the printing and editorial sides who made bloody sure they were unflappable and the job got done. It was a team effort by a lot of people. I got the kudos for it, but I think George Crosbie is probably the unsung hero, particularly in regard to copy organisation and advertising copy management. If I got any credit it was because I was prepared to work every hour of the day and night for the next nine months to get the bloody thing to work. And I did. It was hard going. We were lucky too because some of the equipment we bought had been used and modified and corrected. We came about three years into the system when a lot of the bugs had been taken out of the equipment. I was often asked what mistakes we made. The main one was we paid for the increased computer-assisted productivity in the caseroom and wages went up. Then both office and editorial, which were not yet computer assisted, looked for parity. We saddled ourselves for five years with extra non-recoverable costs. The early '80s were tough times.'

Two of the senior members of the family, Commander George Crosbie and Thomas Crosbie, did not live to see the new era in print technology and computerised typesetting. They died in 1972 and 1973. Senator James Crosbie presided over the event as chairman.

Ted handled labour relations during the critical periods of change in the '70s and '80s. He was a tough, shrewd and fair negotiator. Even his greatest critics tended to view him benignly because they respected his expertise and knew he always had the best interests of the newspaper at heart.

He says the firm's record of good labour relations can be traced directly to the influence of John Leland, the company secretary. Leland, a small dapper man, joined in 1923 and spent 55 years with *The Cork Examiner*. Among his duties, he signed expenses for reporters and photographers, and scrutinised them carefully. When a photographer once submitted a docket to cover lunch with a contact, Leland questioned the expenditure. The claim for lunch was entered under the heading of 'entertainment'. The photographer explained that he had to treat his contact to lunch for a good reason. 'If it was supposed to be entertainment, wouldn't it have been cheaper to take him to the pictures?' asked the company secretary.

'John was the most honest man I've ever known,' says Ted. 'The staff didn't realise to what extent he fought with the family on their behalf. In other words, he might have appeared to be strict on things like expenses, but if he thought for a moment that the family or boardroom were being unfair on someone he fought like a tiger. Our good industrial relations in the difficult periods of the '50s and '60s was because John set the parameters for myself and anyone else in the family involved in labour relations. I genuinely think that this is the biggest tribute I can pay him. The reason, frankly, why we got through all the periods of change from the end of the '60s onwards – and, okay, it cost us money and we were doing really impossible things way ahead of everyone else – was because John had set down those principles of fairness. The chapels knew that while John was there, together with his assistant Donal Moloney and myself heading up industrial relations, we rarely did something that we shouldn't do. I used to love labour relations. I'd have a feel for what was going on in the business because I'd be talking to people all the time. I also think that a lot of the trust had emanated from my own father who was a great human being in his own quiet way.'

There have been close shaves – but the Crosbies always kept the presses rolling. One exception was when journalists nationally took action in 1972 in support of the late Kevin O'Kelly of RTÉ. The reporter was jailed over a radio interview with Seán Mac Stiofáin, the Provisional IRA Chief of Staff. The stoppage interrupted a near-perfect record. 'I was very cross because we lost an edition,' recalls Ted. 'We hadn't lost an edition since the machinery was broken up. I didn't like losing an edition. Remember, I'd often been here until 10 in the morning when things were rough getting the last papers off, but we never lost an edition.'

Ted had to roll up his sleeves when summoned from his bed on a stormy night on 12 January, 1974. The storm had knocked out electricity supplies. 'We had a 24-page Saturday *Examiner* to get out,' he recalls. 'I came down in the height of the storm. We reduced the size of *The Cork Examiner* for the country edition from 24 to 8 pages, which was all the small 68kw emergency electrical plant could handle. We got out, anyway, with an apology on the front page. By the time we had 55,000 off, the ESB came back and we went back to the full 24-page paper. That was a night to remember, I can tell you.'

There were nights, too, when Ted and his boardroom colleagues bristled with pride at superb productions that conveyed the biggest stories – among them an explosion on the French tanker, *Betelgeuse*, in Bantry Bay that killed 50 people in January 1979, the first papal visit to Ireland in September of that year, and the World Cup exploits of the Irish soccer team during the summer of 1994. On the night when a terrible tragedy visited Bantry, *The Cork Examiner's* West Cork correspondent, the late Jim Cluskey, beat the clock to get the news to Academy Street; he filled the front page which had been cleared to make way for his exclusive on-the-spot reports.

A special edition, *The Examiner on Sunday*, rolled off the presses to cover the visit of Pope John Paul II on 30 September, 1979, with run of paper colour photos of the event, and also to report the Irish World Cup victory over Italy at Giants Stadium in New York on 19 June, 1994. It was the first newspaper in Ireland to be printed in colour. *The Cork Examiner* went on to become the first six-day paper to bring in colour on a daily basis.

The papal visit marked the pinnacle of the career of Larry Lyons, who accompanied the papal party on the Aer Lingus 747 that touched down at Shannon Airport. Larry had his moment of glory when the Pope greeted each of the journalists on board the flight. Typically, his encounter with His Holiness was the talk of the press corps. Larry had been given some medals by his wife in the hope that they might be blessed by the Pontiff. When his opportunity arrived, Larry fumbled in his pockets for the medals but produced a handful of coins instead. The Pope, oblivious to the shiny discs in his hand, gave his blessing. A photograph taken by former *Examiner* photographer Michael Olney recorded the moment for posterity.

The cheer that went up in the office on Saturday night, 18 June, 1994, when Ray Houghton sunk World Cup favourites Italy in a famous 1-0 victory, raised the roof. Ted recalls that memorable occasion for other reasons, while everyone worked flat out to produce the Sunday paper. It was also the night of the pensioners' Mass and supper in the office. Amid the euphoria, the pensioners mingled with the staff on duty and, not surprisingly, bottles were opened. 'You had this strange sight of retired machine room men, full of drink, wandering around the office as we tried to print that paper,' he recalls. 'I remember one talented electrician, who shall remain nameless, who got at the beer that night. I personally booted him out from behind a cabinet where he somehow got it into his head that a fuse was going to blow any minute.'

Examiner journalists became the first in the country to input their stories directly into a computer system in 1986 with the introduction of Linotype System Six. It marked a significant shift away from tradesmen controlling the process towards the distribution of electronic functions to the journalists and advertising staff. It marked a huge sea change for the journalists: no longer was the newsroom a noisy place as reporters clattered out their stories on typewriters. The typewriters were swept aside to make way for computer terminals on every desk. In those early days, the eerie silence of the room was occasionally broken by a stream of expletives from an older hand who pressed the wrong button and lost his story. 'There was a lot of interest in System Six, and it came in very fast,' says Ted. 'It was a good workhorse and served us well. We learned a lot from it.' After less than a decade, System Six was being phased out and despatched to the dustbin of technology when Electronic Page Make-Up (EPM) simplified the process even further. Once again, the journalists had to learn new technological tricks of the trade. Ted led the advances as chief executive during the period from 1982-83 until 1993 when he was succeeded by George's son, Alan. At the same time, Ted had a seven-year spell on the PA board until 1986, and stayed on as a consultative committee member for another four years. Donal Crosbie – who was a patron of the arts, bon viveur and immensely popular with the staff – died in 1990 after a long battle against cancer.

The newspapers were changing too. The *Evening Echo* was converted from broadsheet format to tabloid in 1991 to stem declining circulation and, building on progress achieved in 1995 and 1996, launched a Limerick edition in 1997. The morning paper underwent the greatest transformation: layout was improved and, in a deliberate policy move to increase circulation nationwide, 'Cork' was dropped from the title in 1996 and it became known simply as *The Examiner*. The greatest tribute to *The Examiner's* print technology came in 1996 when the company got the contract to print the Irish edition of the daily *Times* and *The Sunday Times*. The irony was certainly not lost on Ted Crosbie, whose great grandfather had once been refused a job on *The London Times* for being a Catholic. 'I must admit that it gave me a certain amount of unholy glee,' admits Ted.

Ted's world fell apart in October 1996 when his wife, Gretchen, died in a road accident while she was driving from Dublin to Cork. They were a close couple, and a united family. Gretchen was a widely loved warm woman and well-known in the city for her charitable work, especially for terminally-ill cancer patients and the Royal National Lifeboat Institution. Ted was helped through it all by the support of their six children: Suzanne, Elizabeth, Tom, Andrew, Edward and Sophie. 'To be honest, I had a bad six months afterwards,' he says. 'But I've been absolutely blessed with a magnificent family. They have sustained me, and I hope I have sustained them. Look, I'm an optimist. You never know what's around the corner. I've been very fortunate in that I've had a good life.'

Ted, who now holds the title of Chairman, Examiner Publications (Cork) Ltd, has no intention of retiring or sailing off into the sunset - not just yet anyway. 'The management is in very good trim,' he says. 'I'll continue working, but in a different way.' He remains hungry for change: to lay the foundations to secure the paper into the twenty-first century. He is excited about the possibilities opened up by the Internet and electronic publishing. 'I like the thought of the immediacy,' he says, 'in the sense that if something happens in Patrick Street we don't have to wait hours before we tell people about it. I think we can do it and do it well. The notion that anything happening after the *Echo* comes out is no longer relevant until the morning paper has got to change.' Other priorities will be to put a greater emphasis on marketing, since there are now other substitutes for newspapers, and also the practical necessity to replace the press eventually. As regards circulation, he'd like to see *The Examiner* back up to 75,000 before he retires. Also, of course, he wants to see the paper retained in the hands of the Crosbie family. 'My greatest wish,' he adds, 'is that when the Lord takes me into the next world and I meet the various generations of the family, they don't wag the finger at me and say, "you're the bugger who lost it". Though I'll excuse the next generation that possibly poisonous chalice. One cannot rule from the grave!'

JOE LYNCH

LIVING WITH LYNCH

WELL, Holy God, *Dinny Byrne* is half-Corkman, half-Spaniard. Glenroe's most famous resident has an identity crisis: Cork and Spanish influences compete to shape a personality known to millions of Irish people all over the world. Truth to tell, the Cork influence is strongest. What would *Miley* make of it all?

The mask is lifted. *Dinny Byrne* is really Thady Cronin, a great character who lived and died in Blackpool, Cork. Thady left an indelible impression on his young neighbour, Joe Lynch, at Seminary Road. Thady was a familiar sight to youngsters growing up in the late '20s and '30s. He liked to stand at his doorstep or on the corner and watch the world go by. He was a self-taught expert on many subjects, but mostly on the weather. He looked up at the sky and could predict when it was going to rain, almost to the minute. Whenever Jack Lynch, a future Taoiseach, and his pals headed off for the playing fields, they asked Thady for the forecast. 'Mr, Cronin,' they began, 'what'll it do today?' Thady looked upwards, sniffed the air and cautioned: 'I'd bring the old groundsheet, lads, I would.' Joe once made a point of listening to the weather forecast on the wireless. 'Sure, it's not going to rain until Wednesday,' he told his neighbour, with some certainty. Thady had the last word. 'I know that, you know that, and the good Lord knows that, but wouldn't any fool bring his coat when 'tis raining.' That was his style. Thady died at the age of 100 years and four months on 7 November, 1964.

One of Joe's pals was Thady's only son, John 'Kid' Cronin, who later became a boxer on the tough professional circuit in England. Kid Cronin protected the younger boys against bullies. Joe was walking home from the theatre one night when the Kid came to his rescue. 'I remember ambling along, all dreamy after the theatre,' he says. 'A fellow came up to me near Sunday School Lane. Kid mistakenly thought he was assaulting me, so he buried him with a dig. And then he convinced the fellow he'd had a fainting fit. Kid was a wonder.' Many years later, after Joe Lynch became *Dinny Byrne* in the top-rating RTÉ serial, *Glenroe*, he met Kid Cronin who, for the last 20 years of his life, was masseur to the Cork senior hurling and football teams. 'It's my father you're doing,' Kid told Lynch. And he was right. It was.

The Spanish influence that shapes the other part of *Dinny Byrne* comes from Pepe Mendoza, an equally wise old man with his own outlook on life. He was one of the richest men in Alicante, 'who owned everything in sight and even had his own airplane'. Lynch met Mendoza shortly after he bought a home in Spain, and they became close friends. Lynch studied the Spaniard's mannerisms. 'He was a tough little man who did things his own way,' he says. 'He liked to bring friends up to his luxurious home where he had every kind of convenience and a household staff. If he liked you enough, he'd cook you meat on two sticks over an open fire.'

So, *Dinny Byrne* is a combination of these two great characters: about 60% Thady and 40% Pepe.

Joe Lynch is mightily proud of his Blackpool roots. They're a different breed there, he says: they walk differently with a confident swagger, and a knowing look in the eye. If you're from Blackpool, you know you're good. He doesn't have a bad word to say about the place. He was born on 16 July, 1925, the eldest of three sons. The Lynch family lived at 17 Seminary Road, a couple of hundred yards down the hill from the Bishop's palace at Redemption Road. One of his earliest memories is of Bishop Daniel Coholan, who was also their parish priest, taking evening strolls through the streets and lanes. He was a genial man whose presence always generated excitement among children in the neighbourhood. As the Bishop found himself under siege by 'clean kids as well as dirty and snotty kids', he usually remarked: 'It's alright. Take your time. I can't run away.' The children kissed his ring solemnly. One one occasion, the Bishop caught the Lynch boy by surprise at the corner of Seminary Road and Seminary Terrace. He was sitting alone on the footpath, moulding a small figure into shape from a pile of mud. 'As the Bishop approached, I saw the feet first, then the soutane and the red buttons,' he recalls. The Bishop smiled down benignly and asked: 'Well, Joseph, what are you doing?' The youngster said: 'I'm making a priest, bishop.' He then asked: 'Tell me, would you ever make a bishop?' The boy replied, innocently: 'I don't have enough mud.'

Joe and his brothers were raised by loving parents and a semi-invalid aunt, Moll Delaney, who doted on them. His mother, Madge Delaney, was born in the townland of Ballymagooly, a couple of miles from Mallow, and came from a family of great athletes. She was raised in a strong republican tradition, had nursing experience and knew how to treat wounds and take a bullet from an injured man. She was a 'daring' woman who once brought food, medicines and letters to men on the run, but brought up her sons as pacifists. The Civil War was a taboo subject: they were warned that if they ever mentioned it they'd get a walloping, and often did. In their locality in Blackpool, she was an unofficial voluntary nurse, always ready to offer help or advice to the neighbours. She could be brutally honest too, once saying to a local woman: 'Your child is deaf; you'd want to do something about it.' Relatives who came to Cork for hospital treatment invariably ended up at the Lynch's house on Seminary Road to convalesce under her care. Nothing was too much for her.

Joe's father, Jim, was a red-headed Kerryman: generations of Lynchs lived on farms in the townland of Dromacoosh, in the Kilgarvan area of Kerry, and the last occupant of the family farm was his uncle who refused to speak English for the last 10 years of his life, conversing only in Irish or French to callers. It wasn't the best land in Ireland, 'but there was a lot of it, and piled up in a heap'. There was some foreign blood in the family: Joe's great, great grandmother was a basque woman living in Paris who married one of the Lynch sons. Jim Lynch went to Cork to work as a driver on the railways. He was 'the calmest, coolest man who ever lived' and nothing ruffled him. 'My father was a quiet, gentle soul,' says Joe. 'He was a bit like Taoiseach Jack Lynch in that sense; a quiet man with a steel back.' His skills of diplomacy were frequently used to stop strikes. Jim once thought of becoming a schoolteacher but had a passion for engines and trains. Joe says his mother learned to recognise 'his hand on the throttle' as the trains decelerated at night going into the tunnel at Kilbarry. 'That's Jim,' she'd say. 'He'll be home in 40 minutes.' He was known in Blackpool as 'Spring Heel' Jim because of his light step and loose, countryman's walk; he wouldn't wear out a pair of shoes in a year. He once drove troop trains but then refused on a point of principle. When a train full of British soldiers halted at the station in Oola, Co Limerick, a bizarre conversation was overheard between two of them. 'Oi, Charlie, where we at then?' His comrade shouted back: 'I dunno.' The first soldier snapped: 'What's the matter? Can't you bloody read? Isn't there a sign up there?' Charlie took an eyeful of the station name and replied: 'It says, two big oohs, an L and an A.'

Jim Lynch met Madge Delaney at a dance in Riverstown. They had a lot in common, sharing strong republican views and interests in Irish language and culture, music and song. When they married and settled in Blackpool, they fell foul of Bishop Cohalan, (whose 36-year episcopate had begun in 1916), because of their republican activities. Years later, when the eldest Lynch son became head altar boy at the North Chapel, the bishop always introduced him to others by saying: 'This is Joseph, my altar boy. I had a bit of a row with his mam and dad but we're all friends now.' The Lynchs had an 'open' house: friends were welcomed to music sessions at night. Madge had a fine contralto voice and loved singing at every opportunity. Jim was an accomplished accordion player, but played in public reluctantly. Joe recalls 'a lot of dignified people' calling for an evening's music and 'we'd sit as quiet as mice'.

Joe describes himself as a boy with buck teeth, red hair, squint eyes and glasses. He was spoiled rotten by his aunt Moll, who lived with them, and by his mother. They always had him 'turned out like a little doll'. Aunt Moll, a small pretty woman, was well educated and she started to teach him at home from an early age. By the time he went to the North Presentation Convent school, he could already read and write and knew his tables in Irish and English. He could even serve Mass in Latin. Other schoolboys teased him: 'He's lucky. He's got two mammies.'

They were great churchgoing people in Blackpool: his mother went to mass every morning; on Sunday mornings all the families paraded in their best clothes to Blackpool Church or to the North Chapel, with the children walking out front followed by parents behind. All the Lynchs were altar boys, the pride of the family. The people of Blackpool were decent, hardworking folk who watched out for each other. Growing up in the parish in the late '20s and early '30s 'gave you a warm, comfortable feeling, as if you were cocooned from the harshness of life'. It was an idyllic childhood: of course, the Lynchs never saw a poor day because Jim earned good money on the railways.

The streets and lanes were peopled by great characters who developed their own values. There were 'fine, manly fellows' who settled a score with their fists. The rules were simple: a fight was a fight and the combatants shook hands afterwards. No messing. In this pocket of Cork's northside, there was respect for the Gardaí too, because they were just as much a part of the community.

Everybody respected Eugene Monaghan, a tough but fair garda whose presence alone was enough to stop a fight. He rarely, if ever, had to book anyone for an offence. When he came into view, the scrap was halted temporarily as one spectator shouted: 'Hey, hey, hold it lads, it's Eugene, cut it out.' A story did the rounds that when Monaghan retired and surrendered his notebook the pages were blank. Lynch recalls another garda, Walsh, who was posted to Watercourse Road station and immediately became known for his distinctive gait. He walked with his head held high, bristling with pride. He was christened the Pride of the Beat. Years later, Lynch met him standing outside the gates of Trinity College Dublin. Walsh was broken-hearted. 'How are you, boy?' Lynch asked the garda. 'How am I?' replied Walsh. 'Just take a look at me. I left Blackpool and I was never the same since. They sent me to Wicklow. They're like bloody savages down there compared to Blackpool.'

Young Lynch was a 'puny little runt' when he started school at North Presentation Convent. He was a pudding to be bullied – but a kindly nun came to his rescue. He impressed the teacher with his knowledge of tables on his first day at school, and promptly got a hammering from jealous classmates afterwards. He was left with a black eye and a bloody nose. He refused to name the culprits because his father always taught him never to tell tales, saying there were 'too many people in Ireland blowing the whistle'. So he kept his mouth shut.

Next, enter Sr Mary Evangelist, a hefty Tipperary woman with a round genial face, a ruddy complexion 'and the loveliest blue eyes I ever saw'. She taught him his first valuable lesson in life: how to fight. In fact, she spent an hour and a half with him around the back of the chapel, passing on the basics of street fighting: keep your elbows in, punch short and crisp, and only hit when you see something worth hitting. 'I was never scared of anybody after that,' recalls Lynch. 'I took my lumps and gave them back as hard as I could and then it was all over. She was a wonderful nun; witty and clever and full of common sense and she lived to 98.'

At North Monastery Christian Brothers School (CBS), Lynch was top of the class academically; a good, steady worker and exams were no bother at all. He was a good singer too and a valued member of the school choir that won prizes at the feis; being a singer meant that he 'got away with murder'. He left 'the Mon' on scholarship to Blackrock College in Dublin where he was educated by the Holy Ghost Fathers.

There are fond memories of Fr Joe Corless who realised Lynch had a fine tenor voice and gave him every encouragement. He got a few tips from John McCormack, who was acclaimed as the greatest lyric tenor of his time and who made over 500 recordings. Academically, he came under the influence of Dr John Charles McQuaid, the staunchly conservative Archbishop of Dublin, who was the only Irish bishop to come from a religious order. He had been Dean of Studies and President of Blackrock College and taught ancient classics. Lynch studied English, Greek and Latin under him. He says that Dr McQuaid was a magnificent teacher, fair-minded and always made students feel as if they were important by addressing them as 'Mr'. 'I had a great time there,' he recalls. 'There was a great international bunch of fellows there at the time. The Holy Ghost fathers were liberal men because they were a young order.' Lynch was a keen all round sportsman: a 'useful' rugby player, soccer player, athlete, and also on the first school cricket team to win the Leinster Cup in 1941.

Joe Lynch was a classically trained actor at an early age: as a small boy he came under the influence of Fr James Christopher O'Flynn. The great Fr O'Flynn, who was curate at the North Cathedral from 1920 to 1946, had a love of Shakespeare from his Maynooth days and passed it on to the youngsters of Cork. He also had an abiding love of Irish song, story and dance. He started teaching Shakespearian acting in the choir room of the North Cathedral and then founded the Cork Shakespearian Company. The home of the company was known simply as the Loft, situated under the shadow of Shandon. Lynch, like many other boys, had his first introduction to the theatre in the upstairs room.

After hearing confessions on Saturday evening, Fr O'Flynn liked to walk down Mulgrave Road where he encouraged anybody who listened to him to attend rehearsals at the Loft. Lynch went along every Sunday morning to recite lines from Shakespearian plays. 'I have lovely memories of those mornings up near the butter market,' he says. 'There was a crowd of fellows shouting Shakespeare, sometimes in a Cork accent, like, and you could hear the Butter Exchange Band practising in the background.' Fr O'Flynn and his company staged Shakespeare at the Opera House; they had set a record in 1928 by presenting eight plays in one week. All the players were amateurs who worked in many diverse jobs around the city. One of the apprentice players was the late Edward Mulhare from High Street who began his career in the first Opera House pantomime and became a star of the American stage and screen. He played the leading role in *My Fair Lady* on Broadway, made a series of movies including *Von Ryan's Express* with Trevor Howard and Frank Sinatra, and then starred in two hit TV series, playing Captain Daniel Gregg in *The Ghost and Mrs Muir* and Devon Miles in *Knight Rider*. Lynch got his first taste of broadcasting thanks to Fr O'Flynn – at the age of nine. In 1934, the priest brought him and other boys to the old Women's Gaol at Sunday's Well to sing Irish songs on the Cork radio station, 6CK, which had started broadcasting there in 1927. Young Lynch returned to the airwaves on many other occasions to sing songs, recite poetry and even Shakespeare in the unlikely setting of the gaol which had become an all-female prison in 1878 and closed down in 1923. Later, Lynch even did a live performance of *Othello* with Fr O'Flynn's boys. He was also in charge of sound effects, and had to improvise when it came to ringing the alarm bell of Cyprus. He took an iron bar in the gaol, hung it on a piece of rope, removed one of his shoes and 'gave it a whack'. A reviewer wrote later: 'Brilliant production from Cork, most enjoyable, but the alarm bell of Cyprus should be ashamed of itself.'

Those early experiences of drama and broadcasting proved to be a strong asset at Blackrock College. After passing the Matriculation in 1941, he opted to return home to study speech and drama under James Stack at the Cork School of Music. Stack had also been a pupil of Fr O'Flynn in his younger days, and later studied drama in New York alongside the late Burgess Meredith, an actor who gave his life to the stage and screen. They became lifelong friends. Many years later, Lynch met Meredith at Dublin Airport. 'They tell me you're one of Stack's boys,' said the veteran actor who, in later years, played alongside Sylvester Stallone in the *Rocky* movies. Stack was the real acting man of Cork who kept theatre going in the city for years. He filled the Opera House during the war years 'when we had it to ourselves and even got to the stage where the queues went all the way back to Patrick Street'. Lynch was among a coterie of stalwarts whom Stack 'could hang any play on'. Stack taught at the school for over 30 years: his contribution is honoured today by the James Stack Memorial Scholarship in Speech and Drama. Lynch had a solid Shakespearian training and was primarily a straight actor in those days. Stack paid them what seemed like a fortune for their professional work at the Opera House.

While studying drama and performing, Lynch had a number of day jobs: the most interesting, and most entertaining, was his role in the engineering department of Cork Corporation during the war years. He had no engineering qualifications, of course, but that didn't seem to matter because he got the job done. It was an unenviable mission: in charge of a gang of labourers with a reputation for toughness who left two previous bosses as broken men. They were rotational workers deployed from the labour exchange, aged 35-55, who preferred to work on the docks rather than use a pick and shovel. Lynch, the new boss, used psychology to win their confidence and get them to work. In the end, these fearsome hard men would have done anything for him.

The inevitable trouble started during their first morning on the job, as he supervised them laying concrete around Collins Barracks at Military Hill. One of the gang spotted a boat docking in the port; word spread about it and shovels were abandoned. Lynch watched the mass exodus from his small portable office. When the gang returned some hours later, he didn't budge or raise his head. They had expected a strong ticking off, but didn't get it. Eventually, one of the men knocked on the door of the office. Lynch went outside and they surrounded him. 'What are we going to sing today, lads?' asked the boss. 'How about *The Banks*?' They were embarrassed. One of them shouted: 'Aren't you going to dock us?' Lynch said: 'I know you're dockers, you lazy bunch.' The spokesman persisted: 'No, we mean are you going to dock our wages?' 'Why should I do that?' asked Lynch. 'Sure we were all off the job,' came the reply. 'Get away out of that,' said Lynch, pretending to sound surprised. 'You weren't, were you?' Then he returned to the office and shut the door. They never had a boss like him before.

Next, one of the real tough guys asked for a quiet word. 'Hey, boss,' he began. 'I'm courtin' this girl, like, and if I'm late of an evening, can I change my clothes in your office?' Lynch replied with a smile: 'Of course, Mr Kingston. Why not.' On another occasion, the gang asked for time off for one of the lads, who went by the nickname 'Narrow Back'. He had a talent for locating cigarettes at a time when they were 'scarcer than hen's teeth' during the war. A spokesman put forward their proposal: 'Narrow Back can get all the cigarettes he wants. He doesn't say where and we don't ask too much, like. Would it be too much to ask, like, if Narrow Back got time off to get us the cigarettes?' Lynch agreed to give him the next morning off to collect the gang's orders and get the precious goods. It became a practice in other Corporation gangs afterwards. Lynch's experiment in worker relations paid off handsomely. 'These fellows were working like mad for me by the time I was finished with them,' he recalls. 'You see, they were content and had a smoke as well. They worked their own way.'

Among other jobs, Lynch was assistant manager, and then promoted to manager, of the wine department of Murphy O'Connor wholesalers, a long established wine, whiskies and spirits firm. It was nice being surrounded by all the fine wines, even though he didn't touch alcohol at the time. After winning promotion, his first job was to recruit all the men into the union, so their salaries went up overnight. Lynch also drove trucks and worked as a lemonade salesman. During his time as a soft drinks salesman, he met a fast-talking American in a city hotel. 'You're a likely looking kid,' said the Yank. 'How would you like to take on the agency for *Coca Cola*?' Lynch conveyed the offer to his boss who poured scorn on the idea. 'That American shit,' he said. 'I wouldn't touch it.' The boss ended his days in a poor house.

Lynch's heart was in the theatre or in a broadcasting studio. He turned down two offers in the sporting world: the chance to play for Swindon in

1946 after being spotted by a talent scout, and the chance to join the sports department of the *Sunday Independent* in 1948. During the intervening year, he became a full-time actor, 'in spite of myself'. He was among the first actors employed by the new Radio Éireann Repertory Company in 1947, paving the way for other Cork actors including Niall Tóibín from Redemption Road. Lynch was a step ahead because he already had radio experience. He was treated initially as the naïve country boy. One of the older actors asked him: 'Listen, sonny, when did you start acting on radio first?' Lynch replied: 'Try 1934.' He nearly dropped dead with shock. Lynch joined a team of fine actors and some great characters including Jack Stephenson, George Green, Thomas Studley, Joseph O'Dea, Ginette Waddell and Una Collins with whom he sang in later years. It was a good apprenticeship under the direction of Micheál Ó hAodha, who later recommended Lynch to the Abbey Theatre. They did up to four plays a week on radio, including the hugely popular Sunday night play. 'It was the biggest attraction in Ireland,' he recalls. 'People adopted the habit of putting out all the lights in the house, sitting down by the fire and listening to the play.'

Lynch's talents as a tenor were showcased in a new programme in 1949, *The Balladmaker's Saturday Night*, along with soprano Una Collins, baritone Martin Dempsey, and bass Seán Ó Siocháin. It was inspired by Ó hAodha and scripted by Bryan MacMahon. Later, scripts were written by Sigerson Clifford and Brendan Behan. Inevitably, Behan joined the singing too; people thought he was sensational. The success of the show gave Lynch the opportunity to sing around Ireland, England and Scotland. 'They couldn't get enough of me,' he says. 'I was doing what I do best, singing songs, with the least trouble.'

Radio work, concerts and variety spots had raised his profile. He won an *Irish Times* radio award. In 1951 he joined the Abbey Theatre. 'They had no Playboy so they took me in,' he recalls. 'I played it for about 15 years after that.' He was the highest earner in the company: paid £10 a week flat rate, and the closest wage was £7 a week. Still, he could make more money in a night of cabaret than a month at the Abbey. He wasn't happy at the Abbey, a 'bit of a joint', although he played some terrific parts. He shared a dressing room with Harry Brogan and Micheál Ó Briain; life with them was one big laugh. That same year he landed his biggest radio hit in *Living With Lynch*, a comedy show which made him a household name in the pre-television '50s. It was written by Michael McGarry and Dermot Doolan. Lynch was the star of the show, joined by Charlie Byrne, Ronnie Walsh and Pamela Duncan.

They were backed by talented musicians, among them drummer Seán Wilkinson who later left to work for Dean Martin in Las Vegas and ended up in Hawaii. Lynch never saw the script until the day of recording. Some of the scripts, he says, were ahead of their time. There was a lot of stuff about outer space. 'We recorded it ourselves, brought it into Radio Éireann in a box and let them take it or leave it,' he recalls. 'Ó hAodha was good enough to let us do that. He was a self-effacing man; in fact, it used to annoy me that he was so self-effacing.' *Living With Lynch* enjoyed the highest listenership until 1956. The show was staged in the Theatre Royal later on and smashed box office records. 'It was quite an achievement,' he says, 'considering there were only four of us on stage.' RTÉ producer Bill Keating later tried to revive the radio show for a television series in 1976, reuniting Joe Lynch and Charlie Byrne. Although the new recordings were 'terribly funny', the series was never screened.

The young actor fell in love and in 1952 married Marie Nutty, a 'good-looking redhead who could sing as well'. She had three Feis Ceoil gold medals, two more than him. They had been introduced in the home of Senator Michael Colgan, a patron of the arts, at Glandore Road, off Griffith Avenue, where he held court for musicians and actors on Sunday mornings. His future wife had Cork connections too: her brother, Bob, was a gaelic footballer who played full forward on the St Finbarr's team that won the Cork County Championship in 1956. The Lynchs had two daughters and a son: Linda, Emmy and Marc.

His career took off in all sorts of ways: singing and playing the tin whistle, stand-up comedy, making records and a lot more besides. Versatility was the name of the game. As soon as his career was launched in one direction, he took off in another. In his own words at the time, 'the action is always in transit'. He covered the circuit of halls throughout England and then chased the big bucks in America. He even had a Top Twenty record in the British Hit Parade.

Lynch was asked by an American interviewer if it was true you couldn't get a drink in Ireland on St Patrick's Day. Not quite. You could get a drink at Baldoyle racecourse or else at the RDS where an annual dog show was held. Behan once made a memorable appearance at the RDS show. On that occasion, Lynch was acting as a marshal for the day. Sir Stanley Harrington, a nice old gentleman whom Lynch knew in Cork, approached him, trailing six small dogs held on separate leashes. 'Sir Stanley was telling me he had picked up a few prizes,' explains Lynch, 'when Behan staggered out in front of me, full of drink. He struggled towards me, got caught up in the dogs and fell flat on his arse. He roared,

"Jaysus, Lynch, what an awful place to bring dogs". When I told that story in America people nearly died laughing.'

Lynch took his first drink at the age of 31, in the company of Behan at the Tower bar. He remembers saying hello to Welch poet Dylan Thomas, who was seated alone near the door. Thomas had a cherubic looking face and 'looked like a ruined angel'. Lynch struggled to finish a glass of beer. It tasted awful. After the last mouthful, he noticed a dead snail at the bottom of the glass. He called over the publican to inspect the glass. 'Joe, there'll have to be a law about this,' remarked the boss. 'You're not suing me,' joked Lynch. 'That thing was dead before I got to it.'

Lynch talked his way onto *The Ed Sullivan Show*, the hottest property on American television. It was the 'big one'. Sullivan's people were signing up Irish actors for a 'special' from Dublin. Lynch wasn't told about the plans, but heard that 'someone who shall remain nameless did a deal for all the Irish actors to be paid £100 a head and their expenses'. Lynch was furious. 'So I went off to America next week to do something about it,' he recalls. Nobody got to Sullivan without being vetted by Mark Liddy, the 'tough guy' behind the show. Lynch called him on the phone and put on a distinguished English accent. They loved accents in America. 'Dear boy,' he began, 'I've come over from Great Britain and I want an audition with your Mr Sullivan. Do you think it's possible?' Liddy said: 'Why don't you come over tomorrow morning and find out, anytime between 10 and 11.' Lynch said: 'Just to show good faith, I'll be there at 10 sharp.' Lynch turned up next day and admitted he had used a phoney accent to get an audition. 'You bastard,' said Liddy. 'I suppose you better go in and see himself.'

Lynch landed a singing part in the Dublin show. He sang *Cockles and Mussels* walking down Moore Street in a white trench coat. 'All the auld ones on the stalls were smiling at me,' he says. 'They all knew me because when I was a kid at Blackrock College I'd cycle down there and chat to them.' The TV crew wanted to do something different during the interval between songs. Lynch suggested that he pick up an apple. The director, who gave all the orders, wanted the scene to look real: he told Lynch to give sixpence or a shilling to Rosie, the fruit seller. 'What d'ya mean give me sixpence or a shilling?' said Rosie angrily as she turned on the director. 'Listen, mister, I've had enough of you right up to here, you long streak of misery, telling this poor boy where to go and what to do. That boy knows where to go and what to do. Listen, I've cousins all over America, and there's nobody taking money off that child. If I took money off him, they'd never talk to me again.'

Lynch started making films and appearing on television in the '60s, juggling careers as an actor and singer. He was one of the first people to win a Jacob's Award in 1962; among those early winners were the late Hilton Edwards and Charles Mitchell. He won a second Jacob's award in 1977; this time in the company of Brian Farrell, Joe Mulholland, Eamonn Morrissey and John O'Donoghue. In 1964 Lynch played a Nazi-trained IRA man, dropped by parachute into Ireland during the Second World War, in the movie *Night Riders*. It was filmed on location in Dublin and Kildare. The big star was American actor the late Robert Mitchum, whom Lynch describes as a gifted, complete actor 'who could do it standing on his head'.

Then there was the time Lynch 'blessed' Richard Harris, Alec Guinness, Robert Morley and Timothy Dalton. The 'blessing' ceremony happened in a canteen at Shepperton Studios in 1970. Lynch was playing the part of a priest in *Loot*, a movie directed by Silvio Narizzano and also starring Lee Remick, Richard Attenborough, Milo O'Shea and Dick Emery. It was an old-fashioned, door-slamming farce from Joe Orton's stage hit. During a lunch break at Shepperton, Lynch walked into the studio canteen, still wearing the black clerical garb.

He was greeted by Limerick-born Harris who was wearing full battle dress for his part as Cromwell in the movie of the same name directed by Ken Hughes. 'Lynch, come over here and bless me,' demanded Harris loudly. Lynch duly obliged and ordered Harris down on his knees; he knew the ritual from his days as an altar boy in Blackpool. To his surprise, Harris got carried away with the joke and summoned other cast members, seated at various tables, to be blessed as well, among them Guinness, Morley and Dalton. It was a 'howl'.

Lynch wrote the music for another movie, a thriller called *Johnny Nobody*, in 1961, starring and also directed by Nigel Patrick, the debonair British leading actor with a long list of stage and screen credits. Lynch made an ill-fated venture into film-making in 1973 when he formed a company to make an Eric Sykes written movie called *You'd Better Go In Disguise*. The money ran out and the film was never completed. He believed in its commercial worth, but failed to interest any big financial backers in his project. 'It's sad to see it lying there after all the work everyone put into it,' he remarks. 'We failed on the last hurdle and lost a few bob on that.'

Lynch was now commuting between Ireland and England; he was never short of work, either on stage or in front of the cameras. Television made him a national name across the water. He had his own show,

Holiday Showground, in which a young comic, Ken Dodd, made one of his first appearances on television. Dodd came on dressed as a mad Mexican: he sang *Grenada* while trying to blow the bobbles out of his eyes at the same time. It was the series, *Never Mind The Quality, Feel The Width*, which really established him in Britain as a household name.

Lynch played the Irish half of an Irish-Jewish tailoring establishment. The show ran from 1966 to 1971 and topped the ratings for three of those five years. 'The odd thing is that we were the number one show,' he says, 'yet we were never invited to any prizegiving functions or award ceremonies. Maybe it had something to do with the mix of Jewish and Catholic religions.'

He returned to the cabaret circuit again. This time around, many of the stage managers thought he was chancing his arm at something new by doing a musical act. 'They thought I was just a television actor, and didn't know that I'd been singing all over England in clubs and halls for nearly 30 years.'

Lynch played memorable roles in RTÉ productions too: among them Eugene McCabe's *King Of The Castle*, screened in 1977, which had won the Irish Life award for best new play back in 1964. It was the story of a wealthy cattle dealer and farmer, Scober McAdam, and his failed efforts to father an heir with his new young wife. The TV version was superbly directed by Louis Lentin. Lynch played *Maguire*, a mischievous farm labourer who persistently needled *Scober*, (Niall Tóibín), about his impotence.

In April 1977, Lynch made a sentimental journey back to where his acting career began, the Cork Opera House, where he guested in *On The Bandwagon*, a light hearted variety show. Next, it was off to Cannes for some episodes of the TV series, *The Saint*, and he played a Corsican gangster in another movie.

Lynch says all the stories of him being difficult to work with, of rows and walkouts, are exaggerated. Only people who've never worked with him make those accusations. 'I'm a baby,' he says. 'My rule is never fight on a set. I got my temperament from my father who was the calmest, coolest man who ever lived.'

At the same time, he stands up for what he believes in and won't compromise to suit popular tastes or convention. In a showdown, he won't walk away. The actor was outnumbered when he publicly castigated the 'fanatics' behind the revival of the Irish language during the first major debate about the issue on *The Late Late Show* in 1965. Lynch, who speaks the language fluently, criticised the revival movement as long as there was one starving person in Ireland. He described the fanatical movement as a 'nod towards Mecca by little hitlers'. There was war in the studio. He had a go at the Gaelic Athletic Association, (GAA), as well, accusing them of taking the mantle of Irish freedom 'onto their rather narrow shoulders'. He recalls that the GAA representatives 'left in a body like the Kremlin crowd'. Lynch stood his ground. 'The only one who backed me that night was Garret FitzGerald, tooth and nail.' He recalls: 'I was flying. I tore into them. I said they were doing terrible damage to the language. One fellow called me a mug on the show.' Lynch remembers that as Seán Ó Siocháin left the studio afterwards, he came over and remarked to him: 'You're a terrible man so you are!' Throughout the years, versatility kept Lynch's career on track: he was capable of playing straight characters, often brilliantly; but also a gifted comedian and a trained singer and musician. He sang in Carnegie Hall and the Royal Albert Hall. If Joe couldn't do it, it couldn't be done.

For a new generation, who never knew of his past acting glories, Joe Lynch became *Dinny Byrne* in 1983. Everybody loves Dinny: the stubborn old farmer who limps his way around *Glenroe*, keeps a watchful eye over *Miley* and *Biddy* and lives by his own homespun philosophy. Rural communities embraced the character: every small town and village has a *Dinny Byrne*. It was an easy role for Lynch because he grew up with a *Dinny* too, who lived in his neighbourhood in Blackpool. Lynch says he was happy to take the part, in spite of being the second choice. 'I immediately invented this limp to slow me down because I was always a fast mover,' he recalls. 'I simulated a bad hip, which I studied, and people were really convinced. Eventually it was decided I should have the operation. So I had a simulated operation. After that happened surgeons all over Ireland were up to their asses in people looking for their hips done – it became the vogue.' Ironically, real life mirrored the script: the actor suffered hip pains and had to undergo a hip replacement at the Adelaide Hospital in Dublin in spring 1997. He jokes that he literally grew into his part.

Wesley Burrows, who devised the series, along with Brian MacLochlainn, the first series producer, gave Lynch *carte blanche* to develop Dinny's personality. Tommy McArdle is the present series producer of *Glenroe*, which was rated number one for 29 weeks out of 36 in 1999/97. The 97/98 series will equal the longevity of *The Riordans* in being 15 years old. Burrows, he says, is the craftiest writer in the world, 'a marvellous man to draw a character'. They chose Kilcoole as the fictional village of *Glenroe*. Today, there is a steady flow of visitors to the locations used by RTÉ including Dinny's cottage and Biddy and Miley's farm.

Glenroe was first shown in September 1983, overshadowed in the ratings by *The Late Late Show*. The serial began to hit the No.1 spot regularly from 1987. There were Sunday night audiences of over one million people, or over 31% of the population. *Glenroe* achieved its 200th audience of over a million in January 1996. Three programmes in the history of the series had audiences representing over half the population. *Glenroe* was beaten for the top ratings only by *The Late Late Toy Show* or The World Cup. There have been five onscreen weddings, three funerals and 13 pregnancies. The scriptwriters have risked some controversial storylines to mirror changes in Irish society over the years.

Like all soaps, the characters are weekly visitors to homes throughout the land. They are real; no flight of fantasy in a writer's imagination. Lynch is *Dinny Byrne* wherever he goes in Ireland. That won't change. He is frequently cornered by sheep farmers and asked for advice about breeds. After The Irish Derby at the Curragh, the actor found himself sandwiched between two farmer brothers in the lobby of a hotel in Newbridge. One implored Lynch for some words of wisdom. Next, he turned to his brother and said: 'There you are; *Dinny* said it. Jaysus Christ, I'm tellin' you straight, Eugene, you'll have to get out of them sheep. You've the wrong breed altogether. I'm begging you now.'

Lynch may be *Dinny Byrne* in Ireland, but he is known as 'Señor Bang Bang' in Spain. His idea of heaven on earth is a hideaway in the Spanish province of Alicante. For many years a hectic work schedule meant commuting between his home in Surrey and Dublin. He likes to steal away to his house in Alicante where people think he is famous for gangster movies. 'The local boys think I'm like John Wayne because I used to shoot people in the films,' he says.

There are still some unfulfilled ambitions: to make another movie or two, and attempt a parachute jump. Whatever about the movie aspirations, the jump may be harder to achieve because of his family's understandable reservations. His dream is to leap from a plane, and when the chute opens he plays a tin whistle all the way to the ground. 'I'd love that mad freedom.'

Throughout his career, a lot of people have shouted at the Corkman: 'You'll never work for me again.' Yet he was the first person they turned to in times of trouble. This familiar retort has inspired his epitaph. A few carefully chosen lines end simply: 'Here lies Joe Lynch, an actor, and he'll never work for any of you again.' That way, he'll have the last laugh.

SONIA O'SULLIVAN

AGONY AND ECSTACY

SUPER Sonia is the track animal: a single-minded obsessive with an insatiable appetite for success. Everyone knows about the blood, sweat and tears – the triumphs and disasters of Ireland's most celebrated track athlete. This steely determination brought her within a whisker of an Olympic medal at Barcelona in 1992, and made her a World and European champion. But the Atlanta Olympics in 1996 plunged her into the biggest crisis of her career. The nightmare re-visited her at the Athens World Championships in 1997. Amid the broken dreams and, frequently, under a cloud of controversy, her instinct is to run and run. Whatever happens, she will always do it her way. But that's not the full story...

There is another Sonia O'Sullivan though, rarely seen in the portrayal of her as a hard-bitten globetrotter whose only home is the track, swallowed up in an endless routine of transatlantic flights, airports and hotels rooms. She knows people see a hardness in her; she says that is only on the outside. There is a young woman who shares the hopes and disappointments of others her age; who likes to do other things apart from chasing medals. Things that might seem trivial, but important nonetheless. She likes reading, listening to music, pottering around her garden, cooking, eating out and going to the pictures. Even a champion likes to settle down with popcorn and watch a good movie. And there is the pleasure of drinking good coffee at her favourite Italian restaurant in London. She finds mooching about the kitchen of her home near Hampton Court to be particularly therapeutic. 'I love to experiment,' she says. 'I assemble cook books, get all the ingredients and make food that's good for you: lots of pasta, rice, fish and chicken dishes. I like to think I'm not a bad cook.'

She knows that the curtain will fall on her athletic career one day, when there will be plenty of time to bake scones. She'll get married and raise a family. The idea doesn't frighten her at all. 'Of course I want a normal life eventually,' she says. 'I want to show that I can run once a day and then get on with a normal life. I don't have any objections to getting married and having babies. I have to meet the right person first, though. I'm not sure where I'd settle down and bring up a family; probably not Cobh, because if you spend seventeen years of your life in one place you want to live somewhere else. London is great at the moment, but I'm not sure if that's the right place either. We'll have to wait and see. A lot depends on who I'm going to spend the rest of my life with. I definitely don't want to be by myself forever.'

Sonia's sights are still set on an Olympic medal at Sydney in 2000, preferably gold. She says she won't stop running until she achieves the grand prize. The Atlanta calamity forced her to take stock of her personal and professional lives. She came through with a new personal perspective; there is more to life than the track and the cycle of winning and losing races. She doesn't panic when her famous finishing kick deserts her, rather moves forward to prepare for the next race. Sonia's Greek tragedy at the World Championships showed she was still off-track, after a disappointing '97 season. Whatever happens, she'll continue running.

It took a long time to come to terms with what happened in Atlanta when she was beaten by a urinary tract infection: sensationally dropping out of the 5,000m final and the 1,500m heat fading away before her eyes. The sickness meant she never had a chance of producing a world class performance. The sporting post-mortem dogged her for months afterwards. 'It still annoys me when people think that I'm hiding something from everybody,' she says. 'In a way it doesn't matter what was wrong with me. I can't change it. Even if I'd won, that didn't necessarily mean I was going to have a good year in '97.' Something was still very wrong with Sonia.

The clutch of World and European gold and silver medals, among other awards, as well as her records, had once made her the flag bearer for a new generation of Irish runners. She was crowned the greatest Irish track athlete since Ronnie Delany, who won gold for Ireland in the 1,500m at the Melbourne Olympics in 1956. She was hailed as the undisputed queen of middle distance running in 1995 when she raced into the history books to become the women's 5,000m champion of the world at the Ullevi Stadium in Gothenburg, Sweden. She had delivered on her impressive pedigree, and the expectations followed her all the way to Atlanta a year later.

Nowhere were the expectations greater than in her home town, Cobh, where people have rejoiced in her famous victories and shared the heartbreaks. Sonia is wrapped securely in their affections – win or lose. When she won Ireland's first ever European championship gold medal in the women's 3,000m at Helsinki in 1994, local shopkeepers set up miniature shrines in their windows. On the day she became a world champion at Gothenburg, Sonia's late grandfather, Michael Shealy, was given a standing ovation in John Mansworth's pub. The town fell silent when the chance of an Olympic medal at Barcelona slipped from her grasp.

Cobh basked in the reflected glory of her victories on the track. Sonia restored local pride and raised spirits at a time when Cobh usually made the headlines for all the wrong reasons. Irish Steel, the biggest local employer, limped from crisis to crisis, and the air of depression was palpable. She brought a touch of glamour to a town that last saw glory days during the era of transatlantic liner traffic.

The Sonia O'Sullivan story is all about true grit, determination and truly awesome self-discipline. An independent streak guided everything she did, going back to her schooldays and early track career. If somebody told her there was no need to do a second training run of the day, she'd go and do it anyway out of spite. There are many tales of her grit: running through the rain and through the snow while others faltered; running in defiance of colds and flu that smothered her during her early teens in Cobh. Nobody was harder on Sonia than Sonia herself.

From as far back as Sonia can remember, she was running: first to and from school, just like the Kenyan runners. It was about a mile from her home at Wilmount Park, Carrignafoy, to St Mary's primary school. Lunchtime was the most testing dash. 'We only had an hour,' she recalls. 'So, the sooner you got home the more time you had for your dinner. It had nothing to do with running as such, I just wanted to get home quickly. I used the play telegraph poles along the way; racing the cars to the next pole.'

The future world champion was born on 28 November, 1969; the eldest of three, with a sister, Gillian, and brother, Tony. Her mother, Mary, whose maiden name was Shealy, came from Cobh. Her father, John, came from Dublin and served in the navy at Haulbowline. He used to go away on the ships, and Sonia recalls the excitement in the house when they got postcards from him in Killybegs. She remembers his uniform with shiny buttons. When any of the children were sick and home from school, Mary O'Sullivan hauled one of his heavy navy overcoats from the hot press and put in on their beds. 'It weighed a ton but kept you nice and snug and warm when you felt freezing cold,' says Sonia.

At St Mary's, the indelible memory is of the nuns: the Sisters of Mercy who carried bells in their hands to keep order and get the children into line going into their classrooms. Sr Rosario took a particular interest in the progress of the youngster, having taught her mother before her. She remembers Sonia in third class as an amiable little girl, 'so unassuming you'd hardly know she was in the room'. Sr Rosario encouraged the early running efforts of Sonia and the other infants who competed for lollipops as prizes. She nurtured her efforts too in the Community Games. They have exchanged cards and letters over the years.

Sonia got serious about schoolwork, and about running, during her secondary years at Cobh Vocational School. She was always in a hurry, and often had to be told to slow down and walk along the corridors to her next class. She was happiest on the field of play; the teachers knew they could rely on her to make up a team whether camogie, volleyball or basketball. Jim Hennessy, one of the teachers, organised much of the sports activities and he brought Sonia and other students to Cork County Vocational Schools Sports, Munster Colleges and Irish Colleges championships as well as cross-country championships. 'Sonia was in a very good junior group and had great comradeship and motivation,' he recalls. 'She was a little gem. I can still see her training on her own in the field. She was dedicated and always wanted to do better the next day.'

In her early teens, Sonia began to train in the fields of Ballymore Cobh AC after school. She joined the club because she and her friends wanted to go to discos there at the weekends and the end-of-year awards. That's how it all started. She'd run any distance, usually 800m or more, and was 'hopeless' at 100m. She went away with the club at weekends to Midleton and Carrigtwohill; it was only down the road 'but it seemed as if we were going miles away'. Club members at the time remember her as a 'handy runner'. It was frustrating, though, that the other girls kept beating her at the sprint events. At 15, there was no extraordinary talent bursting forth. Someone told her in town one day she'd be good at cross-country running. She didn't even know what it meant. Her natural talents first surfaced in cross-country; the longer distances suited her.

She represented Cork in the BLOE, Irish juvenile athletics board, Championships, and took her first Munster Colleges cross-country title while still in first year. Jim Hennessy drove her to the cross-country event in Dungarvan. 'On a Saturday morning when people were going off to GAA and soccer matches, he was taking one girl to a cross-country race,' she recalls. 'He used to meet me at the school at nine in the morning, and then it was off down to Dungarvan.' She trained and ran with schoolpals Deirdre O'Mahony, Christine Butler and Lisa O'Donovan.

She developed strong self-discipline to balance the demands of homework and training. After school came an hour's training, and then home for tea before knuckling down to homework at precisely six o'clock. 'I had this rule and stuck to it,' she says. 'I had to be into the homework by six. I'd eat quickly, then go into my bedroom and close the door.'

The family frequently felt the wrath of Sonia's regime. She'd turn down the TV volume and order silence in the house. One evening, her brother, Tony, was playing pool with friends in the garage. They were creating a loud racket. Sonia marched out and swiped the cue ball and black ball from the table. 'The real reason I did that was probably because I wanted to enjoy myself too but felt that homework had to come first,' she says. 'I felt that if I had to study and be serious then everybody else had to be serious as well. It's the same when I go training now. I can be very intense beforehand, but when the training is over I'm a totally different person.'

Sonia wanted to be the best in her class, and at the same time find space to do other things outside school. 'I wasn't going to study forever,' she says, 'although I decided to put in the time and get the work done.' Geography and Home Economics were among her favourite subjects. To this day she can name all the rivers and mountains in Ireland. Home Economics was enjoyable because she got the chance to cook and bring home her goodies. Sonia became expert at making scones.

Sonia's home study regime paid off for the Intermediate Certificate in 1985 when she collected four As in Commerce, Science, Geography and Home Economics.

Sonia liked a challenge, whether running cross-country or picking potatoes for pocket money in Cobh. Sonia was like any girl of her age, playing with her friends in the park, until she put on the running gear. She had found her niche, and the single-minded pursuit of excellence took over. Neighbours soon discovered that she'd refuse a lift home if they spotted her running along the roads. Even when struck down by a particularly nasty flu one winter Sonia kept on running. Her evening runs were punctuated by extreme fits of coughing. She tried to hide the sickness and didn't tell anyone because if she was kept home from school that meant missing running too.

The first important breakthrough came in 1985 when she won the under-16 BLOE track title in the 1,500m and was runner-up in 800m. She had gone to Mosney for the Community Games finals at the age of 14, and also represented her school. She won the schools' cross-country title: both the junior and senior races, becoming the only athlete to pull off that double. 'I'd won a national championship and I hadn't really been training properly,' she recalls. 'I realised it wasn't too difficult to be up there winning medals.' She called a local coach, Sean Kennedy, who would play a major role in coaching her over the following eight years up to the Barcelona Olympics. She asked him for a training programme. He said he needed to know what she'd been doing already on her own. She told him she didn't really know; 'just running, like'. 'Sean started to write out programmes for two weeks at a time,' recalls Sonia. 'After a while I knew I was always going to do things my own way because he'd write out something for seven days but if I had to go somewhere or do something I'd just switch the days around and do the hard day today and the easy day tomorrow. To be honest, I even do that now. I run how I feel rather than on the basis of what someone tells me to do.' Kennedy's biggest task was to keep the youngster under control. Sonia was doing hills and steps on top of her usual training routine.

Unlike her younger sister and brother, Sonia wasn't particularly outgoing. She preferred to concentrate on studies and the rigours of training. She went to discos with her friends, occasionally, but wasn't keen on the rituals played out under the bright lights. She usually made up an excuse that she wasn't allowed to go. To her friends, it seemed to be a 'big deal' to go to the disco. 'You'd wait for the guys to ask you to dance. There'd be a group of girls on one side and the boys on the other. Half the time we just danced together and didn't bother with any of the boys. The lads probably thought I was a bit weird; all this girl does is run around a field all day.'

The year 1987 was a big one: Sonia left school with excellent Leaving Cert results and her dedication to training paid off. She won the BLE, Irish governing body of athletics, national senior cross-country title, the youngest ever to do so at 17, beating title-holder Mary Donoghue and a star-studded field. Nobody considered her a medal prospect. Sonia beat the favourite, Caroline Mullen, who had returned home from America with some impressive victories. She sprinted away from the top contenders with 600m to go, and they failed to match her power and strength. Looking back, Sonia had only aspired to be in the first 10 and says she never expected to win the race. The victory cleared the way to run on the Irish team in the World Cross-Country Championships at Warsaw. However, Sonia was studying for the Leaving Cert and, with French and Irish oral exams being held around the same time, she decided to give it a miss. During the summer, she delivered a blistering performance in the Cork City Sports at the Mardyke, winning the 3,000m in a time of 9.01 and knocking 26 seconds off the Irish junior record. It was the second fastest time in the world by a junior that year. 'I think people were stunned by the time,' she says. Sonia powered past a field which included Liz McColgan of Scotland, the world 10,000m champion.

Later, she travelled to the European juniors in Birmingham but a stress fracture in her leg forced her to withdraw. She thinks the fracture was caused by training. 'I've had quite a few of them,' she says. 'It was probably due to the fact that I was running quite a lot while still growing and that puts a lot of stress on your bones.' In fact, she suffered extreme frustration with stress fractures for some time after she'd started an athletics scholarship at Villanova University in the US, the academy of athletics.

John and Mary O'Sullivan were delighted with their daughter's achievements, although they weren't quite sure what the future held for her. 'My mother was always worried about what I was going to do with myself,' says Sonia. Her cup was overflowing with success – literally. She collected all her medals in a cup, and later transferred them to a jug. 'It was like having a jar of pennies and two pence pieces, except these were gold, silver and bronze medals,' she says.

An athletics scholarship in the US seemed to be the next logical course of action. Sonia picked Villanova in Philadelphia which had offered her a scholarship. Her father thinks she liked the idea of becoming the first Irish woman to go there. Sonia flew out at Easter for a brief visit to Villanova. Her first experience of the States was a revelation. She was collected at JFK airport in New York by two other students who introduced the Irish girl to the Big Apple. Villanova was impressive: it had top class facilities, experienced coaches and international-standard competition that athletes were starved of back home. Sonia met coach Marty Stern and decided to return to the business college there in August.

She says: 'The big thing from my perspective was that I'd be able to train with other people there, whereas at home I was doing everything by myself. It just seemed better to go to America because you go to school in the morning and go training in the afternoon. It seemed a lot simpler than going to UCC or Limerick and having to get your own time for training.'

Back home, Sonia was enjoying celebrity status in the summer of '87 after her national victories and a great performance at the Cork City Sports. She spoke of her ambition to run for Ireland at the Olympic Games. Her heroine was Zola Budd. 'All I ever wanted to do since I started running was to make it to the Olympics,' she said at the time. 'After my run in Cork the other night I suddenly realised I could get there.' The Leaving Cert was a piece of cake: out of eight subjects she got seven honours and a pass in Physics. She detested Physics but loved Geography, Accounting, Domestic Science and Biology, in which she got an A grade.

On the day she left for Villanova, the drive from Cobh to Shannon Airport seemed like the longest journey in the world. It wasn't easy for John and Mary O'Sullivan to watch their 17-year-old daughter fly off into the great unknown.

Villanova was exciting in the academic sense: she studied for a degree in Accounting and Business Studies and got the chance to take a range of other subjects besides. Once again, study came easy to Sonia once she put her mind to it. But Villanova wasn't so much a nursery for athletics, more a factory where she lost her way during the first two years at a time when she continued to be dogged by injuries. She was coached by Stern but continued to be advised from home by Kennedy. The first year was tougher than expected: she felt she was being run too hard and found it difficult to adjust to the Villanova system. At the same time, she was put through rigorous cycling and swimming programmes to keep her free of injuries. 'The training was quite competitive because the girls were really good,' she explains. 'For the first few years I was hopeless. I should have done much better. But I kept getting injured and things didn't go right and it took me two years to sort myself out. As soon as I did, I knew after one run that I was going to win races and run fast. It became easier after that.'

Sonia was never a party animal, but felt compelled to join the social circuit early on in order to make friends. 'The first time I went out I was very intimidated by the Americans,' she recalls. 'They want to mother you because you're away from home. Eventually, you've got to stand on your own two feet and figure things out for yourself. I think I could deal with anything by myself now.'

After her second year at Villanova, she came home to work for the summer behind the bar at the Rob Roy in Cobh. She learned how to pull a pint and enjoyed the craic in the pub. There were plenty of late nights, and she seemed to be living it up for a change. Like all mothers, Mary O'Sullivan had niggling worries about her daughter's future. 'She was forever chasing me around,' says Sonia, 'asking "when are you going to get a job?" and "what are you going to do with yourself?"' During that summer, Sonia ran about six miles every day, but doesn't think she was sufficiently fit. She decided to try a 5k road race in Killarney, and surprised herself. 'I ran a fairly decent time and couldn't believe it,' she recalls. 'I decided I could do better and started training again. I went back to America and trained really hard and won their national cross-country. That was really the turning point.'

For the next two years, Sonia decided to go it alone. Training plans were faxed to her by Kennedy, and she'd fax back her times. Sonia told Stern what she was doing: she felt instinctively that she was right and they were wrong. The results vindicated her stance. 'In the last couple of years I paid back what I'd been given in the first years,' she says. 'You do feel that you've been supported and given all this education and you owe something to the college.' She won five NCAA titles for Villanova: two outdoor 3,000m, two on the indoor track and the Cross-Country Championship in 1991.

Sonia sat at the side of the road and cried when she finished ninth at the European Championships in the Croatian town of Split in 1990. Still, she had set a new Irish record of 8:52:65 for the 3,000m. She decided not to run in the World Championships at Tokyo in 1991, but to concentrate on the World Student Games at Sheffield where she took gold in the 1,500m and silver in the 3,000m. Her victory at Sheffield was well publicised in Ireland. 'People at home made a big deal of that win,' she recalls. 'It was the first time I was met by crowds at the airport, coming home with medals.' Sonia's dedication to her studies at Villanova paid off, too, when she graduated with first class honours in Business Studies and Accounting.

By the spring of '92, Sonia had become the first Irish woman to notch up a world track record, scoring the best indoor time for the 5,000m in Boston. In June, she improved her 3,000m best from 8:52.65 to 8:39.67 in a defeat over Elana Meyer in Holland. On form, at least, Ireland had a medal winning prospect at the Barcelona Olympics that year, and the weight of expectation fell on the Irish golden girl. Sonia qualified for the 3,000m final: Cobh held its breath and ran every metre with her as she led the field all the way home. John and Mary O'Sullivan had watched their daughter do well in the heats, and reckoned she could finish in the top six or even better. Typically, John had made his way down a few rows to be closer to the track before the gun exploded. He was a bundle of nerves and shouted: 'Hang in ... hang in.' With over 200m to go, a burst for glory by British runner and European Champion Yvonne Murray expired and Sonia took the lead. She was on her own. She didn't know what to do and couldn't handle it. The dream ended. She was overtaken by the two

Russians on the finishing straight, and then lost to Angela Chalmers of Canada for the bronze medal. It took a while to put the bitter Olympic disappointment behind her. Within a couple of months she had beaten the three runners who outclassed her in the 3,000m final.

Even though there were tears in Barcelona, Sonia rates her first experience of the Olympics as a career highlight. 'It was special to be part of the Olympics team,' she says. 'We went away to a training camp beforehand and that was great fun. Even if I'd won in Atlanta in 1996, it wouldn't have been the same as my first Olympics. We had a good team. We all hung out together; everybody had the aim of running our best.' Cobh was *en fête* for Barcelona '92. When Sonia eventually came home, she was 'amazed' that people were so proud of her in defeat. She wondered what it would have been like if she won an Olympic medal.

Sonia came into the '93 season a superior athlete. By now, Kim McDonald, an influential broker in sport, had taken over as her agent and coach in London. Sonia had signed up an advertising contract with Heinz (Ireland) and also linked up with sponsors Reebok, the top international sports goods manufacturers. She ran a magnificent 3,000m at the Bislett Games in Oslo in 8:28.74, leaving behind Murray and Meyer among a top class field. It was the seventh fastest 3,000m in history, and just six seconds away from the world record.

Optimism levels soared going into the World Championships in Stuttgart a month later: Sonia seemed on track for gold in the 3,000m. Then came the Chinese takeaway. The three Chinese 'springers' outfoxed her in the last two laps and Sonia again trailed in fourth place. Another bitter disappointment. 'Just forget about it,' advised her father through the fencing after the race. 'No,' replied Sonia. 'I won't forget about it.' Sonia was angry, and came back to the track six days later to take silver in the 1,500m. The ovation for her in the stadium surpassed that accorded to the gold medallist, Dong Liu of China. Her parents were at the stadium in Stuttgart to savour the moment.

Sonia returned to the glory trail in September to win the 3,000m at the Grand Prix finals at Crystal Palace in London from Murray. She finished second in the mile just over an hour later and ended up second overall behind Sandra Farmer-Patrick of the US. Ireland's greatest middle distance runner was given a heroine's welcome home to Cork and Cobh on 21 September. Travelling from London with her sister, Gillian, Sonia was given an unofficial flyover of Cobh by the Aer Lingus pilot. Cork's greeting – Well Done Sonia – was illuminated in giant letters over Patrick's Bridge. She was whisked to Jury's Hotel to collect a record-breaking tenth Cork Sportstar of the Month award to add to her two overall Supreme Awards. Then it was off for an open-top bus ride to Cobh.

In July 1994 the 24-year-old showed she'd lost none of the previous season's form to become the first Irish athlete to break an outdoor world record by clocking 5:25.36 at the 2,000m in Edinburgh. Murray, the reigning European 3,000m champion, finished second in 5:26.93 to break her old British and Commonwealth record. Regina Jacobs, the US 1,500m champion, came third. It was Sonia's race: with 200m to go she turned on the style, powered her way around the final bend and pulled away down the finishing straight. It was her third successive victory, and her second world record after breaking the indoor record for 5,000m at Boston in 1991. A week after Edinburgh she smashed the European 3,000 record with a superb 8:21.64, beaten only by the Chinese.

Sonia carried the favourite tag for at least one gold medal going into the European Championships in Helsinki in August 1994. She did the business, winning gold in the 3,000m to become the first Irish athlete to win a European track title. She shadowed defending champion Yvonne Murray from the start and stayed on her shoulder until 180m from the line. Her famous finishing kick took over and she shot away to win in 8:31.84. The euphoria was captured in a memorable picture of John O'Sullivan embracing his daughter, which made the front pages across Europe. It always amazes Sonia that he gets so close to the track in order to be there for her, win or lose. 'I know he's always watching me and wants to know that I'm okay.'

Sonia was over the moon. 'A lot of people were doubting me,' she said, 'but I knew I was in great shape. If I was going to lose it would be by making a mistake. Coming home with a medal is one thing. Gold is something else.' At home, Mary O'Sullivan, who preferred to see the video recordings of her daughter's races after the excitement had died down, broke with tradition to watch the race live on television with her son, Tony. Cobh went bananas. There was a rousing rendition of the national anthem in Mansworth's pub as Sonia stepped up to take her gold medal during the awards ceremony on TV.

The omens were good going into the World Championships at Gothenburg in August 1995. She had trained in Melbourne to reach peak fitness for the 5,000m final. There were winning performances in Oslo, London and Nice. The people's champion displayed her formidable talent on home ground at the Cork City Sports. She showed she was ready to take on the world by setting the fastest 1,500m time of the season in Monte Carlo, with a new Irish record of 3:58.85 – the first woman to break four minutes in the 1,500m that year. The O'Sullivans, and everybody in Cobh, again jumped for joy when she outclassed a world class field, including the record holder, to take gold in the 5,000m final. She saw off the challenge of the Portuguese runner, Fernanda Ribeiro, in a nailbiting final lap. She ran away from the world record holder and 10,000m champion to win convincingly in 14:46.47 – the sixth fastest time ever and her second fastest. Immediately afterwards, she was plunged into controversy for not carrying the Irish flag. She explained she was exhausted by the race and wasn't fit to carry a flag; the first flag offered to her by her father was too heavy. Whatever about the flag row, Super Sonia was hailed as the undisputed queen of middle-distance running. Gothenburg was the dress rehearsal: roll on Atlanta '96 for the 1,500m and 5,000m double.

It should have been a fairytale script for the golden girl: the greatest prize of all, an Olympic gold medal, to sit beside her World and European Championship medals. Nothing could have prepared Cobh, Ireland and the sporting world for the disaster about to unfold. First came a bizarre humiliation for Sonia: she was forced to strip in the stadium tunnel before her 5,000m heat, out of her sponsor's Reebok gear and into the official Irish kit, manufactured by Asics. The unnecessary episode was the result of a dispute between the Olympic Council of Ireland (OCI) and BLE, over what manufacturer's gear she could wear. There was no time to return to her dressing room and she had to change in public. Sonia went into the tunnel leading to the track with the Asics gear in her bag, knowing she might have to change in a hurry. People spoke of humiliation; she thinks that's too strong a word. 'The only thing that makes me angry looking back was the actual process of taking the numbers off one outfit and putting them on another. That's one of those sticky things you get nervous about before a race. I went to the 5,000m on the understanding that I could wear the Reebok gear. There's no way I would wear it if I had any reason to believe that I wasn't going to be allowed wear it. I brought the Asics gear with me because I felt that if I had nothing else to wear then I could be disqualified. Kim told me to wear Asics but I said I was wearing the Reebok gear. I'd made up my mind and wasn't changing it.' Sonia is adamant that the much-publicised tunnel incident had no long-term effect on her Atlanta performance.

The gear controversy was a trivial sideshow compared to the real problem for Sonia: her health. She thinks the problems started a fortnight before she arrived at her training base in Philadelphia on her way to

Atlanta, most likely in her races in Nice and London. She ran the fastest 3,000m of the year in Nice. She won again at the 5,000m in London, the final rehearsal before Atlanta. She didn't feel good, but decided to think positively for Atlanta.

The final training session with Marcus O'Sullivan in Philadelphia did not go well. She ignored the warning signs. 'Maybe I just didn't feel as sharp as I should have done,' says Sonia. 'There wasn't really any doubt in my mind that I was going to be okay. I thought maybe this was just normal leading into the big race. I think it was obvious to Kim McDonald, Frank O'Meara and Marcus O'Sullivan that I wasn't perfect. They came to the track and watched me everyday. We were in a position where the Olympics was in a week's time. They're not going to tell me, "you look terrible". That wouldn't solve anything.'

Sonia had to stop twice to go to the toilet during her usual run on the morning of the 5,000m heat. She had diarrhoea, but dismissed this as last-minute nerves. During the heat Sonia found herself struggling, unexpectedly, against Sarah Wedlund when she broke from the pack. Just like her heat in Gothenburg a year previously, Wedlund went out to break the field.

Surprisingly, on this occasion Sonia had to work very hard to close the gap. She managed to sprint over the last 200m to win the heat. The race took a lot more out of her than it should have. She was bathed in sweat at the end. She put it down to the humidity. 'I knew I didn't feel good,' she says. 'There should never have been that gap.' On the night after the heat she awoke covered in sweat and had to change the bedclothes.

On the morning of the 5,000m final, Sunday 28 July, Sonia went for a run with Frank O'Meara, the Irish 5,000m champion. He noticed she was going to the toilet more often than usual. He asked her if something was wrong. She said her stomach was slightly upset, but nothing to worry about. She didn't consider the slight diarrhoea to be a big deal. She recalls: 'I was stopping every 10 minutes. I thought to myself, "before the race you're nervous, this is typical". You hope little things that seem like minor problems don't grow.'

Sonia knew she was in big trouble from the first lap. Hundreds of flag waving fans were stunned when she walked off the track with just over two laps remaining. The gold medal that should have gone to Sonia went instead to the Chinese runner, Junxia Wang, who ran away from Pauline Konga of Kenya after the world champion left the track.

Sonia had struggled through the slow early laps, with the field lapping at 75 seconds through the first four circuits. When the leaders threw in a fast lap of 65 seconds, the full extent of Sonia's disaster was plain to see, now left struggling in 10th position. The sixth lap slowed again to 74 seconds but it was too late for Sonia. She eventually went from 13th to 15th position at the rear of the field. She decided to cut short her agony, disappearing down the tunnel with over two laps to go. She could see that officials on the sideline were staring, and sensed they felt sorry for her. She didn't need 'this kind of sympathy crap'. She wanted to escape and get ready for the 1,500m. 'I went to run into the tunnel but they weren't going to let me in,' she recalls. 'I just kept running. They wanted to take me into the medical room. At first I didn't want to go in. Then I realised it was the safest place to go to try and get myself together before I faced people.' Sonia emerged into the chaos of the 'mixed zone' of athletes and accredited personnel where she was hugged by her father. 'I can't stay here,' she told him. 'I've got to go. You're going to bring everybody over here to me.' He tried to console her. 'She is very upset,' he told reporters. Kim McDonald, her agent, was also waiting in the wings.

Sonia knew that everybody wanted answers, but she didn't even have answers for herself. A driver was waiting to whisk her away. She decided to run with McDonald through the streets back to the house where she was staying. She didn't stop once. Emotions were freed. 'I was crying on and off at different points,' she recalls. 'I knew obviously there was something wrong, but I figured maybe it's a 24- hour thing and I'd start all over again. Before I got home I decided I'd run in the 1,500m.'

Everybody wanted an explanation. The first clue came when she sent an intriguing fax message to the Irish team in the Olympic village after quitting the race. The fax found its way into the public domain: the Irish media seized on her admission that she had a 'little problem with the Big D'. They interpreted, correctly, the 'D' as diarrhoea.

Within 24 hours she faced the media at a press conference convened by Olympic Council of Ireland President, Pat Hickey. She had an upset stomach that caused diarrhoea going into the 5,000m final. Yes, she would be running in the 1,500m. Then she became embroiled in the wrangle between the Olympic Council and BLE over the gear change controversy. In hindsight, she thinks it was a mistake to have been there for the entire press conference amid all the flak.

It happened again in the 1,500m heats on Wednesday, 31 July. She warmed up with Frank O'Meara, who felt she was sure of surviving the heats. Once the gun went, Sonia knew she'd lost it. 'I was hanging on,' she recalls. 'I had a heavy feeling in my legs. It wasn't a normal kind of tiredness. I was stuck to the track. There was no bounce at all.' She fell behind at the bell and was well out of contention long before the finish. It was a disastrous final 400m: the field pulled away from Sonia, now struggling at the back, and she finished second last. 'This is the end,' she told reporters, with tears streaming down her face. 'It certainly felt like the end of the world at the time,' she now says. Looking back, Sonia says it would have been much easier to handle if she had been overcome by a more dramatic illness. Next came the theories. Sonia had her heart broken. Sonia had been cursed. Sonia had her food poisoned. Sonia caved in, psychologically, under the weight of expectation as swimmer Michelle Smith enjoyed a gold rush. If anything, this spurred her on even more: she thought if Michelle could win then maybe she could too. The tall stories were amusing at least, particularly the one about being pregnant. 'I was rolling around the place when I heard some of them,' she says. No, the physical sickness didn't have a psychological base. She'd been to the Olympics before, and nearly came away with a medal. She knew what to expect at Atlanta.

Observers said the medical condition should have been spotted sooner, and treated earlier. Sonia says: 'This was a huge occasion. Two days beforehand you don't go looking to see a doctor because what if he tells you that you can't run?'

There were accusations of bad management: some claimed Smith had been better managed than her in Atlanta, and Sonia's personal relationship with McDonald got in the way. Sonia stands by McDonald, who took flak in the press. He advised, but she called the shots. 'Look, I am my own person and I make my own decisions. I don't need somebody telling me what to do on a daily basis. Kim manages my races. When it comes down to racing the bottom line is I do what I want to do.'

McDonald had been her agent and coach since Barcelona. The relationship got closer. She recalls: 'He managed Frank O'Meara and Marcus O'Sullivan. Things followed on from there.' He entered her life around the 1992 Olympics. 'That was when I first met him and he started putting me in races. Then he started advising me on coaching and racing. He did this a lot after the Chinese in Stuttgart when I was determined that I was going to go out and run as much as them and as hard as them and as far as them. He never stopped me from doing anything like that. There was absolutely no problem between us going into the Atlanta Olympic Games. It helped enormously that we were such good friends.' Their personal relationship ended, as well as his coaching role, after Atlanta. He still acts as her agent.

It took a long time before Sonia could even talk about the Olympics without tears coming to her eyes. She genuinely thought people at home would treat her differently after the Olympics failure. The mail poured in from Ireland: a mountain of letters and cards from well-wishers. Children sent over their medals. When she returned to Ireland she found the same affection. Sonia's outlook changed: time to lighten up. 'I had to accept what happened as unchangeable,' she says. 'There was no point thinking about what if I won two medals or what if I broke a world record. The letters and cards made me realise that people wanted me to win again. It wasn't the end of the world.'

The sensible step might have been to sit out the rest of the season, to take a complete break for three months. She ignored this advice. Sonia was back training within days and racing within a few weeks. She wanted to get back on track, and find out if the old magic was still there. It wasn't. The Grand Prix final in Milan proved the point. The competitive juices were still flowing. Sonia enjoyed a comeback victory in the road mile in Honolulu where she ran 4:26.43. She was feeling great and felt the old form returning. The win in Hawaii was just the tonic before she left for three months of training in Australia at the start of 1997.

Three world championships lay ahead in '97. Sonia took silver in the 3,000m at the world indoor championships in Paris. She ran the near perfect race – but a mistake in the last bend allowed Gabriela Szabo through on the inside and the Romanian powered on to take the gold medal and retain her world indoor crown.

Sonia had a poor showing in the women's world cross-country race in Turin, after leading for nearly half of the race. Bronze medals marked the best ever placing by an Irish women's team. But there was heartbreak for top hopes in pursuit of individual medals as Catherina McKiernan, four-times silver medallist, came seventh and Sonia came ninth.

She won the first Grand Prix meet of the year in Olympic Park, Melbourne, taking victory in the 5,000m against relatively moderate opposition. But her early season form collapsed once the Grand Prix events got underway. It was not to be the season of renewal she'd hoped for. Sonia trailed in a distant tenth in a 1,500m race at Sheffield behind Britain's Olympic silver medallist, Kelly Holmes, who triumphed with a new British record at 3:58.07. Sonia's 4:11.52 was one of her slowest 1,500m races. It was seen as a serious setback to her preparations for the world championships. After the dismal performance at Sheffield, Sonia pulled out of the 5,000m at the Bislett Games Grand Prix in Oslo in July, the same distance at which she won a world championship gold medal at Gothenburg in 1995. Sonia's loss of form forced her back to the training track to re-think her strategy for the world outdoor championships in Athens in August where she would defend her 5,000m title and also double up at 1,500m. Blood tests were ordered in the hope of finding a reason for the loss of form. There was one bright note, on home ground in June, when she held off the challenge of American champion Regina Jacobs to win the women's 2,000m at the Cork City Sports.

Sonia's Greek tragedy showed the old magic had deserted her. It was like a re-run of Atlanta. Again, the world saw the image of a pallid, sweat-streaked athlete struggling to find answers. Again, her hopes of glory evaporated in a haze of controversy. 'It's supposed to be a sport; it's not about that sort of behaviour,' she told RTÉ's Tony O'Donoghue in a remarkable interview after the women's 1,500m final on Tuesday, 5 August. The race had ended for Sonia after she became embroiled in a three-way tussle with Swiss girl Anita Weyermann and Regina Jacobs of the US on the final straight. At the bell, Sonia was perfectly placed for a final thrust to the line. Suddenly, Weyermann burst through with both elbows flailing: she clattered into Jacobs, who was now in front of O'Sullivan. Next, Sonia put her hand out in an effort to stay on her feet and got caught up in Jacob's singlet. Sonia couldn't recover from the upset and came home in eighth place. She was furious at Weyermann. And Jacobs was furious at O'Sullivan. There were extraordinary scenes on the way to the tunnel afterwards. Jacobs felt that O'Sullivan had cost her a gold medal, and told her so. She confronted the Irish athlete and struck her hard on the back. Sonia insisted that her act of grabbing the American's singlet in the race was accidental. Then the RTÉ cameras caught the moment when Sonia spotted Weyermann and shouted that it was she who should have been disqualified. The 1,500m debacle scotched hopes of a double medal haul at the Athens championships. It was the worst possible approach to her defence of the 5,000m title. Sonia lost her crown when she flopped in the semi-finals of the 5,000m on Thursday, 7 August. It was all over – again. Sonia had ignored the advice of her trainers who wanted her to take a break. 'I accept there is something wrong,' she remarked. 'I just don't know what it is.' The jostling incident in the 1,500m final may have been a convenient crutch; now the truth about her condition could not be avoided. Whatever happens next, one thing is for sure: she is not a quitter. No way. In fact, in retrospect, she is quite philosophical about it: she feels 'sometimes you have to take risks because otherwise you would never know'.

She is ready to put the '97 season behind her and prepare for the European Championships in Budapest in 1998. Super Sonia likes to say that she has yet to run her best race. The next shot at Olympic glory will be in Sydney in 2000. She'll keep on running until her moment arrives. 'Everything I do is going to be geared towards Sydney,' she says. 'There are few Olympic champions around. But there are lots of world champions. It's much easier to be a world champion than an Olympic champion. I'd be happy if I had an Olympic medal. Definitely. If it didn't happen though it wouldn't be the end of the world. Running is what I do, and what I do best, but I know now that there are other things in life. I'd like people to remember me as not just a good runner but as a good person too. I don't want to be forgotten as soon as I stop running.' As they say down south, 'there's no fear of that happening, girl.'

EILEEN NOLAN

FIRST LADY OF THE STAGE

'APPLES for sale,' cries the old woman. It's a trick: the evil queen is disguised as she returns to the cottage of the seven dwarfs with a poisoned apple to kill Snow White. The queen takes a bite and then offers the fruit to her. By now, the children are shrieking in the audience. 'It's the queen,' they chorus. 'Don't eat it.' Their emotions are fired by the fate of Snow White, the fairest one of all. Amid the crescendo of ear-splitting screams, a small boy shouts up at Snow White: 'Spit it out, she's trying to choke ya.'

The childrens' outrage is always real, whether directed at the queen in *Snow White*, the wicked witch in *Hansel and Gretel*, the wolf in *Little Red Riding Hood* or the giant in *Jack and the Beanstalk*. The innocence of children caught up in the good-versus-evil battles of Christmas pantos never changes through the generations. Nobody can ever predict how the small minds will react to live theatre.

Just ask actors Billa O'Connell and Paddy Comerford, two veterans of pantos at the Cork Opera House who've been the ugly sisters in *Cinderella* on many occasions. Once, as Billa climbed into bed with Paddy, he was reprimanded by a little girl in the audience. 'You never said your prayers,' she said prissily. Ever since, the ugly sisters made sure to pray and bless themselves. On another occasion, the children were in a frenzy as Billa gave Cinderella a tongue-lashing, and told her to forget about going to the ball. Billa shouted at the audience: 'Mind your own business.' A boy left his seat in the third row, ran up to the foot of the stage and roared back: 'Shut up, ya fat fool!'

Nothing surprises Eileen Nolan, founder of the Montforts stage school and matriarch of the theatre in Cork for over three decades. Her name is synonymous with the stage. She is a mother figure for generations of young people to whom she bestowed a love of performing. She put thousands of youngsters on the stage. Today Eileen and her team teach speech, drama, dancing and singing to the children of former pupils. She calls them all her 'family'. That affection is genuine. For the children under her wing, to be in the Montforts is simply part of growing up in Cork, as natural to them as the daily ritual of school or sport. It is a way of life. And that's the way it's always been. They will tread the boards of the CAT Club, Everyman or Opera House and make their mammies and daddies proud as punch, even if they do fluff a few lines. 'I've always felt that I could relate particularly to the younger children,' she says. 'In the CAT Club last night I could feel that the children were drawn to me even though some of them had not met me. I could see it in their eyes looking over at me if they needed a little bit of help.'

Pantomime brings out the best in the children both on and off the stage. 'To watch children in the audience at a pantomime is unbelievable because they take it so seriously,' she says. 'Even in the CAT Club, where the panto production is much smaller than the Opera House, some children will come out and sit in the bar with their mummies because they're afraid of the giant or the witch. Sometimes they won't go back inside. They think this is real. We tell them that the good will always win over the bad. When we explain that to them they don't feel too bad. They love talking back too. We had a sponge fight this year and everyone had great fun throwing sponges at the giant and knocking him out. They clapped and cheered when the giant was beaten. The children are still as good today as when I started the Montforts. People talk about kids becoming more precocious, sophisticated and maturing earlier. They're still wonderful to work with. The innocence is still there. Pantomime is a tradition that will never die.'

There is a treasure trove of funny stories. Eileen was once intrigued to watch a small boy, dressed as a mouse, about to walk on stage carrying a detached tail in his hands. When she asked the boy about the tail, he replied: 'My mommy told me I'm not supposed to wear my tail because the cat bit it off.'

Every show has its memorable moments. Things can and do go wrong. On the opening night of *Mame* at the Opera House, the curtain swished open across the stage and broke all the glasses on a cocktail cabinet. 'It seemed disastrous at the time but we got over it,' recalls Eileen.

A love of music and the theatre was fostered by her parents. Eileen's father, James O'Brien, was involved in the Fr Matthew pantomime company at a time when six or seven pantos were staged in the city. She was the eldest of five daughters and grew up with their father going off to rehearsals. Sundays were special during panto season when the cast regularly visited their home. 'It was really terrific,' she recalls, 'because we were getting the stars into our house. My home was driven by a love of music and theatre, so it was the only road I could take.' Eileen's mother, Frances, was leader of the Cork Symphony Orchestra and gave music and drama lessons. She followed in her mother's footsteps and joined the Symphony Orchestra; she played with the orchestra at symphony concerts and the ballet for six years. She decided to join a dramatic group. She trained as a speech and drama teacher and qualified with Trinity College, London, and also holds an Irish diploma from Sion Hill. Although she had played violin with the orchestra, 'my vision was to be up there on the stage rather than down in the orchestra'.

Then Cupid's arrow struck her during drama shows at the old CYMS in Cork. 'Tony was a member of the gramophone circle at the CYMS and also involved with backstage. I saw him standing at the back of the hall with a lovely dog,' says Eileen. She got to know the owner and they went to various dog shows together. She bought Tony his first German Shepherd and he bought her a poodle. They were married on 22 July, 1959.

Eileen was teaching the girls of South Presentation Convent and developed choral verse-speaking groups. She fused into one unit two groups – the girls of South Pres and boys of Presentation College. Under her direction each group had won awards at feiseanna in Cork and Dublin. She brought them together to perform as a mixed choral verse group at the Cork Choral Festival in 1962, and for years afterwards they were the only choral verse group at the festival.

They travelled to festivals in England and also began to make a name for themselves in concerts at home. The big turning point came on 26 July, 1964, when they performed in a concert for the nuns at the Mercy Convent in Rosscarbery. After the verse speaking, the nuns called for a song to keep the show going and the group broke into *'Don't Let The Rain Come Down'*. Michael Casey produced those early efforts, and the notion of a singing group was conceived under his musical direction. They were christened, appropriately, after the name of Eileen's house, Montfort. 'I had drama classes, speech classes, choral verse and now we began the singing with Michael,' says Eileen. 'As well as doing the schools I started classes as well.'

The Montforts would become her family in every sense. 'I love children. I knew I couldn't have a family before I was married. I said to myself, "are you going to sit down under this and moan about it or are you going to do something about it?" Tony was with me all the way and very supportive. We just decided that this is what I was going to do in life. Thank God it's worked out.'

The Montforts' theatrical chapter opened in 1965 when they did a revue at the Fr Matthew Hall. When the new Opera House opened a small group of Montforts – five boys and five girls – provided a chorus for *The Jack Cruise Show*. They were busy doing the chorus for two of the city's pantos by Christmas '66: *Red Riding Hood* at the Fr Matthew Hall and *Cinderella* at the Opera House. Every year since, the Montforts have been part of the Opera House panto. Through the pantos the Montforts worked with some well-known names in showbusiness including Tony Kenny, Billy Boyle, Angela Farrell, Alma Carroll and Sandie Jones. Locally, there would be lasting friendships with Billa O'Connell, Paddy Comerford and the inimitable Cha and Miah, Frank Duggan and Michael Twomey, all of whom were gifted showmen and wrapped in the affections of Cork people. Everybody loves Billa, who first tread the boards in *Cinderella* at the old Father O'Leary Hall on the Bandon road in 1948. He has played a dame ever since, and panto is his life. The funnyman donned the robes of academia in the summer of '96 when he was awarded an honarary MA at UCC in recognition of his contribution to the theatrical life of the city. For Cork people everywhere, Billa is truly one of their 'own', and cherished.

The story is told about a group of Scottish tourists who were staying at the Imperial Hotel and who wanted a good night's entertainment. They asked the hotel porter to suggest a show in town. They were delighted to hear him say that 'Billy Connolly' was appearing in cabaret at Jury's Hotel on the Western Road. After finding front row seats in the hotel's cabaret room, they were surprised to see a stranger walk out on stage. There was no sign of Billy Connolly. One of the Scots turned to a local man seated next to him and asked: 'Where's Billy?' The Corkman couldn't understand what all the fuss was about and said: 'Sure that's him ... Billa ... that's our Billa.'

Two loveable characters, Cha and Miah, came to symbolise Cork, just like the Montforts. These Leeside philosophers have been advising the nation ever since Twomey borrowed his office porter's cap and coat and became 'Miah' for a street interview on RTÉ's Newsbeat programme in 1969. Twomey was partnered by Frank Duggan who became Cha, his sidekick, and the Cork pair with attitude had a regular spot on Hall's Pictorial Weekly. They were first to christen Jack Lynch 'the Real Taoiseach'. And he was their No. 1 fan. Invariably, when either Twomey or Duggan are recognised on the streets of Cork, each one is referred to by both names. 'Look, there's Cha and Miah' becomes the familiar remark when either one is spotted. After sculptures of two characters peering skywards were installed outside the County Hall, people dubbed them the 'Cha and Miah' statues in their honour.

The Montforts also came under the influence of an English producer, Jimmy Belchamber, who first got them to move and sing at the same time and who cultivated individual talents. The Montforts did a lot of work with the late Jack Cruise at The Opera House. Jack Cruise and Maureen Potter were household names in the '60s – two panto greats. The Montforts were the first amateur group allowed to work with Cruise's professional company in Cork. Eileen Nolan remembers him as a formidable, strict performer. 'He was a perfectionist,' she says. 'He was a funny man on the stage but quite a serious man off the stage. There was no way that he would allow anything to happen on stage that wasn't fully disciplined or prepared. Everything had to be just right. He wasn't grumpy, but he wasn't the funny man all the time.'

The Montforts began a five-year association in 1967 with *The Swans Shows* and the gang from Bridewell Lane. *The Swans Of The Lee* shows, billed as 'a riot of laughter, song and dance', attracted a huge following at the Opera House. When they went into the Swans as a chorus, their lack of experience showed. They got a ticking off from theatre critic, Robert O'Donoghue, who wrote a Saturday night review in the *Evening Echo*. 'We'd wait in fear and trepidation because his reviews were always quite sharp,' says Eileen. 'We all accepted that the man knew what he was talking about. His columns were always good and we learned from him. After one of our first shows he said the Montforts sounded beautiful but looked like Bo Peep searching for sheep because we didn't know how to move. From there on I decided to do something about that.' Eileen wanted a group that could dance and sing. 'We moved into dancing because I figured that if one had to run a stage school, one could not be true to the meaning of a stage school unless you had singing, dancing and drama.'

While busy with the Montforts, Eileen was also teaching in schools. 'When I started first as a teacher I was wandering around for an hour here and an hour there. I swore that if I were to do something with the business I would have to give jobs to people that would be worthwhile. I would employ them rather than they doing what I had to do for years, going around begging for an hour. When I started I used to work for an hour in Lismore, an hour in Cappoquin and an hour back again in Lismore.'

She had a profound influence on a new generation in the '60s. She was known as an elocution teacher, travelling to schools in the city and county, entering her pupils in local feiseanna and even directing them in school plays. One of the boys at Turner's Cross national school who came under her spell would end up in Hollywood as an internationally-acclaimed film designer.

'I think Eileen Nolan is the reason I'm here today,' says Bob Crowley, who designed the Oscar-nominated movie, *The Crucible*, starring Daniel Day Lewis. 'No one ever tried to spot talent until she came along. Every Wednesday afternoon, she would waft in wearing brilliantly bright clothes, exuding colour, glamour, perfume, even sex, only I didn't know it then. It was like Joan Collins entering a nunnery. This hour with Mrs Nolan cost a penny and it was the best penny's worth ever spent. She gave us an alternative to the drudgery, the routine, the artistic deprivation.' Bob Crowley made it into the bigtime as a set designer: he has designed numerous productions for the Royal Shakespeare Company, the Royal National Theatre and Covent Garden; operas and ballets in every major theatre and opera house in Britain and Europe; and now Hollywood movies. Crowley has also won numerous Olivier and Tony awards.

Meantime, Michael Casey had stayed with the Montforts until he went to RTÉ in 1967 but remained available to write arrangements. Cathal Dunne took over, later going to Dublin to further his career in composing and recording. In 1971, there was another milestone for the group: they were asked to join the cast of the *Summer Revels*. The Montforts were 'bookends' to each half of the programme with their own 'spesh' in the second half. Michael Twomey, producer of *Summer Revels*, recalls memorable scenes down through the years including the Scottish scene in 1973, the Hollywood scene in 1977, *Rhapsody in Blue* in 1978, the Cockney scene in 1981, *42nd Street* in 1982 and the Junior Montforts in *Oliver* in 1979 and *Annie* in 1980. 'Each year some fine individual talents emerged,' he says. 'Not only did they do their own thing but several Monts appeared successfully in many sketches.' They sang and worked with Dave McInerney, Billa O'Connell, Paddy Comerford, Marie Twomey and Cha and Miah. It was through *The Revels* that the Montforts met two other valued friends – London choreographer Larry Oaks who arrived for *The Revels* of 1975 and also Ronnie O'Shaughnessy who joined as musical director in 1973. Michael Twomey fondly recalls the Montforts' presentation of *The Wizard of Oz* in the Opera House at Easter in 1973. The producer was Jimmy Belchamber with choreography by the late Joan Denise Moriarty; guest artists in leading roles included Dave McInerney, Paddy Comerford, Dan Coughlan and Elaine Stephens. 'As a show, *The Wizard of Oz* has often been described as pure magic and in the hands of the Montforts that's exactly what it was,' says Twomey.

The Montforts' American connection began in 1972 when the Little Theatre of Jefferson City, under the direction of Fr John Long, arrived in the Opera House to stage the modern musical, *How To Succeed In Business Without Really Trying*, which the Montforts were invited to augment. 'We really felt so awful, like country cousins,' says Eileen. 'These were young Americans who had tremendous experience in make-up and hairstyles and everything else. We learned a lot from them.' In 1978 the Montforts were invited to Jefferson city to rehearse *Pippin* for presentation in the Opera House. Fr Long was a 'hard task master'. When Eileen decided the Montforts should tackle the daunting job of producing *West Side Story* in the Opera House, Fr Long and choreographer Ed Wesley offered a helping hand. They followed with *Hello Dolly* in 1980 and *Oklahoma* in 1981, with Fr Long again as producer. The following year, the Montforts made a return trip to the US – this time for song and dance classes.

Through these years the Montforts were a versatile bunch of performers. They did radio programmes from the Cork RTÉ studios as well as TV adverts; made a record; performed at Blackrock Castle banquets and in concerts around the country; sang at weddings and performed in two films – a promotional project for B & I Line and the Montforts formed the main body of extras for an RTÉ television production of the Frank O'Connor Story.

They had made their TV debut on *Reach for the Stars* in 1972. The long list of TV credits included Tony Kenny's Christmas Show in 1977; a TV show from the Opera House for the opening of RTÉ2 in 1978; the highlight of TV work was in the *Rock Nativity* in 1980 starring Tony Kenny and Johnny Logan, with music by Tony Hatch and Jackie Trent and choreography by Larry Oaks. In 1986, the Montforts performed their first concert at the National Concert Hall, with the National Concert Orchestra and soloists Austin Gaffney and Joan Merrigan. They returned to the Concert Hall on two occasions. It was also the year they staged their first production of *Camelot* at the Opera House. The big shows were expensive because they had to pay for the choreographers and musical directors. The Montforts staged smaller productions at the School of Music such as *An Evening with Cole Porter and Broadway*. The shows continued into the '90s with *Annie*, *The Best Little Whorehouse in Texas*, and Jurys Cabarets. Eileen says two of her best shows were *Camelot* and *West Side Story* at the Opera House.

Yet, whatever the highlights over the years, she knows that 'in this business you're only as good as your last show. What's gone is forgotten. What matters is the present.' The Christmas Panto continues to capture the young imaginations, both on and off the stage. It means months of practice and, of course, a great commitment from parents during panto season.

Today, the Montforts reach communities throughout Cork city and county. Speech, drama, song and dance is taught in studios at Ballincollig, Ballyvolane, Blackrock, Carrigaline, Carrignavar, Clonakilty, Douglas, Fermoy, Empress Place, Leitrim Street, Mallow, Midleton, Wilton and Turner's Cross. There is a nursery school in Ballyvolane. In addition, Eileen and her team of 12 teachers teach speech and drama in 15 primary and secondary schools. There are junior, intermediate and senior performance classes in the Montforts representing the best talents drawn from her network of studios. 'Some people who come to dance classes will never make accomplished dancers but they just want to be involved,' says Eileen. 'That's fine and we always encourage them. But if you want to have performance classes then obviously you have to pick the best from the studios. So these students have a second class in the week where we work on their performance. You have an overall group that would be better than your normal dance class. They are used in the dance week at the Opera House, for special displays and the Opera House pantomime.'

While the heart of Cork beats to a different tune, the army of Montforts are put through their paces in the studios. The outside world is forgotten – temporarily at least. 'This is something the children love,' says Eileen. 'It's a positive thing and makes for good citizens. I worry when I hear a parent say, "well, she can't come this year because she's going into first year". I believe they are taking away something that's very special to the children. After all, with drama or sport you're training children how to cope with leisure time. I feel that if their leisure time is taken care of by something that they really love then they're not going to get into trouble. When their exams are finished they don't know what to do and can be led astray. Sometimes I feel quite sad about that.'

Nobody can ever predict what path in life former Montforts will take. The 'extended family' is littered with success stories: those who pursued professional stage careers in Ireland or abroad; those who went on to assume leadership positions in society; those who simply became good citizens and good parents themselves later on.

It is a source of great pride to see former Montforts achieve success professionally: some have made it to London West End Shows such as *Les*

Misérables, *CATS*, *Phantom of the Opera* and *Guys and Dolls*; others are teaching or directing in America, Europe and the Middle East. By chance, Eileen switched on BBC TV Gershwin Night while at home one night in Ballyvolane to discover a former pupil, Michael McCarthy, singing in the finale. Former Montforts keep in contact from all over the world. 'On Christmas Eve, my phone starts ringing at 2 p.m. and doesn't stop until about 3 a.m. on Christmas morning,' she says. 'They are my family. They are all wonderful.' Eileen was proud as punch when two of her students – Elaine Symons and Norma Sheehan – passed auditions and won coveted places at the Royal Academy of Dramatic Art (RADA) in 1997.

In spite of all the accolades, Eileen never pursued huge commercial success in the way that *The Riverdance* concept was translated into a mini-industry. There was no grand game plan to conquer the world stage. 'Of course, it would have been nice to have had a *Riverdance* show and go to Broadway,' she says. 'I have no regrets. I went where my roads took me. Remember, I never went out to achieve all of this. I just went with what seemed right at the time; if it worked, well and good, if it didn't, then too bad. I'd have loved to have made it to Broadway. But we did play in America. I've always felt that if we went into the professional theatre, it might take away the kind of family relationships that I've worked on through the years. If we did go into the business professionally, we would have lost some of this. If you go professional, then it's got to become a tougher business and you're going to hurt people ... the iron fist in the velvet glove. I always think of people's feelings. I wouldn't like to hurt anybody.'

Her life has revolved around theatre, teaching and children. That's the way it's always been, and that's the way it's going to continue. In the stage school, she is delighted to have raised the standard of dancing to the same level as speech and drama. But there's still a lot more to achieve. For one thing, she dreams of having 'a really beautiful custom-built studio in the city where we could all be together with all the classes and wardrobe, costumes and everything under one roof'. The school is currently divided into a number of locations across the city.

Eileen scoffs at the idea of retirement. It's a life of deadlines, first night nerves and challenges. She is also on the board of the Cork Opera House. 'I couldn't imagine myself sitting around doing nothing,' she says. 'I'd get itchy feet if I wasn't with the kids or working on a project. I probably do too much and there never seems to be enough hours in the day.' A few years ago, Eileen and Tony built a house overlooking the sea at Courtmacsherry in West Cork; it is their little piece of heaven. They relax there in the company of close friends, particularly the McCarthy and

Adams families. Looking back, she has no regrets, apart from never mastering the piano. Cork's First Lady of Theatre would like to be remembered 'as someone who was very caring, helped as many people as I could and who brought happiness to everyone'.

For the Montforts, the theatre lights will never dim as long as young imaginations are fired by the excitement of drama and as long as there are wicked witches, evil queens, hungry wolves and fearsome giants to be slain.

NOEL C. DUGGAN

GOOD EVENING, MILLSTREET!

'GOOD evening, Millstreet ...' There was high drama in the Green Glens Arena: a fairytale script for Dublin bank official Niamh Kavanagh who sang her way into the hearts of Europe with *In Your Eyes*. Ireland were on course for a fifth Eurovision crown. The UK entrant, Sonia, singing *Better The Devil You Know*, had threatened to spoil the party. In the end, the result hung on the votes from Malta, the last of 25 national juries to give their verdict. Niamh needed only 2 points to win. But if the host country failed to score and the UK got the top score of 12 points then the winner would be Liverpool's Sonia. The Maltese jury sealed the fairytale: 12 points for Ireland and 0 for the UK.

One image captured the elation of that incredible Saturday night in Millstreet on 15 May, 1993: the sight of Noel C. Duggan raising his arms in victory and hugging the then Taoiseach Albert Reynolds amid a background chorus of Ireland's World Cup anthem, *Olé, Olé, Olé*. Noel C had confounded the critics to bring the Eurovision song contest to his showjumping arena. And we won.

A lot of things could have gone wrong, but mercifully didn't. Noel says he's always scared whenever he gets his teeth into a big project. That's a good thing, though. His grandfather, Andrew, a great businessman, used to say you must have confidence in yourself to achieve anything but you must always have sufficient doubt in your confidence to ensure that you achieve it.

Noel was certainly scared during Eurovision week. So scared that he had a recurring nightmare about the 12,000 screws in the roof of the arena, which had been built only two years previously. Some of the screws would pop and, with a heavy shower, rain drops would seep through the roof and fall on presenter Fionnuala Sweeney before a TV audience of 300 million. 'I had that nightmare for ages,' he recalls. 'I could see it vividly. If any of the screws popped or if any were missing and a hole was left and if it rained like hell, the water would come down on the stage on Fionnuala. The press would have a ball out of it.' The nightmare threatened to become real during voting on the big night when a hailshower struck Green Glens. Noel nudged his wife, Maureen, and said: 'Oh, my God.' It was a close call: the heavy rain didn't fall until after midnight when the show was over. Sure enough, on the following morning, he checked and found a few drops around the stage area.

Although Noel says he's not a particularly religious man, he believes that his 'humble connection with the Almighty' brought him through Eurovision and other 'cliff-edge' enterprises. His faith is strong: what he calls a straight line to the Man Himself and the Mother of God. His mother once taught him a prayer that he's amended to suit his purposes. It ends by asking God for protection against tragedy, disaster and enemies. Noel recited the prayer several times a day during the run-up to Eurovision. 'When the real pressure is on,' he says, 'I would go into a room, put off the light and close the door and talk things out with God.' On other occasions, in times of trouble, he has prayed aloud when the arena is filled with sound and nobody can hear him. He set the stage for heavy rockers *Pearl Jam* shortly after a Co. Cork schoolgirl was crushed to death at a *Smashing Pumpkins* concert at the Point Depot in Dublin in May 1996. 'We were very worried, scared of our lives.' He was on the frontline handing out water across the barriers to the young people. 'I was praying all night long out loud to myself.'

In spite of all the begrudgers, *Eurovision '93* was a master stroke for Noel C, Millstreet and rural Ireland. It all started when he watched Linda Martin sing *Why Me?*, the winning song at *Eurovision '92* from Sweden. At home in Millstreet, he took an envelope from the mantlepiece and wrote to RTÉ, offering his arena free of rent. For a while it was regarded as a standing joke; the Dublin 4 brigade dismissed Millstreet's claim as impertinence. As soon as Noel C made up his mind that he wanted Eurovision '93, 'hell or high water wasn't going to stop me'. He had to fight his way 'through *The Marian Finucane Show*, *The Pat Kenny Show*, all the other radio stations, the D4 outfit and the rag newspapers up there'. After his letter to Montrose, there was no reply for two months. He was frustrated by the delay. It was the impossible dream – or so it seemed to everybody except Noel C. Duggan.

There is a smile and glint in the eye as he recalls that David versus Goliath battle. He says he was spurred on after a Dublin journalist challenged him on *The Marian Finucane Show* about the inadequacies of Millstreet: the twist handle telephone, the local garda station closing at six o'clock and insufficient electricity generation. RTÉ would need fibre optic cable, said the journalist – but Noel had never heard of it. He decided to secure agreement from all relevant agencies on everything that needed to be done if RTÉ gave him the nod for Eurovision.

To take the contest outside Dublin for the first time would be a huge gamble. Noel had the perfect answer for those misgivings. He reminded RTÉ it was the same distance from Dublin to Millstreet, 170 miles, as from Millstreet to Dublin 'and we do it all the time and don't make any big deal about it'. He recalls: 'RTÉ were putting all these things before me, saying "we can't because ..." I was getting them all wiped off the list one by one. Maybe people like the ESB and CIE were agreeing to everything because they thought I wouldn't get Eurovision.' Millstreet railway station was given the second longest platform in Ireland outside Dublin. The final obstacle in his path was the stage: a set of 2,500 square feet, made of polycarbonate, underlit by thousands of zig-zagging lamps, 95 feet across and sloping up to 38 feet. RTÉ told him their set had been designed and his roof wasn't high enough. They needed four feet under the stage to accommodate the lighting. 'I have the plan for that,' said Noel. 'We'll dig out four feet out of the ground.' RTÉ had 'no more excuses but they kept us on tenderhooks until the very last moment'.

He got the first inkling from Gay Byrne during October '92. 'Before RTÉ told me definitively, Gay was on to me and asked if I would be ready to do a radio programme. He had Joe Duffy down here for a link-up. That was before it was announced. Liam Miller, the Eurovision executive producer, rang me up and said they were coming down to make the official announcement to the press.' It had been a 'hard battle' with Miller, whom he describes as a great professional and a friend for life. He says he will always be grateful to Miller, to the then Director General Joe Barry and every member of the RTÉ Authority. The local population of 1,500 embraced Eurovision enthusiastically. One local wag, thrilled with RTÉ like everyone else in town, remarked that they had the 'neck of a tractor tyre' to choose Millstreet.

Noel C. Duggan and his team had a seven-month countdown to make it all happen. He laid down some markers. First, he didn't want the international juries saying 'Good evening, Dublin' or 'Good evening, Ireland' – rather, it had to be 'Good evening, Millstreet'. Second, he wanted a horse theme in the opening film sequence, which proved to be a stunning curtain-raiser. Third, he suggested a mountain dance concept for the centre-piece, given the historical significance of Sliabh Luachra in the locality. His own ancestors had come down from the mountain during the Famine. However, producer Liam Miller said there wasn't enough time to develop that concept. Instead, former Eurovision winners Linda Martin and Johnny Logan filled the interval slot, with Johnny joined on stage by the junior and senior students of Cork School of Music. Noel is convinced to this day that his mountain dance idea sowed the seeds for the Riverdance act at *Eurovision '94* in the Point.

The scale of the operation began to dawn on them, 'because up to then we were taking it all a bit in our strides'. Yet, in many ways RTÉ found relatively little difficulty in staging the contest at Green Glens because the complex was ready and waiting for them. Millstreet already had a world-class facility on its doorstep. And it was already cosmopolitan. For years, Noel had been developing international showjumping in the town. Indeed, he says that bringing the first international horse show to Millstreet in 1979 was actually harder to achieve than Eurovision. The five-acre covered equestrian centre, including the main two-acre arena, would have been capable of hosting an indoor All-Ireland hurling final. Staging an international showjumping event of huge logistical proportions made the song contest seem like a piece of cake – well, almost. For Eurovision the jumping arena had to be transformed into a giant television studio. It was a superb technological feat for RTÉ. And there was certainly no electricity shortage, 'we got the power connected from Whitegate and Tarbert and around the building here; enough to blow up the whole town it was so strong'.

Amid all the hype, the transformation of a town was taking place; a community galvanised into action to show the rest of rural Ireland what could be achieved. There was a minor controversy two days before showtime when BBC newsman Nicholas Witchell compared the Green Glens complex to a cowshed. Witchell later wrote a letter of apology to Noel. The best 'apology' though came in the form of a 12-point voting boost from the UK jury for Niamh Kavanagh. The Irish win after a nerve-jangling finale launched the greatest party ever seen in the town.

'You'll only beat that if Jack Charlton wins the World Cup with the Irish team,' exclaimed Albert Reynolds. Ever since, tens of thousands of people visit Green Glens to see for themselves where it all happened. '*Eurovision* was an awful thing for us to suggest and a terrible thing for RTÉ to agree to but it worked out brilliantly in the end,' reflects Noel.

Eurovision '93 confirmed Noel C. Duggan as the champion of rural Ireland and Millstreet as its model of inspiration. Former Taoiseach Jack Lynch, who was among the 3,500-strong audience at Green Glens, told him in a letter afterwards that the *Eurovision* achievement 'will be a personal monument to you'. Four years on, his mailbag remains heavy with letters of praise, poems written in his honour and invitations to speak to rural communities around the country. These are all kept in his office at Green Glens.

The gospel according to Noel C is that if it can be done in Millstreet it can be done anywhere. He likes to quote a Chinese proverb that the longest journey begins with the first step. Rural Ireland is neglected by Dublin. 'But I don't blame Dublin,' he says. 'I blame ourselves. A lot of towns and villages are asleep. They're afraid. They think it's their rightful place in life to be dilapidated, to be neglected and to have the potholes. They're rising up now. More than anybody will ever know, Millstreet has given the message loud and clear to all rural Ireland and even to small communities in inner cities. The people must get up off their backsides, believe in themselves and go get it. Everything is going into Dublin. You only have to drive to Dublin to see all the money that's being spent on the roads. The money has been coming from the European Community and diverted to Dublin where the majority of the votes are. There is an old saying that little people in big places can make it difficult for big people in little places. For instance, a mickey mouse civil servant behind a big desk in a big job in Dublin can see Millstreet, Macroom, Cahirciveen or Claremorris or wherever and he can draw a line across it and say "that doesn't matter". But if the decision is about Newlands Cross or Clondalkin it might be passed straight away. I've found a lot of that through my life. This town was so quiet fifteen years ago you could play a score of bowls on the street and you'd affect nobody. It's quite amazing what's happened to Millstreet.'

The revitalisation of Millstreet was a personal crusade, driven by his own strong sense of identity and family history. *Eurovision* left Millstreet with new shopfronts, better roads and a new pride. The local community council has achieved more than any other statutory council in the land.

Eurovision was never going to be an end in itself. Two years later came another fairytale Irish victory at Green Glens. This time the eyes of the world were on bigtime boxing as Noel set the stage for the WBO super middleweight championship between Steve Collins and Chris Eubank. Noel C had pursued a major boxing event with characteristic zeal. He had tried to get a big fight after hearing about the collapse of a programme in Hong Kong. He failed in that bid but had better luck when he turned in a different direction. He convinced British promoter Barry Hearn to take the Eubank-Collins fight to a town of less than 1,500. 'I had very little trouble talking Barry into this,' he remarks. 'All I had to do was get him here; convince him that he should come. My venue did the talking. He arrived in Cork airport at ten past twelve and he was here at ten past one. At ten past two he was convinced.'

Next, mighty Sky Sports plugged the world into Green Glens for a two-hour live telecast. Collins delivered the fairytale script and outboxed Eubank to take the title in another dream finale for the Irish. Noel C relished the excitement: he stood just outside the ropes as 8,000 people roared themselves hoarse. When the fight ended he jumped into the ring and said to the Irishman, 'Steve, I think you've won it.' Collins replied: 'Noel, I know I've won it. Now what about a pony for my kids.' Later, Noel C was mobbed by people congratulating him; it was as if he had won the title himself. Someone remarked it was toss-up whether Noel C and Millstreet combined got more publicity than Collins himself.

The business philosophy is blissfully simple: calculated risk-taking, common sense, a reliance on gut feeling and thinking fast on your feet. Albert Reynolds once played by the same rules to build a ballroom empire and house the showband explosion. 'I've often sailed close to the wind,' says Noel. 'I've often tread in dangerous grounds like a fool where a wise man wouldn't go. But to do what I've done and where I've done it you have to take chances.'

Noel C sailed close to the wind on many occasions since he started a Sunday Gymkhana in 1973 that grew to become an annual international outdoor show by 1979 which lured stars like Harvey Smith, David Broome, Eddie Macken and the Whitaker brothers to Millstreet. A love of horses is in his blood, going back six generations. It all started when he bought a promising show jumper who was difficult to handle. Iris Kellet suggested he should send the horse to the British rider, Harvey Smith. Noel C made the call. 'Chuck him in a wagon and send him across to Liverpool,' said Harvey, and a lifelong friendship had begun. 'Harvey has done more for Millstreet than any person alive,' says Noel C.

The Millstreet Horse Show was the realisation of a dream: Noel C and his friend, the late Captain Austin Woulfe, then head of the Equestrian Federation of Ireland, wanted to stage an international event outside Dublin. After the first show, Noel C went further to persuade the International Equestrian Federation to stage the European Junior Show Jumping Championships in Millstreet. 'After six months, I got a call one day and they said, "you have your wish",' he recalls. 'I remember putting down the phone and saying to myself, "what in the name of God am I going to do now?" There was no hotel, no guest houses. I didn't have a fine indoor venue like today. There were no toilets on the grounds worth talking about. We had nowhere to host the opening reception for 16 nations.' Noel C turned to the people: the community council set up a sub-committee that met every Saturday night in his home. *Match of the Day* was switched off the television while they drank tea and made preparations. The town was given a facelift. Accommodation for 500 guests was organised in local homes. Millstreet Community School, located beside the showgrounds, was converted into a temporary hotel with beds provided by the army. The horses were stabled in nearby farms. 'That was the most incredible thing that had ever happened in Millstreet,' he reflects. 'That was even more acute than Eurovision when it came. You see, by the time Eurovision came around we had put a lot of big things behind us from a very low beginning.' Noel C told everyone: 'The best is yet to come'. He meant it.

The shows were now generating invaluable publicity for the town, and the community wisely exploited the potential to attract industry and create indigenous jobs. The first Millstreet show attracted 150 people and 50 horses. Today, the event draws up to 25,000 people and 2,000 horses and ponies. It attracts riders from four continents and 20 countries.

Noel C had to think fast on his feet one day in August 1983 at Shannon Airport when a dozen horses from Libya were loaded onto boxes for the journey to the show at Millstreet. The Libyan party included riders keen to get international experience, led by Colonel Ali Futuri who was a friend of Libyan leader Gadaffi. 'There had been a great buzz for days before as word spread that Gadaffi's horses were jumping in Millstreet,' he recalls. A rumour even went around that the Libyan leader might turn up. However, the Libyans' arrival nearly turned sour when they got bogged down in a dispute with customs officials at Shannon. Col Futuri was threatening to stop the Libyan plane from being loaded with meat for export and also threatening to fly back to Tripoli with his party. Noel C overheard the argument, and decided to act quickly. He slipped out of the terminal building and told his men to head for Millstreet with the horses. By the time the dispute was being sorted out the horses were already crossing the Limerick-Cork borders. The Libyans went on to compete at the show, and Col Futuri praised the warmth of the Irish and the friendship of Millstreet.

The lowest point was undoubtedly the fire that destroyed part of the equestrian centre during a summer show in 1987. Once again, it was time for some fast-thinking. Noel C was woken by the gardai who called to his home in the early hours. 'They told me to come quickly, the place was on fire.' Flames were shooting high into the dawn sky. There was panic everywhere. The visitors, who were staying in caravans and tents on the grounds, let loose 370 horses to escape the flames and some were later recovered up to 27 miles away.

'I remember walking around that morning in an awful state,' he says. 'I was everywhere. I put on some clothes over my pyjamas. I was all wet from the fire hoses. I remember saying, "Oh God, why did you do this to me?" I thought this was the end for sure.' The fire started at 4.45 a.m. after chip pans, left on overnight, blew up. By 7 a.m., some 20,000 sq feet of buildings were reduced to rubble including offices, restaurants, bars and trade stands, in spite of the best efforts of five fire brigades. By 7.30 a.m., Noel C was on the phone to the then Minister for Defence, Paddy Power. He told him: 'Minister, it's a national disaster, I want the army field kitchens.' By 10.20 a.m., the army were cooking breakfast in the grounds. All the horses were collected and returned.

The outdoor competition went ahead – just three minutes late. The Duggan family and a group of locals surveyed the damage, went away and prefabricated a new building which was delivered, erected and sheeted in time for the indoor event at 7 p.m. that evening with 30,000 visitors in attendance. The day, and the show, had been saved.

Noel C had triumphed over adversity. Now he doggedly pursued grants over the next three years to create a world class centre for the non-thoroughbred Irish horse. 'I was fighting the system to get grant aided for a horse-breeding, training and marketing station as an alternative farm enterprise. I had to go to Brussels to get grants and Brussels had to tell Ireland to support this project.' The result was a £4.5 million pounds complex including an indoor arena complete with seating for over 5,000 people, restaurants, hospitality boxes, corporate entertainment and trade stands area. The complex also boasts the longest bar in Ireland at 100 metres. The indoor arena extended the showjumping season into the winter by accommodating indoor shows.

By 1993, the complex was home to two international horse shows a year. The indoor arena is the jewel in the crown; purpose built for showjumping but easily adapted to other uses. The Green Glens complex has been described as an astonishing monument to the horse. It also includes an advisory service, laboratories, breeding advice, breaking and training facilities and marketing services. Noel C wanted to improve the blood lines of the Irish non-thoroughbred horse. He invested large sums of money in half-breeds. The showjumping attracts buyers for horses bred in the area. He's a good judge of equine stock and mixes easily with the farmer breeders and rich Arab horse buyers. The story of how he bred Mill Pearl from a supposedly barren mare about to be sent to the slaughter is legendary. Mill Pearl went on to compete in the US equestrian team which won a silver medal at the 1988 Seoul Olympics, and subsequently valued at £2 million.

It is a story of Home Town Boy Makes Good in a Big Way. The kind of rags-to-riches script that would do justice to any soap opera or hero movie. It goes like this: Five generations ago, during the 1840s famine, Noel's great grandfather, Cornelius Duggan, with his four sons and their 16 horses, moved from Sliabh Luachra on the Cork-Kerry border to work on the railway line being built to connect Dublin and Kerry. Sliabh Luachra was a place of poets and musicians and some of the longest-living people in the world. Cornelius – endower of the C in Noel's name – set up the general hardware and builders' providers store in 1851. One of the sons, Andrew, Noel's grandfather, got the idea of using horses to transport goods and passengers to and from the new railway station which had the advantage of being on the main road between Cork and Kerry.

Andrew, who married late in life, took on the business; he sold wine and spirits and had the agency for a fearsome brew called The Bandon Wrestler. He lived to the age of 97. 'I was my grandfather's favourite,' says Noel C. 'I was to be his follower, the hardware merchant. The seeds that he sowed in me are only being harvested now.' The Duggans flourished. Millstreet flourished too; a town on the butter route, along which dairy produce went from Kerry to the butter market in Cork.

Back in those early days Millstreet was overshadowed by the legacy of landlordism in the form of four estates that surrounded the town. The arrival of the motor car in the '20s sounded the death knell for the horse: Millstreet died with the horse. From being the pivot of goods traffic from Kerry to the port of Cork, it was turned into a desolate island in the '20s when two main thoroughfares were constructed – 10 miles to the south on one side and five miles to the north on the other. There were 20-30 outstanding businesses there at the time; 'those families were better off than the merchants of Cork but they sat in their glory and allowed the town to die'.

'The town slept for 50 years,' says Noel, who vowed to become its saviour one day. 'We had an old public house and a hardware shop and I used to hear my grandfather talking to the customers and friends from the country who used to come in on market days and fair days, and he used to be lamenting about the great town that Millstreet was up to about 1920 and how it deteriorated. I always had this ambition that one day I would bring the town back to what my grandfather said it was like at the turn of the century and that is what I have done.'

Noel C was born on Christmas Night 1933. He was 13 when his father, Cornelius, died at the age of 47, and the second eldest of 11 children. His father had been running the business. His death was a major upheaval. Noel C left school without sitting an exam to try to support the 17 people living in their home and take over the family's 18-acre farm. 'I learned how to do everything,' he recalls. 'I ploughed with a pair of cobs, grew potatoes, cabbage and carrots, ploughed open drills and I was destined to become a farmer.'

At 15, he sold a third of his stock, a cow and a heifer, got £30 and left home in 1950 to serve his time as an apprentice in the hardware trade at Athleague, Co Roscommon. He had to pay his employer for the privilege of working 12 hours a day for six days every week. His day began at 5 a.m. first exercising the horses belonging to the parish priest, Canon Barney Keane, and then launching into 12-hour working days at the shop. For nearly two years he worked for nothing and ate alone. 'I was 5ft tall and weighed seven stone but I was hardy and I carried 10-stone bags on my back,' he says.

Less than two years later, Noel C returned to Millstreet, suffering from a hernia. By 17, he had taken over his grandfather's business. He borrowed £40 from the bank to set up his hardware enterprise in April 1951. He hired a local pick-up truck for 30 shillings, drove to Cork Iron and Hardware, an old company his grandfather used to deal with, and bought £35 worth of nails and buckets and broom handles. The mission wasn't complete until he went to Leaders in North Main Street and bought a shopcoat. At 7 a.m. next day he put the stock outside on the footpath with a big sign, 'Baths and Buckets Now in Stock'. He had nothing else in stock, 'but whatever they wanted I sent my brother out the back door fast up the town to the other hardware shop to buy it'. Millstreet was a dying backwater, bypassed by the Cork-Killarney road. It wasn't unusual to see 'two rival flocks of geese going from one end of the town to the other'.

When he reopened his grandfather's shop, 'it was looked on by the locals as *Eurovision* was by the Dubs'. Neighbours thought it was doomed to failure. 'They laughed and they scoffed and they mocked and they talked at the corner.' But he says: 'I was successful from day one because the second day was better than the first and the third day was better than the second. I worked like a slave day and night.' He rode seven miles on a bicycle to make his first delivery – 10 rolls of wallpaper. The bicycle was substituted in time by a horse and cart, then a tractor and trailer and then a pick-up truck. Today, he drives a Mercedes. 'In those days it was unusual for a hardware shop to deliver,' he says. 'I bought an old truck and when I closed down at night I would drive around delivering by moonlight. I worked like a slave and the business grew to supply all aspects of farm supplies and hardware.' In 1960 he progressed into farm buildings and graduated into structural steel. A protracted strike in a structural steel company in Co. Carlow brought opportunity; he was asked to supply steel to meet contracts the company had already entered. He decided to begin fabricating his own steel and his structural steel business was born.

That year he met his wife, Maureen Corkery, a nurse, "a lovely red head" from one of the oldest families in the area. She was a 'sound woman and without her none of all this would have happened'.

Gradually over the years, the empire began to take shape; by 1973 Noel C was comfortable in business, so he wanted to do something for Millstreet and to revive the horse industry. He dreamed of one day having the first international horse show outside Dublin. In time, he bought the four 'landed gentry' estates that hemmed the development of Millstreet into a long and narrow corridor and kept the railway station a mile from the town. As long as these four estates remained intact, they would ensure that no development could take place around the town itself. So he decided to buy the four of them. The estates were once 'no-go' areas. 'One could have been shot in the old times on this land,' he says. 'If we came out of school in the evening and played on these grounds there would be a big investigation next day. If you owned up to it you got your backside kicked, and if you didn't own up to it you got your backside kicked anyway.' One day, landlordism would fall under the youngster's hand. One of the former estates is now the Green Glens complex on a spread of 50 acres. He called it Green Glens after his favourite song, *The Green Glens of Antrim*. Drishane Castle was the last of the four estates to fall to Noel C.

The business has expanded over the past quarter of a century to become the most successful in the region. Structural steel is a key part of the business. His 50 horses roam on a 475-acre farm. He insists that all his successes are rooted in his time as a hardware man. 'Without the hardware shop there would be no Green Glens'. The Duggans will celebrate the 150th anniversary of the hardware business in the year 2001. Noel C himself marked 46 years in business on 5 April, 1997. The success story is due to 'hard graft and commitment to a family-run business'. It's a source of pride and joy that the seven companies are wholly owned and run by the Duggan family with no outside shareholders or investors. All four offspring are involved in the businesses. Barry looks after the structural steel business; Martina, Gena and their mother, Maureen, run the hardware side; Thomas and Noel manage the Green Glens and equine interests. As Noel C puts it: 'It's all for one and one for all.' The annual turnover for the companies runs into millions of pounds.

For the man once dubbed Ireland's answer to Ross Perot, the sky is the limit. 'I could get the door of the White House open to me or I could get the door of the Vatican open to me,' he says. 'I've achieved it to the White House.' When Noel C read about President Clinton's upcoming White House Conference for Trade and Investment in Northern Ireland and the border counties of Ireland, taking place in Washington from 24-26 May , 1995, he figured that was the place to be. However, he didn't have an invitation, and couldn't get one. He rang the US Embassy and Department of Foreign Affairs. 'Nobody wanted to know me; this wasn't for somebody from Millstreet.' Frustration mounted when he heard about all the 'experts' going to Washington. From his Green Glens office on the evening of 6 April, he dialled directory enquiries and asked for the White House telephone number. The operator thought he was joking. 'You're six days too late,' she said. 'Fools' Day is gone.' When Noel C insisted, she put her supervisor on the line. 'You're trying to cod us,' she said, but gave him the number eventually. Like a lot of people, Noel C has plenty of friends in high places; but it's what you do with them that counts. He put through a call to Republican Senator John Warner, whom he had hosted at Millstreet during an Irish stopover around the time of the Gulf War. No problem. The invitation came to Noel C within 24 hours.

The rise and rise of Noel C isn't all about making money; his past, present and future revolve around Millstreet and its people. 'I don't want to die a multi-millionaire,' he insists, 'but neither do I want to die in debt. I don't want to fail, so everything I do must be profitable. My grandfather used to say to me, "if you work hard enough at not becoming broke, you've a good chance of becoming a millionaire". Hunger is a great sauce; hunger for achievement and hunger for success. My life isn't about preparing for the stock market. I don't want to be a Kerry Group or Waterford Crystal. For me it's not all about making money. For me it's about resurrecting and revitalising a community that was dead. My crusade was to regenerate the town where my great grandparents had success for many years but died broken hearted because the town had gone down so badly. I'm a man at peace with myself for having achieved that. I wouldn't want to do anything else but what I've done, where I've done it, and the way in which I've done it. That makes me a happy man. When people shake my hand and thank me for what I've done that's worth more to me than a million.'

He is constantly striving to publicise the town, attract attention, visitors and investors. Everything is possible for a rural community if there is an indomitable will. Recognition for his achievements came with an honorary degree from the National University of Ireland; Bord Fáilte made him an honorary ambassador for Ireland; he won People of the Year awards and a clutch of other citations. There are always begrudgers, of course. One begrudger wrote and circulated hate-mail letters during early July, 1995, alleging that he owed money. Noel C was outraged. He says he knows who wrote the letters. 'It was totally malicious and poisonous, done out of jealousy.' He likes to borrow Brendan Behan's blunt message for the begrudgers: 'f them.'

The lifestyle of the Duggans is comfortable rather than extravagant. No jet set frills. 'You'll see no yacht moored for me; no helicopter waiting to take me from A to B. I'll stick to the roots. I don't go sailing or surfing or golfing. My pastime and joy is what I'm doing.' He doesn't see himself as 'a big guy' above anybody else. 'I'm not ashamed to do anything. I'd drive a lorry and deliver a load of steel today if there was nobody else there to do it.' And he means it.

For Green Glens and Millstreet, there are all kinds of national and international events being mooted for the future, one bigger than the next. The credits keep on rolling: from conferences to pop concerts, *Riverdance*, *Disney on Ice*, prestige showjumping, bigtime boxing and conventions. 'Last year 250,000 people came into this building and the nearest traffic light is 22 miles away,' he says with a roguish smile. Noel C is always thinking of new ideas, 'these can come to me while I'm on a plane or when I'm driving a tractor; my mind is always alive with ideas'.

From his early days, he had two secret ambitions: first, to be the greatest gaelic goalkeeper in Ireland and, second, to write a best-selling song. The goalkeeping option was one of few aspirations that went unfulfilled. There's a good song in him, though, waiting to burst forth some day.

The next dream is to develop the local Drishane Convent, a 225-acre property with a spectacular old castle, into a £10 million hotel, health and leisure complex. He bought the convent for £1 million pounds from the Sisters of the Infant Jesus who had a boarding school there. He envisions a hotel, a conference centre, an inter-denominational wedding centre, swimming pools, tennis courts, a world-class golf course and a health and alternative medicine centre. With its own church, Noel C says it will be the first hotel in the country to offer the full package for weddings; couples from around the world can have the ceremony, reception and bed all under the same roof. 'There'll be a landing strip for light aircraft too,' he says, pointing to detailed plans laid out like a military operation on his office desk. 'They'll taxi into here from Heathrow, just a short hop away. A railway line will also take guests to the hotel.' The development is aimed at the Japanese, American and continental European market. 'That's my best and biggest project yet,' he says. 'Once I have that complete, I could bring any kind of event to Millstreet, and not necessarily into the Green Glens Arena. There are no limits to what I could do. My life isn't complete until I have done that. Drishane represents the closing of the circle.' Noel C has an aversion to borrowing and wants to find major investors for the project. 'I wouldn't borrow the money because I couldn't sleep owing that kind of money. I don't want to die prematurely and leave my family with a burden on their backs. So I'll get that job done and when it's up and running I'll have time to breathe.'

Mr Millstreet would like to be remembered 'for what I have done –no more and no less'. His epitaph would read: 'Everybody said it couldn't be done but I did it and did it my way.'

What's more, it was all done under the one roof – Noel C's.

PETER BARRY

GOLDEN MOMENTS

IRON Lady Margaret Thatcher and Corkman Peter Barry had at least one thing in common: they were both the children of grocers. But that's where any common ground ended. The British Premier regarded the Irish Foreign Minister with deep suspicion during the negotiations that led to the signing of the historic Anglo-Irish Agreement in 1985. He says she always regarded him as the 'hard cop' of the Barry-FitzGerald duo. Protocol dictated at Heads of State banquets that Barry was always seated beside Thatcher. He tried to break the ice and turn on the Cork charm many times, but to no avail. 'I was always dying to talk about the grocery trade. She wasn't the least bit interested. I said to her on many occasions, "I'm a grocer's son and you're a grocer's daughter, what problems had ye with the price of sago?" It was no good – she wouldn't bite. It always struck me as very odd that she wouldn't talk about the grocery business.'

The Corkman had memorable encounters with Mrs Thatcher due to his key role in Anglo-Irish relations during the Garret FitzGerald government of 1982-87; he was the primary architect of the Hillsborough Accord, first joint chairman of the Inter-Governmental Conference proposed under the agreement and key player on the New Ireland Forum. 'She had a higher regard for Garret and Dick Spring than for me,' he reflects. 'She had been told, or else formed the impression, that I was an intransigent, unreconstructed fenian. She certainly conveyed that impression to me. I don't think she thought of anybody in terms of liking or disliking. I think she thought in terms of whether they were able to do their job, whether they were on her side or against her. It was confrontational. I don't think she thought of people in terms of say, having a night-out with them because they might be good fun. She thought of people in terms of jobs they did, whether they agreed with her point of view, and if they didn't agree how much she would have to bully them to get them around to her point of view, and where that task was impossible she'd get them out and walk away. She would presume then that you were somebody slightly inferior, were definitely wrong, and there was no point in her wasting any more of her much more valuable time trying to persuade you. We frequently make the mistake here of thinking about British politicians in Irish terms, whether they are good or bad for Ireland. They are there to serve their own country and their own people. We must treat them on that basis. My job was to persuade her, Tom King and other ministers that it was in the interests of their electorate and their people that we find a solution to Northern Ireland that is peaceful. It wasn't to persuade them about the justice of the nationalist cause – you couldn't do that. You'd have to talk to them in terms of their own self-interest.'

Barry vividly recalls the stern look on her face when she spoke about Germany over dinner during the height of the Cold War. US President Ronald Reagan had condemned Russia as the evil empire. Thatcher backed Reagan. She told Barry: 'The only thing we have in common ... the Americans, Russians and ourselves ... is that Germany can never be reunited.' That was five years before Germany was reunited!

On rare occasions he saw the human side of the Iron Lady: she had a habit of falling asleep when European Summits and Anglo-Irish meetings drifted late into the night. 'She'd have started her day at six in the morning and eventually she would just fold. The conversation might be taking place at the other end of the table. She got tired and couldn't stay awake.'

The successful conclusion of the Anglo-Irish Agreement was the climax of Barry's 28 years in national politics, a career in which he held four ministries, served as deputy leader of Fine Gael for over a decade but failed to achieve his ultimate ambition to become party leader and Taoiseach.

He aspired to Foreign Affairs because he wanted a say in Northern Ireland. The tradition had been that the Taoiseach's office handled northern affairs; Dr FitzGerald agreed to give the Corkman a major input if he took the job.

The New Ireland Forum had sown the seeds of the Anglo-Irish Agreement. The Forum Report was a radical document, he says, because for the first time Irish Nationalists recognised the rights of the Unionist community. But the document's solutions were rejected out of hand by Mrs Thatcher in her controversial 'Out, out, out' speech. After a two-day

Anglo-Irish Summit at Chequers between FitzGerald and Thatcher in November, 1984, the British PM turned down the major options of the report by saying: 'A united Ireland was one solution. That is out. A second solution was confederation of the two states. That is out. A third solution was joint authority. That is out.' Her brusque dismissal came as a bombshell to the Irish side. 'After the publication of the New Ireland Report, Garret and I had gone over to talk to her about what was coming out of it,' he recalls. 'She got a briefing on the report but possibly hadn't read it. I think she didn't appreciate the flavour behind it. She just honed in on the three solutions. That was a humiliating experience because she had been badly briefed. Some of her own civil servants were upset by the way in which she used the words ... Out, out, out. They were amazed at the venomous way it came across. They were shaken that she had gone so far because she appeared to be slamming the door in our face. So we went around the back door. We sat down with a group of civil servants on both sides, set up a committee and out of that eventually came the Anglo-Ireland Agreement.'

The accord was signed before the world's media by FitzGerald and Thatcher at Hillsborough Castle on 15 November, 1985. Any change in the status of Northern Ireland would only come about with the consent of a majority of the people of Northern Ireland. The agreement provided for the establishment of an Inter-Governmental Conference in which the Irish government could put forward proposals on aspects of Northern affairs; the joint conference chairmen to include a permanent Irish ministerial representative and the Secretary of State for Northern Ireland; as well as a Secretariat to service the Conference. Fianna Fáil leader Charles Haughey accused the Irish government of having abandoned the national aim of unity, by recognising the legitimacy of the Unionist position, in an international agreement.

Barry maintains it was a significant achievement for an Irish government to get a say in the running of Northern Ireland. The agreement gave nationalists a means of addressing their complaints without violence. It showed nationalists 'they didn't have to depend on the gun to achieve political objectives. I could see that it undermined completely the armed wing of the IRA.' The agreement made the peace process possible, and Barry's early role has always been acknowledged by SDLP leader John Hume.

The Corkman became the Republic's 'man across the border' and a target for extreme unionists. He was condemned by DUP leader Ian Paisley. Anytime the two men met, 'Paisley was barely civil'. On one occasion during the Irish EC presidency, Paisley, as an MEP, was to attend a parliamentary committee meeting in Dublin Castle. Barry presided at the meeting, which was followed by lunch. 'Somebody said to Paisley beforehand, "I see you're going down to eat with Peter Barry." Paisley said, "No, I'm going down to eat Peter Barry".'

In light of the hardline unionist reaction, the new assignment brought risks to himself and his family. He got intelligence to the effect that he was on a loyalist paramilitary execution list at one stage. During the critical Anglo-Irish period of 1986-87, loyalists claimed to have poisoned packets of Barry's Tea. Nothing was found. His family was under 24-hour garda security in Cork. Gardaí set up a hut in his front garden. His wife, Margaret, got abusive phonecalls. To this day she will not open a parcel coming through the letterbox. Barry found the heavy security 'offensive' and told his government colleagues he felt more in danger with the security than without it. When Barry read a newspaper report that the Dutch PM had chased burglars in his pyjamas through his home, he cut out the article and sent the clipping to his justice colleague. 'I said, "if the Prime Minister of the Netherlands doesn't have a bodyguard, why should I living in Cork have a bodyguard?" They just ignored me.'

Nothing in his background could have prepared him for the unionist hostility; he came from a middle-class Cork merchant family and followed his father's footsteps into politics. Ironically, the politician derided by unionists had emerged from the kind of business/rugby background so characteristic of affluent Ulster Protestants. He knew that his new job under the Anglo-Irish Accord would be no picnic, and showed toughness and resilience.

Business and politics were in his blood. Peter Barry was born in Cork on 10 August, 1928, the son of a local grocer and tea merchant. The Barry Tea Company had been founded by his grandfather, James J. Barry, who came down from Ballyhooley in North Cork to be apprenticed as a grocer's curate to Simcox's in Patrick Street. He opened his own shop in Bridge Street in 1901 and a second shop in Princes Street in 1910. James Barry sold tea from the shop and promoted it as one of his specialities. Old photographs of Cork show signs saying: 'Barry's famous 2/- tea'.

It was Peter's father, Tony, who laid the foundations for today's company. Tony, the eldest of eleven, left school early and went into the Princes Street shop where he finished his apprenticeship in the trade. He had been in the Army during the Civil War and came out to run the business. He later closed the shop in Bridge Street to concentrate on the

Princes Street outlet. He was innovative in that he stressed the taste of the tea; he won the 1934 Empire's Cup in London, given by the tea trade and competed for by tea tasters all over the world. He was the only Irishman ever to win it. This confirmed the Barrys as authorities on the quality of tea.

Politically, Tony became actively involved in Cumann na nGael in the '20s and was W. T. Cosgrave's election agent all through the '30s and until he retired in the '40s. He thereby kindled his son's interest in politics.

Young Peter grew up in Cork at a time of considerable poverty and depression in the 1930s. The family home was at Egerton Villas, Military Hill. His earliest childhood memory: a small boy looking out the window on a dark winter's evening, watching the man lighting the gas lamps down Military Hill, seen from Egerton Villas. He also vividly remembers his father sitting at home in his favourite chair, smoking a pipe and reading a book. 'He was one of the most educated men I knew even though he had no formal education. He was chairman of the library committee for nearly 40 years and he read every day of his life.'

Peter went to the Model School on Anglesea Street, made his Holy Communion and went to Christian Brothers College off Patrick's Hill. It was a strict regime for students at Christians. The Brothers had a strong sense of vocation to education; a lot of them were kind and a few had 'a less than firm grip on their tempers'. The leather strap was the accepted form of discipline. Young Barry didn't get the strap 'because, he says 'I was politically trained early on to say the right things!'

He recalls the daily routine: 'I remember the trams going up Summerhill, and we used to walk down Wellington Road to school in the mornings. The Brothers lived in St Gabriel's and they walked from Summerhill up York Street, so you'd look down and if there was a Brother coming up, you knew you were on time, you were ahead of him. There was a next door neighbour of ours, Mr O'Sullivan, who worked in the Yeast Company in Blackpool, and he used to walk down every morning in the '30s; he'd stop, look across and take out his watch and say, "Monaghan's clock is slow again this morning". Monaghan's clock was the City Hall clock and Philip Monahan was the City Manager at the time. Further on, there was a lovely smell of bread past Thompson's that would make your mouth water, and then there was Campbell's Sweet Factory. They made handmade sweets down in Hardwicke Street and you'd go down to get a penny worth of boilings'.

He can remember the *Evening Echo* being sold by boys in bare feet. Also, of course, the shawlies who came into the Barry's shop. 'It was said about my father that there was no point in going to Tony Barry in Princes Street because the women with the shawl, he'd always serve first. I think it's a nice tribute to him.'

He can never forget the poverty he witnessed growing up in Cork. As a member of the Society of St Vincent de Paul, he visited families struggling for survival. 'I remember calling to a family on the Lower Road; there was a mother and father and two or three children living in one room. There was one bed, and no clothes on it. There was a table, no food, and an open fire. It was so humiliating for them. We would not give them money because the thinking in the middle classes at the time was that you couldn't trust them to spend it properly. I squirm when I think of the things I gave my name to without giving enough thought. We gave them dockets to allow them get bread and milk in the shops. It was terrible. We didn't even trust them. The extraordinary thing was that there wasn't a revolution then.'

He also witnessed the flow of emigration. 'The Inisfallen sailed at six o'clock on a Monday, Wednesday and Friday. It was awful to go down there and see young fellas, badly dressed, with their tatty suitcases, mothers and fathers crying as their 18-year-old went away and they might never see them again. These youngsters were on their own; uneducated, no money, and no addresses to go to.'

The Barry's business would have flourished were it not for the war. During the war, tea was rationed and traders bought tea from government-controlled supplies. In 1956, they were free to buy their own tea again from the country of origin. By now Peter was working in the Princes Street shop; at the age of 18 he had left school and began his career as a counterhand and worked his way up through the business.

Peter was fascinated with tea, just like his father and his father before him. By the late 1950s, he did an early exercise in market research. Housewives liked the tea; but they found it too far to go into Princes Street and would prefer to buy it in their local shop. Around that time he sniffed the threat ahead with the arrival of large supermarkets into the grocery trade. An experiment in wholesaling was put into action: Joe O'Mahony, who worked behind the counter in the shop, was sent out to Blackpool in Cork as the target market. It was a success – the first 5 lbs of tea that Barry's sold wholesale. Today, the company, which is run by Peter's son, Tony, sells 6.5 million lbs a year and has a 30% share of the market.

Peter expanded the business and changed the traditional source of tea from Sri Lanka and India to East Africa where tea is plucked all year round. It was wonderful to visit the plantations of Kenya, Tanzania and Uganda, 'standing there with a sea of green in front of you'. Blending is where the individuality of the tea comes in. Peter amazes people with his encyclopedic knowledge of tea; he can identify different tea types by taste.

Barry's tried to ensure that their tea was of a higher quality. Peter modelled the expansion of the company in the same way that market leader, Lyons, organised their business and sold tea. They invested in machinery, transport and premises. Instead of giving discounts and offers though, 'we decided to put the value into the packet'. Today, the Barry companies have a total net worth of £25 million. Peter says he could never see himself selling the firm. He will let his son take his own decisions about the future. 'I certainly won't put any clause in my will saying this business is not to be sold.'

The future statesman reckons he got his first taste of politics when he watched his father chair an election meeting in Patrick Street in 1943. He vividly remembers standing under the platform, peering up at his father as he spoke on behalf of W. T. Cosgrave. He was only 15 at the time. He became his father's right-hand man during his political career from 1954 to 1965. 'I was his political agent. I managed him, suggested what he should do and ran his election campaigns. I think he trusted my judgement. I suppose I learned what an awful life politics is, but it never sunk in evidently!' Tony Barry was a Fine Gael TD for Cork from 1954-57 and from 1961-65; served in the Senate from 1957-61 and was Lord Mayor of Cork from 1960-61.

Peter came into politics through Cork Corporation, serving on the City Council from 1967-73 and following his father's footsteps when elected Lord Mayor for the term 1970-71. He was first elected to the Dáil in 1969 and returned at every election until his retirement. 'Fianna Fáil had been in office for 12 years and I felt that wasn't good for democracy,' he says. 'Fine Gael were at me to stand. I told them I'd stand for two elections. If the government was changed in that time then I'd have done my job. If it wasn't, I'd step aside. I stood in 1969 and Fianna Fáil were re-elected. I stood in '73 and the government was changed.' When filling out a Dáil occupation query form, he described himself as 'tea taster'.

Terms on the Cork Health Authority and the Cork Regional Development Organisation improved his profile in Fine Gael headquarters. In 1969-70, he earned his first Oireachtas position, appointed to the Committee of Public Accounts. When Fine Gael under Liam Cosgrave entered a Coalition government with Labour in 1973, Barry was appointed Minister for Transport and Power. He held the office for three years before moving to Education for the final year of the Coalition. He was appointed Fine Gael deputy leader in 1979. The brief 1981-82 government saw him serve again in Cabinet as Minister for the Environment. He landed the Foreign Affairs job in late 1982 and remained centre-stage alongside Taoiseach Garret FitzGerald until 1987.

Civil servants regarded him as a hardworking and talented minister with a tremendous grasp of his brief. He brought about reform in each government portfolio: as Minister for Transport and Power he founded Bord Gáis; during his time in Environment he set up the National Housing Agency; and in Foreign Affairs he signed the Single European Act and pioneered the Anglo-Irish Agreement.

He says he was his own man, and accepted or rejected the advice of civil servants in the departments. 'The advice was usually pretty good and soundly based. There's an element of truth in the TV programme, *Yes Minister*, where civil servants try to get their own way. For example, the civil servants didn't want the housing agency. I went into Environment with a brief to give a shot in the arm to the construction industry. I had a reluctant department. I convinced a couple of them that it was a good thing. We were only in office a short time, and I got all that through the Dáil and Seanad within six months.'

The Corkman was always regarded as a politician of integrity and honesty; colleagues who served in government with him say he had an inability to compromise when there were occasions as a minister 'when he could have virtually bought votes'. The lack of any ruthless streak was undoubtedly a drawback politically, especially when others in his own party were wielding knives. Critics regarded him as being aloof and arrogant, the quintessential Cork merchant prince – a tag which does not sit easily on his shoulders.

He liked the life of a government minister. 'It was great fun. The thing I liked best were the files marked *Secret*. That's what it means being a cabinet minister. That's where the power is. I use that as a kind of metaphor for being at the cabinet table. You're making decisions in cabinet which affect this country and the lives of the people, maybe for a long time to come. It's a heavy responsibility and a great privilege. You were moulding history. The trappings meant nothing to me. I hated having guards outside my door. I hated having a squad car following me. You'd crave for your privacy at times.' But there were advantages. 'To be honest, I liked being driven on a wet night to a dinner in Cork City Hall whereas if I took my own car I'd have to park away by the bus office and walk. Not having to find parking in Dublin was great.' Anyway, he says you couldn't get a swelled head about being a minister because somebody would stop you on the street in Cork and quickly tell you what you were doing wrong!

The FitzGerald government was run on consensus; as Taoiseach he was more chairman than chief. 'Garret would always listen. If he came in with one idea and thought your idea was better he would have no hesitation in dropping his own. He had enough confidence in himself to allow people around him who were his intellectual equals. Charles Haughey as Taoiseach didn't want any questioning at his own level of his own judgement. So he surrounded himself with people who were intellectually inferior to him. Garret didn't; he sought people whom he could bounce ideas off and who would be able to respond to him. If you look at Haughey's cabinets there were lots of very nice people but they certainly weren't going to challenge anything he was doing.'

The Foreign Affairs portfolio crowned Barry's career and established his statesmanlike image. The downside of the heavy Anglo-Irish workload was that he was able to spend less time in his Cork South Central constituency. He had to balance the demands of international affairs with national politics and local constituency work. On a typical day, he conducted a question and answer session with senior pupils of Ballincollig Community School about the Anglo-Irish Agreement, meet a GAA delegation at his Cork office and drove to Dublin where he worked until 10 p.m. at the Department of Foreign Affairs.

Some critics say he didn't devote enough energy to his constituency. On the home front there had already been huge industrial setbacks in the early '80s with the closure of two of the city's anchor industries, Fords and Dunlops, at a time when he held government office. The success of the Anglo-Irish Agreement was followed by election defeat for the party in 1987. The FG vote and his own vote dropped, but he doesn't relate it to the Agreement. 'There was general dissatisfaction with the government anyway. The country had been through a tough time. We made harsh decisions to bring down the rate of inflation. It's very hard to look after your constituency, especially a five-seater, and look after your job in Dublin as well. People said to me at the time I should have gone to live in Dublin and visited the constituency, rather than the other way around.'

The party leadership twice eluded Barry, and so the prospect of becoming Taoiseach drifted from his grasp.

In 1977, after a general election in which Fianna Fáil had doubled FG's representation, Liam Cosgrave resigned and the leadership of the party came down to a straight contest between Garret FitzGerald and Peter Barry. Barry realised that FitzGerald had the stronger support and withdrew. 'There was a very good chance I would have been elected, but the grassroots wanted Garret. The parliamentary party would not have wanted Garret, and they would have elected me. There was a block in the middle who didn't want me but who were much more opposed to Garret. This block was acting against Garret rather than for me. Therefore, they'd have voted for me. That's not a good basis for leadership. I figured that in those circumstances, I would not have been an effective leader. Garret was the right choice at the time.'

Next time around, Barry expected to win the leadership but lost out to the relatively inexperienced Alan Dukes, after the election defeat of 1987. The Fine Gael/Labour Coalition had broken up on 20 January, 1987, when Labour failed to support Fine Gael's proposed budget. Fianna Fáil returned to power that year without an overall majority and Charles Haughey was appointed Taoiseach.

It was a time for soul-searching in Fine Gael and a new direction. The leadership was a three-cornered contest between Barry, Dukes and John Bruton.

Barry was confident of victory. However, he began to have doubts during the last few days when he heard that some members, whom he thought were voting for him, had changed their minds. 'I didn't think Bruton was in it at all,' he reflects. 'I thought it was between Dukes and me. I was surprised that two people, whom I thought would be supporters of mine, voted for Alan. There's always a grey block. I never counted a majority, but I had counted enough heads that I thought gave me a basis to expect the same proportion of don't-knows would come to me and give me victory. As I say, I got a bit nervous when I heard about these two people in particular. If I named them and you asked them, they'd say "Of course we voted for Peter Barry".'

The result left him 'shook and disappointed'. After the defeat, Peter and Margaret drove back to Cork from Dublin that night. They stopped off to join Dukes's celebration party in Kildare and congratulated him. They went on a 10-day holiday to Sicily. 'I licked my wounds, came back and got stuck in. The worst thing you can do is brood and feel that fate has dealt you a bad hand. If I was honest with myself and could live it all again, I'd see that it was things I did and said to people in the intervening 15 years that lost me votes ... I think Alan probably worked harder on them than I did, although that's not the only reason. He's a highly intelligent, attractive personality with lots of energy. The party just thought he'd be a better leader.'

The Corkman remained philosophical in defeat and supported Dukes and his successor, Bruton, during a time of upheaval and discontent in the party while in opposition. He kept a dignified stance, in spite of the party turmoil and later their poor performance at the polls in November 1992.

Advancing age meant he would probably never get the opportunity of leadership again. Many people in the party have since hankered over what might have been in terms of a Barry leadership. What kind of Taoiseach would he have been? 'I would hope to have been in the chairman, rather than the chief, kind of mould. I would have brought around me people whose talents I respected and give them their head. The North and Europe would have been priorities.' It was not to be. There is no point looking back now. He adds: 'Of course, I would like to have been leader of Fine Gael. I would like to have been Taoiseach. But I'm not carrying a cross around for the rest of my life. Most people in this country have never been Taoiseach. I'm not in a unique club.'

In 1990, he refused to accept the Fine Gael nomination for President. He was asked to contest the presidency by then party leader Alan Dukes. 'I just said, no. I told Alan I didn't believe it was an office to which I'm suited. I said I wanted to stay in active politics at the time.' The refusal may well have cost him any remaining hopes of party leadership. His colleagues' anger was all the more intense after the Brian Lenihan tapes controversy where it was felt that Barry might have punished him more than Austin Currie. Nobody doubts that Barry would have done far better than Currie in the presidential polls which put Mary Robinson into Áras an Uachtaráin until 1997.

As a new wave of youth swept through the FG rank and file, Barry came to be regarded as the elder statesman of the party. The leadership issue was settled; he would never carry the reins of power again.

After the November 1992 general election, Fianna Fáil and Labour formed a partnership government. The 'Rainbow' partners had failed to agree among themselves. Fine Gael's partners-to-be, Labour, were now in bed with Fianna Fáil under Albert Reynolds as Taoiseach. Barry kept his seat but FG's poor performance, coupled with the forming of the FF/Labour, government was the final straw for Barry. On 5 February, 1993, Barry announced his departure from national politics; he would not contest the next general election and was withdrawing from the party's front bench and deputy leadership. 'It looked as if the next election wouldn't come until 1997,' he reflects. 'My prospects of getting into government in the late part of the decade were virtually nil because of my age. I'd be nearly 70. There was no point in blocking a seat here that somebody younger and with more of a future could take up.'

Barry, architect of the Anglo-Irish Agreement, watched from the sidelines as the Hume-Adams talks brought new hope and British Prime Minister John Major joined Taoiseach Albert Reynolds in the search for peace. It led to the signing of the Downing Street Declaration on 15 December, 1993, the IRA ceasefire of 31 August, 1994, and a loyalist ceasefire six weeks later. The 17-month-old IRA ceasefire ended on 9 February, 1996, when an IRA explosion rocked the London Docklands. The ceasefire was restored on 20 July, 1997, with two new administrations in power – Labour under Prime Minister Tony Blair in London and Fianna Fáil under Taoiseach Bertie Ahern in Dublin. Barry believes there can only be lasting peace if nationalists and unionists realise and accept they can't achieve all their goals and must settle for something less in the interests of future generations. 'Both sides have to bend and move away from extreme positions,' he says. 'That's the only way forward.'

Barry's assessment of John Bruton's leadership is that he was a 'magnificent Taoiseach' in the face of scandals which rocked Fine Gael while in government with Labour and Democratic Left up to the June '97 election. He concedes that damage was done to the party and to the wider body politic. Young people don't trust politicians. They don't see the political parties or the Dáil as relevant anymore. 'I realise that young people are disenchanted with politics. I'm 28 years in politics and I've known 400 or 500 politicians in that time. I would say that 95% of them are honest, hardworking people who felt they were doing the right thing for their country.'

Barry played a key role in keeping the Michael Collins letter collection in Ireland. He bought the collection of letters between General Collins and his fiancée, Kitty Kiernan, at public auction in 1995 amid fears that they would be sold outside the country. Barry says of him: 'Michael Collins was forever a visionary.'

The Barry political dynasty is being carried on by his daughter, Deirdre Clune, who was elected for FG in Cork South Central in June '97. His other children are carving successful careers: Tony is managing director of Barry's Tea at the Cork headquarters; Fiona is married and living in Cork; Donagh is a business consultant; Conor was programme manager to then Defence and Marine Minister Sean Barrett during the

Bruton-led rainbow coalition and Peter is working in the tea division of Premier Foods in the UK.

The grocer's son says he has no pretensions about how he would like to be remembered; he would be happy if people said he was a reasonably good human being who did his best. The epitaph would simply be: 'He worked hard and did his best.'

BILL O'HERLIHY

THE PEOPLE'S CHAMP

JUST hold it there, Bill!

Meet the man who can capture the national mood with a facial expression and a few simple words. A look of delight or disappointment can be more revealing than anything his panel might say. Of course he defers to the experts. That's the whole idea. For two decades Bill O'Herlihy has represented the plain people of Ireland in television land; bringing us through the highs and lows of Olympics, World Cups and European Championships. He asks the questions we want to ask but are afraid we might sound silly. You can count on Bill to call a spade a spade. At the same time he's got to keep his cool while everyone else is boiling over with emotion. He does all these things and makes it look easy, which is the mark of a true professional.

Bill's patience was certainly tested many times during the Jack Charlton era when he found the Big Man 'one of the most difficult people I ever had to work with in my life'. He says: 'It used to drive me mad when he put me and my RTÉ colleagues down on television as if we were somehow asking the most banal questions and then watch him smarm his way through interviews with ITV and BBC when they asked precisely the same questions. It was no wonder that John Giles once remarked on air, "I see Jack has done another course at charm school". Jack had a wonderful capacity to use the media to suit his own agenda. And this was particularly evident when Jack appeared on The Pat Kenny and Gay Byrne Shows to promote his own image in a very positive and personal way. When it came to dealing with RTÉ Sport we were an irritant to him. We were asking questions he didn't want asked. He didn't like to be challenged in a football context; when you challenged him you'd get put down so hard at times.

'But that was only one side of Jack. In a different set of circumstances – and I've seen him operate in the PR side of the business – Jack was the nicest man in the world: kind, considerate and endlessly patient.'

When Charlton refused to appear on the 1990 World Cup programme with Eamon Dunphy after Ireland had been eliminated by Italy, a compromise was reached whereby he would be interviewed by Bill for an hour-long Christmas special. The venue was a hotel at Dublin Airport. The interview was going fine until Bill asked questions about management style. Bill recalls the incident: 'I said to Jack, as a supplementary to one of the questions, "what you're really saying is that the reason why we qualified for Italy, as against England, Scotland, Wales or Northern Ireland, was because of management." He said, "I'm not saying that at all. I'm not going to be put into that position by you. What you're setting out to do is to embarrass me with the English media. I'm not going to accept that from you. I want the interview stopped." I said, "hang on, I'm simply asking you a supplementary question, arising out of what you've said." He said, "I'm not going to have you put words in my mouth. Stop the interview." Jack would only agree to continue if we scrubbed the whole section. We had to go along with that because we couldn't go back to RTÉ and say we had only 10 minutes instead of the hour-long interview.'

Bill says Charlton had great strengths and nobody would fail to recognise what he achieved with the Irish team. He would be the first to salute his notable triumphs. 'I suppose I was conditioned by Giles and Dunphy to take a view that Charlton had a great team but he didn't make the most of it. A view was expressed frequently on air by our panelists that Charlton was happy to qualify but not necessarily ambitious enough to win World Cups or European Championships. Charlton would take the view that the team wasn't good enough to win and so to qualify was everything. There was only a certain distance that you could progress and he would say that he achieved the maximum possible. Giles and Dunphy would argue that Charlton's team, at its peak, was one of the best in the world, but he forced them to play a certain way which limited them.'

Off-screen, Bill is a public relations man, and good at it too. Behind the relaxed, easygoing exterior lies a man driven by competitive and commercial instincts. PR has been his livelihood for nearly quarter of a century. His company, Bill O'Herlihy Communications, is one of the busiest in the country with an impressive list of high-profile clients.

Bill O'Herlihy was born in Cork on 27 September, 1938, into a secure middle-class family with strong political and journalistic traditions. The family home was at Glasheen Road in the Fine Gael heartlands of the city's southside.

He was the eldest of a family of six – four boys and two girls. His mother's family, the Horgans, were rooted in the Fine Gael tradition: her father, John, was a TD for the party who served as Lord Mayor of Cork in 1941. His father's family had newspaper ink flowing through their veins. Bill's grandfather, Willie O'Herlihy, had a long career with *The Cork Examiner* where he was in charge of the newsroom as chief reporter, a house title then for news editor.

His grand-uncles were journalists in Cork, Dublin and London, one of whom was reputed to have reported the proceedings of the House of Commons. Bill's father, David, somehow managed to avoid the journalistic bug and ended up in the relative anonymity of local government in Cork. David O'Herlihy worked as a hospital administrator, first at St Finbarr's on the Douglas Road and later at St Mary's Orthopaedic in Gurranabraher, in the employ of the South Cork Board of Public Assistance. He was a workaholic; replaced by three people in the hospital after his retirement. Bill's mother, Mary Frances, known as Minnie, lived for her children. The O'Herlihys were ordinary, middle-class parents, devoid of any pretensions.

'Let's be frank about it,' says Bill, 'they had no money either. My father had a nice white-collar job that wouldn't have been well paid. It must have been difficult trying to raise six children on his salary. They were part of an environment and culture in which the common ethic was that you virtually gave your whole life for your kids. This philosophy sustained them, and many other parents of the '40s.' Since neither of them drank, any extra money was spent on the children. Their social lives were unadventurous: a night out at the pictures or, occasionally, the Opera House.

His father was a familiar figure on the doorsteps at Greenmount every Sunday, collecting for the Sick Poor Society. He was also a member of the Society of St Vincent de Paul, and first launched the Meals On Wheels service in Cork at the Lough Parish.

It was a happy, loving home. 'My father and mother were very happily married,' says Bill. 'They conveyed a terrific sense of love which anchored all our lives and which, I hope, we've passed on to our homes. As a family we were very close emotionally.' They liked to talk a lot. He recalls great debates about the pressing issues of the day across the dining table. He believes that children can change and educate parents and broaden their outlook on life. The process of education is a shared experience.

As a schoolboy at Glasheen National School, and later at St Finbarr's College, Farranferris, Bill O'Herlihy dreamed of becoming a journalist, like his grandfather and grand uncles. He liked English and study came easy to him. He liked sport, too, playing hurling and football for a city club. He started secondary school at the age of 12, did the Inter Cert twice at 13 and 14, and then the Matric at 15. He passed all his exams, although never made it to the Leaving Cert or to college. After going into sixth year, he got the chance to fulfill his dreams. His father brought him into the *Examiner* office to meet the late Tom Crosbie, then chairman of the newspaper.

That meeting in 1954 sowed the seeds of a career in newspapers, television and public relations. He remembers the words of the chairman, who was a genial father figure of the firm. 'Any grandson of Willie O'Herlihy is good enough for *The Cork Examiner*,' he proclaimed. 'When a job comes up, you'll get it.' Just like that. The substance of the meeting was over in minutes. It was to be the only job interview of his career, 'and wasn't even an interview in the real sense at all'.

The budding journalist knew he was in the door; it was only a matter of time. Less than three months before the Leaving Cert in 1956, a letter came one morning from the company secretary, John Leland, who gave 55 years' service to *The Cork Examiner*. A vacancy had arisen in the Reading Room; if he wanted the job he could start on Monday week. 'Mother of God, are you not going to do your Leaving?' asked his mother across the breakfast table. 'What do I need my Leaving for?' he asked. 'I want to be a journalist. I'm not going to turn down this opportunity. I've got my matric so I can go to University later if I want.' Anyway, to send their eldest son to UCC would have been a financial strain on the O'Herlihys. It remains a source of regret to him that he didn't study for a degree by night, even though 'going into *The Cork Examiner* was the best thing I ever did'.

Before his 17th birthday, Bill had already started his working career in *The Cork Examiner* while his friends were playing football and looking forward to college life. Work stunted his sporting development and he regrets not having played more. He was employed first as a copyholder in the Reading Room. It was the place where proofs were read and corrected in the days of hot metal, a slow and monotonous process, yet essential nonetheless. New recruits – described by their boss, Mossie Brown, as 'correctors of the press' – got an invaluable insight into the workings of the entire newspaper. The Reading Room was led by some wise and eccentric characters: significantly, it served as a cradle for youngsters who aspired to becoming junior reporters and sub-editors on

The Cork Examiner and the *Evening Echo*. He did an eight-month apprenticeship in the Reading Room, sometimes working the night shift when he walked home through the sleeping city at 4 a.m. with a copy of the paper under his arm. He spent two months in the Commercial Department and then got his first big break to land a subbing job on the *Echo* under the watchful eye of an austere editor, the late William Declan Mary O'Connell, who had taken the helm in 1955. It was a step closer to achieving his real ambition, to be a reporter. 'I decided not to go to college at night so I'd be free anytime to pursue a reporting career. As things turned out, it took me about four years to get into the Reporters' Room, so I would have been able to do the exams. I lost out.' Still, he had much more money than his friends. He earned £2/10 a week in the Reading Room. The wages were later raised to £3/15 . 'I thought I was made up,' he recalls. 'I was able to live very comfortably on 10 shillings a week. I could afford to have a date, go to the pictures, and smoke. The cost of living was so low that you could do an enormous amount on those wages. I wasn't a drinker, so I had more money on my hands.'

He remembers life on the *Echo* subs desk as 'extraordinarily easygoing'. William Declan O'Connell was a 'wonderful editor': a strict newspaperman of the old school who held the editorship for 12 years until 1967; he demanded high standards and 'was very decent and good to me in many ways'. There were older and wiser hands on the subs desk, among them two memorable characters, Crichton Healy and Walter McGrath. It was an era before competition would impose the pressure and discipline of earlier evening newspaper deadlines. The early *Echo* was printed at four o'clock, and the later edition at six o'clock. After a couple of days on the desk, he discovered that everybody went home for lunch. 'They literally went home; it wasn't just a cup of coffee and sandwich down in Reidy's pub,' he recalls. 'The editor and subs went away at 12.30 p.m. I was left holding the fort on my own from 12.30–2 p.m. during which time all the copy came in. I used to face mountains of copy for that night's *Echo* including all the court stuff.'

The new recruit on the subs desk awaited the return of the editor, William Declan, with some trepidation. The question was always the same: 'Well, have you got a lead for me?' Most of the time he had a lead, 'but if I didn't it was serious'. On one particular day, young O'Herlihy had drawn a blank. There was no lead. He said to himself, 'What am I going to do?' He spotted a paragraph on the wires about a big battle in Indo-China. 'I decided to, well, extend it,' he recalls. 'I got the paragraph and wrote a whole story around it. Of course, it was highly irresponsible when I look back now. Nobody was ever the wiser. William Declan was happy that the job was done that day, but he never knew how. He'd probably turn in his grave if he found out.'

By 1959, O'Herlihy achieved his ambition to land a plum job in the Reporters' Room. His first boss was the late Willie Spillane, the Chief Reporter of the day. He was a gracious journalist, who looked after the junior reporters under his command. He drove them hard but was always fair. As a correspondent for other newspapers, he put extra money their way by asking them to send off some lines from weekend sports fixtures. Spillane was succeeded as Chief Reporter by the late John O'Sullivan, who also wrote the editorials and who had been regarded as a brilliant reporter in his day. O'Herlihy had high regard for the late Tom Barker, who deputised occasionally for the news editor. Tom, a true gentleman of the fourth estate, had a practice of reading the paper before any of the reporters turned up for work. He often peered out from behind the paper to remark: 'Bill, you split an infinitive again.' When he was reprimanded for the first time O'Herlihy replied, innocently, that he didn't know how to split an infinitive. Barker explained the error. 'Funnily enough,' he says, 'that stayed with me for the rest of my life and, to this day, I won't allow anybody split an infinitive.'

It was a time when the clatter of typewriters made the newsroom a noisy place. A good shorthand note was the mark of a professional. Reporters worked long hours, with little time-off, and took the younger recruits under their wing to cultivate their news instincts. O'Herlihy served his time in the courts and council meetings and also on the sporting fields at weekends. Nobody had a better nose for a story than the late Larry Lyons, doyen of the Cork press corps. He was a flamboyant journalist, tailor-made for the big occasion, whether covering the Cork Film Festival, the Olympic Games or mixing with the rich and famous on board luxury liners that docked off Cobh. He was a tall, imposing figure around whom there hung a perpetual cloud of cigar smoke. 'He was the reporter who defined standards among the young fellows. He was a wonderful reporter with a great ironic sense of humour and sometimes a don't-confuse-me-with-facts kind of attitude.' The late Stephen Coughlan and Cathal Henry were among the eminent reporters; both were Chief Reporters during their careers.

It was a breeding ground for top-class general reporters. There were no specialists and no by-lines. The reporters on night-town were expected to take copy down the phone from correspondents and other contributors. They covered news and sport. 'We were multi-purpose animals,' he says. 'We could do anything because our training was very comprehensive and very good.' He can remember cycling the 17 miles to

Coachford on Sundays to cover the Mid-Cork GAA division, hurling and football. 'I never saw anything so tribal as the matches between Inniscarra and Ballincollig at Coachford in the Mid-Cork Championship,' he says. 'I once saw a woman breaking an umbrella over a player's head. There'd be huge fights between the crowd and the players.'

Among his newsroom contemporaries were Val Dorgan, Dermot Russell, Dick Cross, Billy George, Larry Lyons, Sylvester O'Sullivan, Vincent Sullivan, George Cronin and Tom Barker. He regards Dorgan as the best sports and news journalist of his generation. Dorgan had hurled on the same team as Christy Ring, and in later years wrote an acclaimed biography of the maestro. 'Val was in a different league to the rest of us,' says O'Herlihy. 'He was the most comprehensively talented person. He could write to a number of styles; he was a heavyweight operator; and he had a writing skill that was unmatched by any journalist of his era. He was the best writer of gaelic games of his time.'

The newspaper was changing too: for one thing, the long tradition of filling Page One with advertisements, which stretched back to the foundation of *The Cork Examiner* in 1841, ended in 1961 to make way for news.

The Cork Examiner was a 'wonderfully paternalistic organisation' back in those days. There was a tradition of employing the sons and relatives of journalists and printers, and the building was populated by many talented people. '*The Cork Examiner* looked after its people. To be a member of the staff gave you a status that you may not deserve but which was very special,' he says, 'because *The Cork Examiner* was such a part of what Cork stood for. When you became a reporter you had a lifestyle of such variety that I was the envy of my father, family and friends.' In time, O'Herlihy covered soccer for *The Cork Examiner* and *Echo*, having taken over from the late George Cronin in the mid-'60s.

Ultimately, the boy from Glasheen Road had high ambitions: to be the editor of *The Cork Examiner*. In those days, he was 'a really tribal Corkman' who loved living in the city and took great pride in the paper. To become editor would be the epitome of achievement. After 14 years in the job, towards the end of the '60s, he aspired to the editor's chair. 'It was never formally indicated to me,' he says, 'but you get an instinct when you know it isn't an absurd ambition.' Alas, it was not to be.

A combination of circumstances gave birth to Bill O'Herlihy the broadcaster. It was another journalist and friend, Tony Sheehan, who gave him his first experience of the airwaves earlier in the '60s. Drogheda United had applied successfully to join the League of Ireland. Their first match was to be played against either Cork Athletic or Cork Hibernians. Beforehand however, Drogheda were playing a friendly against Portadown on a Saturday. O'Herlihy had a girlfriend in Laytown, Co. Meath, whom he had met on holidays, so an assignment up the country was ideal. He travelled north to assess the Drogheda team in advance of their match against the Cork side. Tony was preparing a *Junior Sports Magazine* insert on Radio Éireann on Saturday afternoon and asked him to participate as soccer correspondent of *The Cork Examiner*. He replied curtly: 'I will in my eye.' But he liked Tony and didn't want to disappoint him. This initial slot led to a series of radio broadcasts out of Cork on the *Junior Sports Magazine* every Saturday. By coincidence, a prominent Cork-based rugby commentator, the late Bill Twomey, best known locally as manager of the Opera House, had been brought back for international matches. It meant that Radio Éireann had nobody in Cork for four Saturdays of the year. So, O'Herlihy was asked to report on local sports events, everything from hockey to hurling.

Around the same time, Radio Éireann were starting a new Sunday sports programme. Again, O'Herlihy was the reporter on-the-spot. 'I was reporting from Cork every Sunday. I was doing some commentary, although that wasn't my forte, and a lot of reporting from the grounds. That led to me doing a lot of radio every weekend.'

At the age of 26, he made his first appearance before the television cameras – thanks to a freelance cameraman working for RTÉ in Cork, the late Roy Hammond. It was a special report for Frank Hall's *Newsbeat* to mark the 50th anniversary of the sinking of the Lusitania with the loss of 1,198 lives on 7 May, 1915, off Kinsale. Hammond asked him to interview a survivor living in Cappoquin. After three days of coaxing, he agreed. 'It was a difficult interview because the poor woman was half-senile,' he recalls. 'I got through it anyway with the help of Roy.' Next morning after the *Newsbeat* report was shown, Hall instructed that O'Herlihy would be their TV man in Cork. He was 'astounded', yet willing to have a go. He freelanced for *Newsbeat* from 1965, working first with Hammond and, later for many years with another well-known Cork cameraman, Joe McCarthy.

His TV work was done with *The Cork Examiner's* permission. 'I never neglected *The Cork Examiner* or did anything that exposed the paper,' he says. 'I never gave any stories to television that I wouldn't have given to *The Cork Examiner*.' There was no grand plan to become a national broadcaster. He simply took his chances when they came along, and even surprised himself. 'You see, all I wanted to do was to measure how good I was,' he says. 'I felt that within *The Cork Examiner* I had succeeded in my objective of becoming a professional reporter doing a competent job. Radio was never a big ambition – much less television. I always took the view that I didn't have the appearance, the presence, the style, or the voice. I had nothing going for me in the glamour boy television sense. What I had going for me though was a very good journalistic background, well trained in *The Cork Examiner*, something which has stood to me for my entire career.'

In spite of any doubts O'Herlihy had about his ability, RTÉ liked what they saw and offered him a contract in 1967 to work as the nation's first television regional reporter, based in Cork. It was a big decision. He was reluctant to walk away from *The Cork Examiner*. So he asked his employers for leave of absence. The request was turned down 'on the grounds that every person who had asked for leave of absence never came back'. They had valued his contribution, and he got the impression that they might take him back if he wanted to return. 'As regards RTÉ, I was in the right place at the right time. I wanted to see whether I'd make it.' Now his talents were exposed not only to the nation but to the current affairs planners in RTÉ as well.

Muiris MacConghail rated the Corkman as the finest field reporter he ever met, and handpicked him in October 1968 to join the *Seven Days* programme at a time when current affairs was being radically reshaped in RTÉ and given a harder, tougher edge. O'Herlihy agreed to join the team on the understanding that he'd be based in Cork. He remembers MacConghail saying there was no problem because he could hop on a plane at Cork Airport 'and anyway they'd want me to cover stories in China and places like that'. He never made it to China. Less than 24 hours after *Seven Days* returned to the screens, he got a call from Sheamus Smith, who was the number two on the programme as assistant to MacConghail and who became Ireland's film censor later in his career. 'Are you with us or not?' he asked. Of course he was. 'Then what are you doing in Cork?' O'Herlihy explained he was to be based in his home city. 'You are in your arse based in Cork,' said Smith. 'You can't work on this programme in Cork. There's a meeting in the morning – be there. And if you want to work with us you won't be going home.' O'Herlihy drove to Dublin in a rage. Another good reason for wanting to stay in Cork was his future wife. By this time, he'd fallen for Hilary Patterson, a Dublin girl who was working with the ESB in Cork as an after-sales advisor and demonstrator.

He says it was never a big ambition to join *Seven Days* because he didn't see Dublin as part of his scenario. 'There was plenty of scope and plenty of opportunities in the Cork television scene for me. I was tempted to see if I could compete in a much tougher current affairs environment. Frank Hall's *Newsbeat* was a soft news features programme. *Seven Days* was a tough programme with a tough editor. The hardest audience you faced was MacConghail.'

O'Herlihy was recruited as a field reporter along with Rodney Rice and Denis Mitchell. A heavyweight line-up was assembled in studio: the late David Thornley, Paddy Gallagher, Brian Cleeve, Brian Farrell, John O'Donoghue and Ted Nealon. It was an array of intellectual talent 'who didn't put up with much bullshit from politicians'. Then O'Herlihy faced the biggest crisis of his career.

He made a programme on illegal money lending on 11 November, 1969, which won critical and public acclaim but also stirred up a hornet's nest. The programme was unique for RTÉ: they used hidden cameras and hidden microphones, which had never been done before. It made for compulsive viewing. It was regarded as outstanding and accurate, until the outcome of a tribunal of inquiry that lasted 51 days and heard evidence from 141 witnesses over the first three months of 1970. It was then the longest public inquiry in the history of the State and cost £200,000. 'I was very proud of that programme,' says O'Herlihy. 'I walked into the tribunal knowing I had done a superb job, and came out 52 days later as a complete gobshite in the eyes of some people.' In hindsight, he thinks the Fianna Fáil government sniffed an opportunity to put manners on RTÉ and wreck the credibility of *Seven Days*. It was a time when current affairs had become the real opposition of the government of the day; all politicians would have been happy to curb the power of *Seven Days*.

In the end, the verdict was damning: the 142-page report by three members of the judiciary, made public on 20 August, 1970, found that the programme was not authentic. It concluded that proper care had not been taken in the planning, preparation, arrangement, production and presentation of the programme to provide an authentic and objective picture. 'You couldn't have asked for a more savage verdict,' he says. 'I would challenge that to the end of my days as being complete nonsense. What had been a top-class programme on day one ended up as a heap of crap on day fifty-one.' O'Herlihy feels that he was made a scapegoat. Afterwards, MacConghail turned to him and said: 'Bill, you know you're finished in current affairs.'

The entire episode was a shattering blow, personally and professionally. It took him years to get over it. He was newly-married at the time and didn't know where his future lay, but Hilary was a tower of strength and kept things in perspective. He knew the writing was on the wall as regards his current affairs career, at least in the short term. *Seven Days* never recovered from the episode and, eventually, ground to an ignominious halt.

He was at a crossroads in 1971 and thought of leaving the station after getting an approach – inspired by the late Donal Foley – to join *The Irish Times*. Oliver Maloney, then director of personnel at RTÉ, told him it would be a huge mistake to quit, that he had too much yet to contribute, and to quit television now would be acknowledging the verdict of the money-lending tribunal. With a year-and-a-half of his contract still to go, he was given an option of departments. He picked sport, much to the chagrin of the department head, the legendary Micheal O'Hehir. When he walked into the department on Monday morning he didn't have a desk, or a chair, and there was no sign of O'Hehir.

His boss returned from racing on Thursday, called the new recruit into his office and said, candidly: 'Bill, I don't want you here because your style is too hard for sports, but now that you're here, you're welcome.'

O'Herlihy made his debut on TV sport reading the 5.55 p.m. bulletin. Viewers rang in to say it was shameful to see someone of his calibre reading racing results. 'I didn't feel a bit like that,' he says. 'Remember, I was married and I had a job. I didn't feel hard done by. I was doing what I liked, sport.'

O'Herlihy believes he brought a *Seven Days* attitude to sport: he wanted to give programmes and interviews an edge; transferring from current affairs to sport was like driving at 100 miles an hour and then entering a 30-mile zone. He brought his characteristic enthusiasm to sport; always full of ideas at planning meetings. Three months later, following one such brain-storming session, O'Hehir put his arm around O'Herlihy and in earshot of everyone proclaimed: 'I didn't want you here, Bill, but thanks be to God you're with us.' It was approval from the master.

Sport was non-controversial; no major issues were being tackled. O'Herlihy tried to drum up debate but, at the end of the day, sports coverage at the time was painfully predictable and he didn't get a lot of job satisfaction. And he knew he was never going to be a commentator. He felt he had achieved his objectives again, and it was time to try something different. He always wanted to run his own business and be his own boss. The chance came his way in November 1972. Young Advertising and O'Kennedy Brindley were dividing up their advertising and PR business in order to concentrate on advertising. They asked the

TV broadcaster to front a new public relations company and gave him the clients. It was called Public Relations of Ireland which, ultimately, would become Bill O'Herlihy Communications. 'They set me up and part of the signing-on deal was that two years down the line the business would be mine,' he recalls. 'It was the perfect way to start.'

PR was a different ball game. It was far more demanding than the RTÉ sports department. 'Because sport was so predictable in RTÉ in those days,' he says, 'there was no pressure. I was working maybe an eight-hour week and now I was translated into a 10-hour day.' He found the adjustment to PR very difficult, primarily because he now felt he had made a mistake in leaving RTÉ. 'I always assumed I was a journalist who worked in television. I hadn't realised that I'd become a television animal and I missed the buzz.'

He can remember looking out the window at home on a bleak day in March and saying to his wife: 'Hilary, what on earth have I done?' After only eight months in the PR business, he went to see RTÉ's Michael Garvey, then controller of programmes, and told him he wanted to come back. 'Have you gone mad?' reacted Garvey. 'You want to give up a business that can be far more beneficial to you than anything else. You're never going to own a television station, you're never going to be DG, you're never even going to be head of sport. Cop yourself on.'

Garvey told O'Herlihy that if he still felt the same way in a year's time, they'd find him a job. He walked out of the meeting a changed man, as if a huge weight had been lifted from his shoulders. 'I now felt that I could concentrate on the PR side in the knowledge that if it didn't work out emotionally more than anything else, I could go back to television.' By coincidence, he got a call five months later from Mike Horgan, one of the sports editors, who wanted him to present a programme. That's how it all began: he would enjoy the best of both worlds, public relations and sports broadcasting.

By 1978, the dual career was taking off: the PR business was expanding with new accounts coming in and he took a regular slot as studio sports anchor, watching soccer with Eamon Dunphy. 'When Dunphy and I started off nearly 20 years ago there was nobody listening to us, nobody watching us, and no commercial break,' he recalls. 'We were in a presentation studio philosophising about all kinds of things: perhaps East Germany against Poland in the European championship and hardly a sinner watching.'

It was hard work but great fun trying to balance two careers. To this day, he loves the contrasts. 'It's great because in the morning I could be advising a company on the communications aspect of an industrial relations dispute, and in the evening I could be on television doing the Champions League.' Surprisingly, he finds the TV work more relaxing than PR. 'I often leave the office jaded tired to go to RTÉ,' he says. 'I'm so stimulated and enjoy television so much that I come out completely relaxed at the end of the day. PR is 10 times more stressful.'

Offscreen, O'Herlihy also became a national handler, a job description that doesn't sit easily on his shoulders. Instead of working against politicians he was now working with them. He had always been a passive Fine Gael supporter and got involved in the party through an early electoral outing of his pal from *Seven Days*, Ted Nealon. When Nealon became party press secretary he set up a communications and marketing team comprising O'Herlihy, Shane Molloy, Frank Flannery, Enda Marren, Pat Heneghan and Joe Jennings. They were the key backroom players who helped the party win an unprecedented 70 seats in the November 1982 general election. The election campaign was organised like a military operation: the strategy group convened daily for breakfast at eight, joined by members of the communications group. O'Herlihy was usually in the press office at the crack of dawn planning the day's media programme.

Fianna Fáil were beaten and Charles Haughey lost office. Dr Garret FitzGerald formed his second administration with the Labour party. The new government had a joint total of 86 deputies, a majority of four.

O'Herlihy was tagged as one of the national handlers under FitzGerald's 1982-87 government. The media invented clichés like 'national handler' and 'spin doctor'. 'The proposition was that we were an unofficial group of people running the country through Garret FitzGerald,' he says. 'That was nonsense. In fact, it was a Fianna Fáil tactic to drive a wedge between FitzGerald and his party by suggesting we were the unelected people who had all the power. The idea was that when the Taoiseach was taking decisions, he wouldn't be living in an ivory tower detached from the people. Our function was to gather the normal intelligence of the market-place and feed it back into Garret. That's all it was; we made no decisions. You were close to the seat of power in the sense that you had access to the Ministers and to the Taoiseach. But you had a very limited role. You didn't have the same influence as ministers, senior members of the party or backbenchers.'

Garret FitzGerald is an 'extraordinary man' with a huge intellectual capacity. O'Herlihy's lasting image of him as Taoiseach is of a humble man: he never wanted any pomp or ceremony and never demanded that people stand up when he entered a room.

During the European Elections, he went on a bus tour with Garret and Joan FitzGerald. When they stopped in one small town, O'Herlihy went into a shop for some refreshments and, to his surprise, the Taoiseach walked in behind him to buy 'minerals for myself and Joan'. It was a typical gesture. When the FitzGerald era drew to a close, the handlers were history 'because we were very much Garret and Peter Barry's men'. Things might have gone differently for O'Herlihy if his fellow Corkman, Peter Barry, was elected leader. He wasn't and O'Herlihy ended a stimulating 10-year association with Fine Gael.

Now he had more scope to concentrate on the non-political side of his PR business. 'Politics consumes all your time and I wanted to build up the business again,' he says. 'You lose out on some things by being associated with one party.' Not all of the alliances made during the FitzGerald era survived: in 1990 he parted company with Pat Heneghan, who had been his long time partner in Public Relations of Ireland and who now runs his own successful consultancy. 'We decided that the time had come to go our separate ways,' he says. 'These things happen.'

He maintained a punishing schedule in developing the business in a new direction while keeping up his TV work at the same time. Occasionally, he found himself in the unique position of presenting TV programmes sponsored by his clients. He says he steers a careful line between pushing his own clients and the TV work.

The PR business had its ups and downs. O'Herlihy had a policy of head-hunting the brightest people. 'I've never been afraid to hire people who are better than me,' he says. 'I love talent, and I love developing talent. That's not the same with other companies in the industry where you find there's a strong person at the top and a series of little ducklings underneath. I always wanted to have a coterie of people who represent excellence in different fields. We're more of a one-stop shop than other companies. It's a multi-dimensional agency that deals not just with public relations but with communications in the broadest sense.'

He admits to being 'one of the world's worst networkers'. He doesn't want to be chasing the 'main chance' 24 hours day, pressing the flesh on the social circuit to win new business. 'Despite all the years I've been on television,' he says, 'I'm basically a shy person. The notion of going out on my own to a lot of functions at the end of the day's work, when I'm feeling tired, and meeting a lot of people that I don't know, doesn't interest me at all. I make no bones about the fact that I mightn't network

– but when it comes down to it, I'm a bloody good PR man and we're a bloody good company with a lot of talented people.' O'Herlihy won the most expensive account awarded in Ireland for years when he won the PR pitch for the LUAS, the light rail system for Dublin, against competition from six of the top PR firms.

When Fine Gael returned to power under John Bruton in late 1994, O'Herlihy had a second coming and his firm won lucrative government contracts, the biggest of them with two cabinet members, the controversial Transport, Energy and Communications Minister, Michael Lowry, and the Tourism and Trade Minister, Enda Kenny. O'Herlihy's PR skills were certainly tested during Lowry's period in office. Ultimately, the revelations about Lowry's business relationship with Ben Dunne forced the Minister out of office and out of Fine Gael.

O'Herlihy believes history will judge Lowry to have been a good minister, far better than people gave him credit for. 'Look, it's a dog's life being the Minister for Transport, Energy and Communications because you're in charge of all the semi-state companies. Michael Lowry was in charge of them at a time when one had to bring them from a monopoly situation into a competitive situation. I found him bright, energetic, quick to get to the heart of a brief and highly political. In the years I dealt with him, I never saw any example of him using his position unfairly or with any malice against anybody.'

The public is fed a lot of misconceptions about the world of PR and spin doctoring. 'The PR business isn't about nudges and winks, tricks and getting journalists on your side by wining and dining them. For a start, PR is about being accurate and truthful in what you say,' he says. 'It's principally about properly understanding the environment in which you're working, looking at the dynamics of that and working out a strategy that suits your client.' He enjoys the business because, 'you're on the inside of a company or organisation, at the right hand of the managing director, helping to make a serious contribution to the development of his or her company. Former US President Lyndon Johnson got it right when he said, it's much better to be "inside pissing out than outside pissing in".'

All in all, life hasn't always been a bed of roses for Bill. Ten days before the Los Angeles Olympic Games, in the summer of 1984, O'Herlihy suffered a mild heart attack. Luckily, he was again in the right place at the right time, surrounded by doctors and nurses when it happened. The day had started on an upbeat note: a final meeting at the RTÉ sports department of the home-and-away team for the Olympics. The head of television sport, Tim O'Connor, talking about the RTÉ Studio presentation, remarked: 'If we had a star system it would be the Olympics starring Bill O'Herlihy. I want you guys at home to give Bill every possible support because the studio must look good.' O'Herlihy, who was sitting at the back of the room, thought to himself: 'Finally, I've made it.' But of course, he hadn't.

The Olympics meeting ended early and he left Montrose for a lunch meeting at the PARC company, one of his PR clients who ran a hospital in Baghdad. Dr Harry Counihan, the head of medicine in Baghdad, was discussing his presentation to be given that night to the Royal College of Surgeons. Bill didn't feel well, with a pain in his chest and tingling down his arm. Counihan picked up the phone and called cardiologist John Horgan at the Richmond Hospital. 'There's a fellow here just starting a heart attack,' he told him. 'I'm bringing him down to you.'

He was discharged from the Richmond after a fortnight and sent home to recover with Hilary and their two daughters, Gillian and Sally, both of whom are now young adults. Gillian has graduated with a marketing degree and is now studying for a PR diploma; while Sally, a national champion and international swimmer, is studying communications at Dublin City University (DCU).

The attack meant that he missed his starring studio role for the Olympics, particularly disappointing because he was to also anchor RTÉ's first breakfast television programme. But he got the green light from Horgan to present the World Cup soccer match between Ireland and the Soviet Union in September. The only condition was that he had to undergo an angiogram immediately afterwards. 'The angiogram was on a Thursday,' he recalls. 'The match was being played in Lansdowne Road on the Wednesday night. I presented the programme and was told later that half the RTÉ crew were afraid I was going to get another heart attack on air. I went up to the Mater that night and checked in. I had my angiogram the following morning.' It was bad news. Horgan and heart surgeon Maurice Nelligan told him he needed a bypass. 'I nearly fell out of the bed,' he says. 'To say I was stunned and gobsmacked was putting it mildly. I had assumed that I was getting better. It didn't even dawn on me that I needed a bypass.'

At first, he refused to consider the heart operation but eventually promised that he would agree to surgery if there were any more chest pains. The pains returned within a fortnight. Surgery was inevitable. O'Herlihy made his peace with God and prayed to be taken through the operation safely. The triple bypass was successful. He remembers waking up afterwards in a ward shared with other heart patients who were either going to or coming from theatre. His chest was 'on fire'. A female patient got out of bed and approached his bedside. 'Excuse me,' she began, 'but aren't you Bill O'Herlihy?' He said he was. 'Can I have your autograph?' she asked. He didn't want to disappoint her and obliged, 'stupid eejit that I was'. Then she returned minutes later and asked for a second autograph for her nephew.

When O'Herlihy switches off his microphone for the last time, he would like to be remembered as 'somebody who never lost his head; who kept his feet on the ground; who recognised he was the luckiest person in the world to have been blessed by a lovely wife and family and who was able to combine two careers; and who never forgot his roots'.

He plans to retire in the year 2000, 'if the Lord spares me', when his contract with RTÉ expires after the Sydney Olympics. A secret ambition is to become Ireland's Alan Whicker: flying around the world to interview the rich and famous in exotic locations. He got a taste of globetrotting when he made *Distant Drum* for RTÉ, a series of interviews with successful Irish people which was sponsored by one of his PR clients, British Airways. 'I think I have the capability of doing something like that and enjoying it,' he adds. 'Or else I'd like to be invited to return for the last couple of years to be the editor of the *The Examiner*.' And he promises he won't be splitting any infinitives.

BRENDAN O'BRIEN

SAVE THE LAST DANCE FOR ME

WHEN showband survivor Brendan O'Brien was barred from another pub in his native city – this time a shabby early morning haunt – he was stopped on the street outside by a customer who recognised the '60s idol. 'Aren't you Brendan O'Brien? Didn't you top the bill in Carnegie Hall?' asked the stranger. O'Brien nodded. 'Are you really barred out of this bloody place? Boy, that's some comedown.'

The former lead singer of the Dixies showband was barred from four or five pubs in Cork city at a time in the early '80s when alcoholism ruled and almost ruined his life. Publicans refused to serve him out of compassion. 'A friend of mine who managed a well-known pub once said to me, "I can't serve you, Brendan. You were my idol. I can't take seeing you like this." I'd have a week's beard, no money and dirty clothes. They wouldn't serve me. They wouldn't like to see me falling around the place drunk. They'd have known me during the better times and probably once danced to the Dixies.'

The picture of a middle-aged alcoholic being carried by ambulance-men from the streets of his hometown seems worlds removed from the career pinnacle two decades earlier when O'Brien and the Dixies topped the bill at New York's Carnegie Hall. Today, he has come to terms with such contrasting images; the struggle with addiction is just part of the agony and ecstasy. He speaks honestly about his torment. The youthful good looks have gone but his eyes still light up when stories of the old days come to mind.

Showbands set the tempo for the swinging '60s in Ireland: Brendan O'Brien was a product of the explosion that catapulted young men from poorly paid jobs to big bucks, from mundane existences to stardom, almost overnight. O'Brien was one of the glamour boys, among the country's first homegrown sex symbols adored by thousands of women. While Waterford's Brendan Bowyer personified Elvis Presley, Cork's Brendan O'Brien imitated Buddy Holly, and the girls loved it.

O'Brien was the youngest of five children; the family home was at Riverstown House, Glanmire, on the outskirts of Cork city. They sold the magnificent country house in 1950, which has since been listed among historic sites, and moved to Military Hill in the northside of the city. He went to school at Christian Brothers College off St Patrick's Hill. He developed an interest in music at the age of nine; he studied the piano, violin and trumpet but opted for the guitar after seeing Elvis' first film, *Love Me Tender*. Like all youngsters, he worshipped Elvis and wanted to sing like him.

By 17, Brendan was playing in semi-pro outfits at local 'hops'. A friend, Johnny Byrne, asked him to join a band in 1958. They modelled themselves on early showbands, especially the Clipper Carlton, and came up with the name, 'The Confirmation Boys', complete with the stage look of red blazers, white slacks and white shoes.

After finishing the Leaving Cert, he took a job in an architect's office at the South Mall in Cork. He put his singing career on hold to study architecture full-time in London around 1959. He got a job as a junior draughtsman with a shoe company based in Oxford Street. He followed the latest musical trends back home: showbands were in their infancy, and the two top name bands were the Clipper Carlton and Johnny Quigley. Brendan had known the Dixies, who were resident at Cork's Arcadia Ballroom on the Lower Glanmire Road.

By 1961, the Dixies were ready to turn professional, encouraged by a successful tour of the North organised by dance promoter Jim Aiken. 'We liked it, and the crowds liked us,' recalls band leader Sean Lucey. 'We decided we were going to pack up our jobs and have a go ... all except one of the fellows. Jimmy Mintern was the other sax player and lead singer at the time. Unlike the others, Jimmy didn't have a trade to fall back on if things didn't work out. Brendan sung one or two songs with us. We decided that if Jimmy packed it in, then we'd bring in Brendan.'

The young Corkman came home for an audition and took a job in the Dixies as rhythm guitarist/vocalist. During a road journey to Galway in the summer of '61, just before they went pro, Brendan asked drummer Joe McCarthy: 'How long do you think we'll last?' He replied: 'Three or maybe four years.' If the band broke up, Brendan knew he'd still only be in his early twenties and could easily return to a day job. His parents, Ellen and Edward, had higher ambitions for their son and didn't like the idea of him joining a band. Brendan jumped at the opportunity.

The Dixies launched their professional career with a two-week tour of England. Cork immigrants in London, already familiar with the band from the Arcadia, flocked to dancehalls such as The Gresham, Galtymore, Blarney and Banba. The dynamic young band packed halls in London, Birmingham, Manchester and Coventry.

Upon their return home, the Dixies went on the road six days a week, playing in ballrooms from Belfast to Ballinasloe, Derry to Dunmanway. Dancing was a religion. The mating ritual switched to the ballroom where the young showbands with their goodlooking frontmen epitomised the glamour and excitement of the swinging '60s. Businessmen built dancehalls at every crossroads to house the explosion and make a fast buck. Everybody wanted to be either in a showband or else dancing to them. The Dixies were in the right place at the right time, on the crest of a wave that spawned 500 showbands employing 4,000 musicians and performing before crowds of between 1,500 to 3,000 a night in 249 major ballrooms. The Clipper Carlton from Strabane had lit the fuse in the '50s, and now showbands overtook the orchestras and big bands.

The Dixies were different. Their manager, the late Peter Prendergast, owner of the Arcadia, had a flair for publicity and made them the best news-makers in the business. No stunt was considered too outrageous. He convinced madcap drummer, Joe McCarthy, to insure his legs for £50,000. He engineered 'personal appearances' for the band in Paris and Rome, sandwiched midweek between bookings at the Oyster Ballroom in Dromkeen, Co. Limerick, The Gresham in Holloway Road, London, and back to Shanagolden in Co. Limerick at the end of the week.

The Dixies were kings of the Arcadia where they held the attendance record for packing in 4,300 on a St Stephen's Night. They worked hard to make a name for themselves outside Cork. 'We really had to do our apprenticeship,' says Brendan. 'Remember when we went pro in '61 we were certainly big in counties Cork, Limerick and Waterford. But we were unknown in Cavan and Dundalk. Instead of having 2,000 in the Arc on a Saturday night we might have 200 in the Adelphi in Dundalk. But we made an impression and the next time round it clicked for us.'

They modelled themselves from the start on the Clippers – particularly the comedy routines – and could rely on solid musicianship complemented by gimmicks and image cultivation. The musical range extended from jazz to rock'n'roll to just about anything the punters wanted to hear. Brendan sang like an angel and carried the music of Buddy Holly to a new generation of pop fans in Ireland. His versions of *Oh Boy*, *Peggy Sue*, *Rave On*, and *It Doesn't Matter Anymore* were all hits. 'We had no singer in particular,' he recalls. 'I wound up a singer and Joe wound up the funnyman. We were really a team. Joe was doing the comedy. Joe made us that bit different because of the clowning. I was doing the singing. Theo Cahill was the backbone of the music. We had an ideal combination.' The young lead singer built up a huge female following. The girls went to watch Brendan, and the boys went to watch the girls watching Brendan.

By 1964, the Dixies were recording and breaking into the Irish charts, and in September of that year came the Carnegie Hall triumph during a two-week tour of the Irish-American ballrooms in New York, Boston, Chicago, Philadelphia, Pittsburgh and Cleveland. When the Beatles caused a riot at Carnegie Hall, the management banned groups in future. The ban was lifted to allow the Irish showband play the second half of an all-Irish bill at Carnegie Hall on 19 September. It was organised by promoter Hugh Hardy who had one of the top Irish radio shows in the US. The Dixies shared a bill with Irish singers and dancers, together with country star Slim Whitman.

Typically, their manager came up with a special postcard in honour of the occasion: it showed the band as passengers in a spacecraft hovering over New York. The Dixies 'brought the house down,' according to *The Irish Echo*. The Corkmen's Association of New York gave them a trophy. The band's welcome home from the citizens of Cork was of a kind usually saved for an All-Ireland winning team. They were paraded through the streets on an open-top bus.

Still, success was measured by crowd numbers, and mighty Carnegie Hall played second fiddle to the bigger dancehalls. 'We played to 2,800 and it was sold out. We never bothered going back there,' explains Brendan. 'Just around the corner was the City Centre Ballroom that would take 4,000 at maybe twice the price, so we used to play there Friday, Saturday and Sunday nights. 'By now, the Dixies were among the richest and most popular showbands: Royal, Capitol, Miami, Drifters, Dixies, Freshmen, Cadets, Mighty Avons, Plattermen and the Clipper Carlton.

Brendan was one of the pin-up idols of the era who left girls weak at the knees, in the same sex symbol league as Brendan Bowyer, Joe Dolan, Butch Moore, Dickie Rock and Derek Dean. The girls worshipped him from the foot of the stage; there was always a sea of outstretched arms and chorus of screams. He was every girl's dreamboat, a hunk who oozed sex appeal. 'It was always dangerous if they caught hold of the mike lead. You'd be whipped off the stage and torn asunder. If you broke a string, hundreds would be looking for the guitar string as a souvenir.'

Brendan was frequently mobbed by fans on the streets of Dublin, Cork and Limerick in the years 1963, 1964 and 1965. 'If you got surrounded by girls they'd start by asking for your autograph, then for your pen, your tie, and then shirt. The guards often picked me up from Patrick Street in Cork after having my clothes ripped off. It was safer to go out at night under the cover of darkness.' Valentine's Day always brought presents from his adoring female fans: usually dolls, flowers and chocolates.

Dixies' manager Peter Prendergast cultivated fan clubs in London, Liverpool, Manchester, Cork, Dublin, Mayo, Belfast and Derry, all run from his office in the Arcadia Ballroom. In 1961, a typical week could start at Seapoint in Galway on Wednesday, the Crescent in Athlone on Thursday, the Adelphi in Dundalk on Friday, the Crystal or Olympic in Dublin on Saturday and the Royal in Castlebar on Sunday night. The band took Mondays and Tuesdays off 'to enjoy our stardom and new found wealth'.

On the road, the Corkmen were the clown princes of showbandland, pulling all manner of pranks. Their madcap humour broke the boredom of hours spent travelling over narrow roads the length and breadth of the country. Rival band wagons were spattered with eggs and flour as the Dixies overtook them in the dead of night. They often marched down boreens playing trumpet, trombone and sax for the cattle at four in the morning. 'I suppose we were a bunch of lovable rogues,' says Brendan. 'A guy said to me once, "the Dixies started a party in '61 and it's still going on".'

The showband elite lived like royalty and enjoyed the trappings of success. 'It was really great fun. I'd be telling lies if I said we didn't like women screaming and throwing themselves at us. We were earning buckets of money. The money was five or 10 times the normal wage. The hotels were brilliant. We were a bit like a successful soccer team: Joe and I scored the goals but we couldn't have done it without the rest of the guys.'

Like Bowyer, O'Brien had a reputation for working hard, and playing even harder. He enjoyed a superstar lifestyle – fast cars, boats, houses and holidays in Spain. His first car was a flash Triumph Herald. He bought his mother a Vauxhall Victor. 'I called home to surprise her and brought her out to see the new car,' recalls Brendan. 'She said, "a bank manager wouldn't be able to afford that." But I said, "Mam, I'm earning more than a bank manager".'

When Brendan got married in the mid-'60s, he bought a large house, 'Leeside', at Tivoli, Cork, and later moved to Glounthaune where he was one of the few with a swimming pool. While driving to Waterford one day he saw a cabin cruiser for sale by the roadside and bought it for cash on the spot. The Dixies were so successful in the early '60s that they owned their own ballroom in the East End of London, appropriately called The Arcadia.

Brendan O'Brien was one of the élite group to have had two records in the Irish Top Ten in 1964. The Dixies were rarely out of the charts during the golden years. They made 27 records. The biggest hit was *Little Arrows* which went to No.1 on 7 September, 1968, and stayed in the charts for 20 weeks. It was a huge seller. *The Dixies* swept *The Spotlight* magazine awards for 1968: they were voted Band of the Year; *Little Arrows* was Record of the Year; Joe McCarthy, Showman of the Year; Steve Lynch, Instrumentalist of the Year; and Brendan O'Brien, Singer of the Year.

The two Brendans – O'Brien and Bowyer – competed for the showband market on stage, but they were the best of pals off stage and would ultimately share an alcohol addiction. O'Brien's achievements are widely acknowledged. In his book of Irish chart hits, broadcaster Larry Gogan rated O'Brien among 36 artistes who achieved most hits in the Irish charts from 1962 to 1983. He had 17 – one more than Bowyer.

Brendan Bowyer and the Royal Showband became the first Irish band to land a residency in Las Vegas, and the Dixies got their big break in 1969. Bill Fuller brought the Cork band to Vegas for an audition held by booking agent Rocky Sennes at the Frontier Hotel where Presley had his first Vegas gig over a decade before. The Dixies got an eight-week residency at the Desert Inn and returned the following year for 12 weeks. They performed three shows a night, six nights a week, followed by parties into the early hours. While performing on stage, it wasn't unusual to see the girls throw knickers and hotel room keys at the Irish musicians. The band was paid $10,000 a week. Bowyer and The Royal were at the Stardust nearby. 'People in Ireland never realised what Vegas meant to the entertainment world. Everyone in the States, no matter how big they were, wanted to play there.'

The Dixies were playing in the same town as legends like Frank Sinatra, Elvis Presley and Tom Jones. They were going to parties with Jones, comedians Jimmy Durante and Jack Benny, and also Sinatra Junior. The Dixies adopted a 'local' everywhere: in Cork it was Handlebars Pub on the Lower Glanmire Road near The Arcadia; in Dublin, The Belvedere Hotel; in New York, The Woodward; and in Vegas, The Flame. Brendan was a drinking pal of actor James Coburn, among a host of celebrities who dropped into The Flame. The Dixies appeared on the *Forest Duke* TV show with Jack Benny and Bobbie Gentry. A photographer friend from Los Angeles, who joined them in the studio later, asked Gentry to pose with the Irish band and she refused to do so. Benny apologised to The Dixies on her behalf. When Durante was introduced to McCarthy, he pinched the Corkman by the nose and said: 'Hey, you've gotta superior weapon.' The Dixies closed the book on Vegas after their 12-week stint in 1970. 'We were making as much money in Ireland, so what did we want going over for,' says McCarthy.

By the dawn of a new decade, showbands were becoming a dying breed. The Royal flagship from Waterford was sinking. Bowyer and his talented partner, Tom Dunphy, jumped ship to form a new band, The Big 8. O'Brien and McCarthy quit The Dixies in January 1972 to form Stage Two. The Dixies found a new drummer and brought in Sandie Jones to replace O'Brien as lead singer. Stage Two were booked solid on the ballroom circuit, and had to refuse work. They had a hit with *Beautiful Sunday* which went to No. 5 in the summer of '72.

The world fell apart for Brendan on the evening of 1 October, 1974, as he sang at a charity dance in aid of the Gurranabraher Handicapped Wheelchair Association at the Stardust Ballroom in Cork. He reached out to adjust the height of the microphone and grasped it with devastating results. The microphone was live. He suffered a severe electric shock and nearly died. The force of the shock threw him backwards about six feet on the stage. He suffered severe burns on both hands and severe thrombosis of the main veins of his body. The accident left him in hospital for three months and wrecked his career. It heralded the end of the showbusiness fairytale and the beginning of a nightmare.

He failed in his High Court action for massive compensation against the Stardust in 1979. He appealed the result to the Supreme Court where the case was settled. The house of cards began to tumble, and he saw his substantial wealth disappear. 'When I lost that court case, I lost a lot,' he says. 'I had invested heavily in commercial property. The cash flow had stopped after the accident. The banks closed in. I had to sell off what I had invested in. In today's terms, I suppose on paper I had close on £2 million between partnerships and my own investments.' He was forced to sell his home, his cabin cruiser, his wife's car and he couldn't afford to keep his son at college. Eventually, all that remained was a building in North Main Street, Cork, where he lives alone today in a modest flat.

Things got worse. Alcohol became a 'crutch' around 1976 when it became clear that his career was finished. Drinking bouts became more frequent; days were lost to binges. At the peak he usually drank at least

24 pints of beer a day, sometimes supplemented with shots of vodka. It got to the stage where he stopped counting.

Early morning drinking became a feature of his addiction in the late '70s and early '80s. 'I would sometimes have to have a drink at seven in the morning to stop the shaking and shivering,' he admits. 'It has to be the worst drug addiction in the world. I just needed a drink like a drug addict needs a fix. That came first and foremost. Nothing else mattered once you had your booze. If you went into a pub at seven, you'd be feeling great by eight. You'd stay until nine or nine thirty and then go to a normal pub where you'd meet people coming in for a coffee at half ten. Having been as famous as the Dixies were, anywhere I went I was known. I'd love sitting on the high stool and telling people about Dean Martin and Jimmy Durante. I'd be talking and talking and before I knew it it would be closing time. If I had the guitar in the car I'd bring it in and sing songs. I didn't really start falling around the streets until the latter days in the '80s when my tolerance was zero. I'm not making excuses but I had a lot of worries. My marriage was in trouble. That broke my heart. I had to educate five children. I had to look after the banks. I had to feed a drink habit as well.'

He says his marriage crumbled over a period of years. It ran into trouble in 1982 and collapsed in 1986. The breakup is still a source of deep regret.

Alcoholism brought such dependency that drink always had to be within easy reach; there were hiding places in the boot of the car or in the wardrobe or bathrooms at home. When the family lived in Glounthaune in 1985, Brendan recalls having a 'stash' in the garden in the event of an emergency. It was a wad of notes and a bottle of vodka, hidden in a wall under ivy. He forgot about them afterwards.

There was one favourite way of topping up alcohol levels in the morning. 'When I was living in Glounthaune, I might call into a local shop after dropping the kids to school. I'd explain that we were having guests in for dinner that evening and needed some wine. That would be at half nine in the morning. I'd take two bottles and knock it back in the car like you'd drink water. I'd go home and that would keep me going for four or five hours with no one in the world, least of all my wife, knowing I had taken a drink.'

There were tricks to getting drink after closing time, and to getting drink when he was broke. After hours drink could be obtained in the hotels – if he had the right excuse. 'I'd go to the Imperial or the Metropole at three or four in the morning, and it could be in the middle of winter on a freezing night. I'd make an effort to look a bit respectable. I'd tell the night porter I was on the way back from Dundalk or Drogheda. Anyone who has this sort of addiction will tell you that after a few pints, you'd feel grand and could go away again. You'd get your wits about you then and could start planning again for the next day.' When the money ran out, friendly publicans put drink bills on the slate. Other alcoholics would come to his rescue if he needed a drink badly enough.

Brendan was often picked up from the street after collapsing into a drunken stupour. 'I did feel embarrassed about falling down in North Main Street and somebody calling an ambulance for me. I'd end up in the Mercy Hospital getting pumped out. The choice in the morning would be to either stop and suffer on for a few days while you detox, or else go out and have a few pints and you'd be feeling grand again.' In the dark days, he was barred out of pubs. They would only accept him back provided he didn't touch alcohol.

He returned to The Dixies when they reformed in 1982. The comeback to the stage was shortlived. The band 'let him go' in 1985. 'I wasn't turning up for gigs. I could be off out in Knockraha or somewhere having a sing-song with the lads. I suppose I'd be too drunk to turn up. Whether you'd like it or not, drink would come first and you become selfish.' O'Brien made another comeback with the Dixies in 1992, but has since been pursuing a solo career.

He made numerous efforts to quit drinking; he had to detox three times a year, usually at St Anne's in Cork or at Sr Consilio's centres in Bruree, Co. Limerick, and Athy, Co. Kildare. He was hospitalised about 30 times over the years. He acknowledges the support given by his close friend, Dermot Murphy, and by his sister, Ita, a former nurse. 'They always stuck by me during good times and bad.'

'It takes me about five days to detox. A minute becomes a whole day when you're in bed sweating and waiting for it to pass. You're afraid of everything. If the phone rang or door banged you'd jump sky high. Your nerves would be red raw. It's a horrible addiction. After five days you're feeling much better and able to have a bath or shower on your own. The shakes are gone and then it's back to the AA meetings. It helps if you can stay in touch with sober alcoholics. There is no cure. I say to myself, "for today I won't drink".'

In spite of the best intentions, he has succumbed many times. 'The drink will tell you, "go on, you're grand". It could be a lovely June afternoon. You might have a hundred quid in your pocket. I could be driving down to East Cork to see some friends. I could quite easily pull into the Island Gate bar and have a pint or two. Then I could drink socially for two or three days. Next thing I'd start avoiding people and wouldn't answer the phone. I'd start going to early morning pubs. It would go from bad to worse. Eventually, you wouldn't be hiding from anyone and you'd go into any pub for a pint.'

The people of Cork learned on 7 March, 1986, that their local hero had served two weeks in jail for road traffic offences. It was a bombshell. *The Cork Examiner* reported that Brendan O'Brien had been given a two-month sentence after failing to pay approximately £700 in fines resulting from contraventions of the Road Traffic Act. He was released from Cork Prison after outstanding amounts were paid by a friend.

'It's quite simple,' he says of the circumstances. 'A friend of mine asked me one day if he could borrow my car. I asked if he was insured. He said he was. He returned the car that afternoon to me. Apparently, the cops had stopped him. Unknown to me, I was charged for having a car uninsured and fined £700 or two months in jail, somewhere in Co. Waterford.

'The Guards arrived up to my house in Glounthaune in an unmarked car and said, "pay the money now or you go to jail". Just like that. I said, "look, I can pay it tomorrow". So they put me into the car and bunged me up to prison. Sean Lucey and a friend of mine paid the fine and took me out. I got no summons, no prosecution, no notification of a court hearing. So I never turned up in court. The court hearing had gone ahead in Kilmacthomas. I knew absolutely nothing about it until I woke up in jail. I couldn't believe it. I admit I had been drinking. When I woke up all I wanted was a drink. I said to another guy in the cell, "Where am I?" He said, "you're in jail". I said, "what am I doing here?" He said, "you came in last night; you were well pissed". I asked to see the prison warden. He knew exactly that I was in there for non-payment of fines. *The Cork Examiner* slapped it across the front page when I was released. Everyone assumed, knowing I'm an alcoholic, that I was slung in jail for drunken driving or something. I was totally wronged again for the umpteenth time.' On the 'inside', everybody knew Brendan O'Brien, and christened him The Celebrity.

A lot of water has passed under the Brooklyn Bridge since Brendan O'Brien went partying with The Dixies in 1961. All the memories are stored between the frayed covers of an old scrapbook which is his cherished possession. The showband sex symbol is now a grandfather. Four of his five children are living in Toronto: Trish, Brendan, Aideen and

Conor. His youngest daughter, Sinead, is living in Cork. Brendan's brothers, Frank and Paul, have lived in Toronto for over 30 years.

Any regrets? 'The marriage break-up was terrible. I never wanted that to happen. Behind all the travelling, the roguery, the making of a fortune and losing of a fortune, I was really a home bird. No matter where we were on a Sunday night, we always came home and I loved coming home, especially to what I would call my married home at Leeside, Tivoli. To come home there, having the two days off, having a lot of money and a lovely wife and young children, I really couldn't ask for anything more. It all went horribly wrong. You can only drive one car at a time and wear one suit of clothes. What's outside all that? Family. The bottom line is family. Ultimately, your home life is most important of all.'

Brendan O'Brien is a survivor – in spite of traumas that would have crushed a lesser man. The magic hasn't faded entirely. When the two Brendans – O'Brien and Bowyer – reunited on stage in Cork during a hot Sunday night in August 1997, it was like old times. He will be remembered long after the dancehall lights have dimmed for the last time.

DARINA ALLEN

SIMPLY DELICIOUS

IT was a chance encounter over the Sunday night buffet at Ballymaloe House. Darina Allen was chatting to guests when a polite Englishwoman asked her advice on food. She wanted something nice, yet light and non-fattening. It wasn't for her but her boyfriend. He was an actor, and had to be careful about diet. 'Oh, what's his name?' asked Darina. 'Hugh Grant.' The name meant nothing to her. 'What sort of actor is he?' she asked. 'He does films actually,' replied the Englishwoman. 'What films has he done?' she asked, to keep the flow of conversation going. '*Four Weddings and a Funeral*.' That meant nothing to her either. 'The girls on the buffet were ready to kick me at that stage,' recalls Darina with a giggle. 'That will tell you how naïve I was. I didn't get to see many films, so I didn't know who they were.' Elizabeth Hurley was 'very sweet'. Hugh Grant was 'charming'. In those days, they stayed at Ballymaloe and roamed around East Cork without being recognised. The hottest properties in Hollywood made several return trips since.

As a rule, Darina doesn't like to name drop, and neither do staff at Ballymaloe House or at her cookery school two miles away. There's murder if anybody lets a name slip. Any stories that hit the press have leaked because a famous face has been spotted in the Shanagarry area. Trying to keep quiet about Hurley, the million-dollar model, and Grant, *The Four Weddings* star whose drive down Sunset Boulevard put him on the front pages, would, of course, be a mission impossible.

Darina has a plentiful store of anecdotes about the who's who brigade; they are told only on the condition that names are hush-hush. Like the wife of one of Ireland's wealthiest men who wanted Darina to teach her how to cook. She had married into a mansion with household staff: the kitchen was off-limits and the cook shooed her away anytime she wanted to prepare a meal for herself and her husband. So she came to Darina for a week's cookery course, 'desperate' to be able to return home and challenge the cook on her own terms.

She was 'terribly, terribly' serious. While making yeast bread one day, Darina caught her staring into the bowl in a state of panic. 'What's the problem?' asked Darina. 'I'm terrified of this tiny little organism,' she replied, on the verge of tears. 'I'm terrified I'm going to kill it and my bread won't work.' The rest of the class were in 'hoots' of laughter. 'The others were housewives who'd managed to get away from their own kitchens for a few days,' says Darina, 'and here was this woman trying to get back in. We had a hilarious week with her in the class.'

Everybody knows Darina – the straight hair, those trademark formidable glasses, cheery smile and a flow of flowery adjectives that can make even a boiled egg sound exciting. The TV cook who held up a steel whisk for the camera, proclaimed it as her indispensable tool, and promptly sent half the country out in search of one just like it. The best-selling author who sold over half a million books in seven years. The mistress of one of the finest cookery schools in the world whose chocolate cake alone would justify crawling to Shanagarry on your hands and knees through broken glass. These days, people drive into the courtyard of Kinoith, the old house where it all started, just to catch a glimpse of her.

Darina's philosophy is uncomplicated. She wanted to take the mystery out of cooking and tell people they could do it too. It's not fancy stuff. It's simple. When she makes a cookery programme she wants everyone to leap out of their chairs, rush off to buy ingredients and have a go in the kitchen. When it works she's overjoyed. She loves feedback and gets a lot because she's so recognisable. Most people say they never had the courage to try a particular dish or recipe until they saw her do it on television. That's a fairly typical reaction. Once, she was even credited with saving a marriage. A woman rushed up to her on Patrick Street in Cork, grabbed her on the shoulder and said: 'I've just got to tell you, Darina, that you're after saving the marriage for me. I could never make bread like his mother, no matter how much I tried. When I saw you making bread on television, I had a go at it. I made him a grand cake of bread and he's only delighted with me now.' That might sound corny, but the woman meant it. Wherever Darina is spotted, people are bursting to tell her about their culinary masterpieces or disasters.

Darina says she never set out to become a household name. There was no grand plan. 'I've never done anything to be famous, that's for sure,' she says. 'It was never something that I strove for nor is it of any value to me in real terms. I was passionate about food. It's amazing, all you need is to be passionate about one thing and anything is possible.'

It is 30 years since Darina O'Connell from Cullohill, Co. Laois, came to Shanagarry to learn about cooking from Myrtle Allen. The Cork credentials were finally bestowed when she got a call from the Real Taoiseach in 1989. It came after her first appearance on *The Late Late Show* to talk about the first series of cookery programmes. She was 'terrified to bits' going on *The Late Late*. But Gay was 'very nice' and made her feel at ease. When she returned to Ballymaloe after spending the weekend in Dublin, she was told about telephone greetings from Jack Lynch. His wife, Maírín, had phoned with a message from Jack, saying: 'Congratulations, Darina, now you're one of our own.' She was thrilled by such recognition. 'I thought that was so sweet of him. I felt very flattered. Now I was being recognised as an adopted Corkwoman.' Life was never the same again after *The Late Late*. Next day, when she went shopping in Dublin she was recognised immediately. 'I could hear people saying behind me, "that's the woman on *The Late Late Show*". When I walked into a restaurant people turned around and stared at me. I found all that attention very difficult at the beginning and wasn't able to cope with it.'

Darina O'Connell was born in Cullohill on 30 July, 1948, the eldest of nine children; six boys and three girls. Her father, Dick, died when she was just 14. Her mother, Elizabeth, is 'an amazing woman'. It was Darina's village and she loved it, situated on the road between Durrow and Johnstown. Blink as you pass through and you'll miss it; it's also a favourite spot for garda speed traps on the Dublin to Cork road. Darina enjoyed a typical country childhood in a village with a strong community spirit. The O'Connells ran almost all the businesses in the village – all things to all men. They had a pub, grocery, post office, petrol pumps, were auctioneers and undertakers and even sold fertiliser. Whatever service was needed by the community, they provided it. They also had some land outside the village. 'I grew up with farming all around me,' she says. 'I helped with all the haymaking and thrashing. That was all part of my childhood. We lived at a time in Ireland when we were all children of the village. We could run into anyone's house and sit up at the table for something to eat.'

At home, there was always cooking going on in the house. With nine children, by the time her mother had finished with one meal, it was time to start preparing the next. Her mother was a very good cook and made bread every day. 'I grew up always having good, simple food around me,' says Darina. 'Nothing fancy, just ordinary food that was good and wholesome. I knew how to make bread because mummy made it every day.'

She was sent to boarding school at the Dominican Convent in Wicklow at the age of 11. She was lonely at first; to go back home just because she didn't like it there was out of the question. So she got used to it. After completing the Leaving Certificate, Darina was at a crossroads. It was down to a choice between horticulture and hotel management. She always wanted to cook, 'but at that stage it wasn't considered the thing to just be a cook or a chef ... you had to do management.' She decided to take a two-year diploma course in hotel and catering management at the College of Catering in Cathal Brugha Street, Dublin.

Darina loved the buzz of the capital and made many friends. There was no great career plan. The idea was to get a good job, find a nice guy, settle down and have lots of children. But she was far more interested in the cooking part of the course than management. Convenience foods were all the rage in the late '60s. She preferred the real thing. "I was in a dilemma,' she explains. 'I wanted to cook really good food. I also wanted to find a restaurant where they were using fresh food and cooking with fresh herbs. It was almost impossible. At the best restaurants – places like The Russell in Dublin and The Oyster Tavern in Cork – their menus were the same virtually all year round. At that stage, people wrote the menu when the restaurant opened and it might be the same 10 years later.' In addition, none of these restaurants wanted to take girls into their kitchens. Near the end of the course at Cathal Brugha Street, Darina was asked by one of the senior teachers, Mór Murnaghan, if she had a job lined up. There was nothing in the offing. They'd heard about a farmer's wife in Co. Cork who was famous for cooking with fresh herbs and ingredients and who'd opened a restaurant in her house.

Darina wrote to Myrtle Allen who sent back a lovely letter. In her reply, Mrs Allen said she had children of Darina's age and offered her the use of a swimming pool and tennis courts. Darina kept the letter. By contrast, most of her classmates got stiff acceptance letters from other establishments telling them to turn up at the tradesman's entrance at eight o'clock.

Darina packed her bags for Ballymaloe House in Shanagarry in 1969. When she stepped out of the car, Ballymaloe looked stunning. It was a beautiful country residence which had been built on to the remains of a Geraldine castle and keep, surrounded by a 400-acre farm. Myrtle and Ivan Allen bought Ballymaloe in 1948. The first person to welcome Darina O'Connell, the new apprentice, was Myrtle's son, Tim. For her, it was love at first sight. 'I thought to myself, "now, he looks interesting". He had long hair, which was very daring at the time. He looked with-it. He was smaller than me and younger. He was very nice and welcoming but didn't really take much notice of me for the summer because he had one girlfriend after the other. It was serious stuff: he literally sometimes put one back on the train and picked up the next one. It wasn't until the winter when everyone else was gone off the scene that I was the only one around and things began to happen. Eventually, we began to go out together.' Tim says that Darina made an immediate impression on him, though he was trying to juggle girlfriends early on. When the last girlfriend was leaving at the end of the summer, she turned to Darina and asked her to mind Tim for her. That was like telling the cat to mind the cream. Darina gave Tim a sense of security; he thought she was confident, optimistic and had a real driving force.

Darina and Myrtle were kindred spirits in the kitchen. Ballymaloe had only been opened a few years when the new apprentice arrived. It was the first of the Irish country house hotels with a growing reputation for fine food. Like Darina, Myrtle hated the convenience food ethos and her cookery philosophy was based on using fresh produce from her own garden and locality and, of course, writing her own menu. In Myrtle, she would find not alone a culinary soul mate, but also a mother-in-law. She was much taken with the Quaker ethic of the Allens. They treated women well, and those qualities were innate in Tim.

Darina and Tim were married in 1970. She was 21; he was 20. They had the joys of trying to sort out a mixed marriage. They decided to have two ceremonies: one in Darina's local church in Cullohill and another in the Quaker Meeting House in Cork. Darina and Tim moved into Kinoith, a late Georgian house built around 1830 which Ivan Allen had inherited from the Strangmans, a Waterford Quaker family. The gardens, once created by the Strangmans from Waterford in the early 1800s, had gone into decline after the death of Lydia Strangman in 1952. The gardens were now a wilderness.

Tim had trained in horticulture and was busy on his father's 100-acre farm there. But farming was going through a difficult stretch. They were determined to make a living out of their new way of life, growing apples, mushrooms, tomatoes and flowers. For the first few years, Darina was content to raise her children and help out in Ballymaloe House. They had four children: Isaac, Toby, Lydia and Emily. 'We had absolutely no money but were happy,' she recalls. 'We were like babes in the woods. We thought we knew everything. We had a little car which Timmy got a present of. But we were getting bad prices and that made horticulture very difficult. That wasn't our fault. The bottom was falling out of horticulture at the time. We didn't have the capital to continue pouring into that side of things. We decided to see what other strings we had to our bow.' Darina and Tim took the overflow of guests from Ballymaloe House for bed and breakfast.

'We'd move out of our own bedroom to make a few bob,' she recalls. 'It was very nice to have people stay over and to cook them breakfast.' Next, they began to convert the farm buildings into self-catering holiday cottages and had a farm shop as well. 'Every penny we made we put back into the place,' she explains. 'We started with one cottage. Quite often a family with children might stay with us for a week or a fortnight and eat at Ballymaloe. We built up a few families who liked to visit. Then we did up another cottage and so on.'

By the end of the '70s, the ingredients of the Ballymaloe success story was falling into place for the Allens. The award-winning restaurant earned an international reputation. Myrtle had started a crusade to recapture forgotten natural flavours while the concept of nouvelle cuisine swept through the smart kitchens of Europe. Her acclaimed *Ballymaloe Cookbook* sold very well and spawned further editions into the '80s. It wasn't so much a collection of recipes, said *The Financial Times*, but a reflection of a genuine and authentic way of life related to the land, culture and produce of Myrtle's country. *Vogue* magazine advised anyone with an interest in Irish food to buy the book. Myrtle opened a restaurant in Paris, *La Ferme Irlandaise* at Place du Marché, St Honore, from which the smells of sizzling Irish rashers and sausages wafted into the morning air. She had also started cookery classes during the quiet winter period at Ballymaloe. Her daughter-in-law helped out with the classes. Myrtle asked Darina to run the classes when she too became too busy with her restaurants. 'I was absolutely sure nobody would come to see me,' says Darina. 'But I loved cooking. So I decided to have a go.' She advertised a series of eight cookery classes on Saturday mornings in *The Cork Examiner*.

Two of the farm buildings at Kinoith had been converted into cottages at this stage and the classes were held in the kitchen of one of them. Well-to-do Cork women drove down to Shanagarry in their Mercs and BMWs 'and we'd hide our bashed up old car around the back'. Darina remembers these ladies fondly because they sowed the seeds of the cookery school.

She toyed with the idea of opening a school at the beginning of the '80s. A Dublin friend suggested she should open a residential cookery school along the lines of the Cordon Bleu in London and Paris which were attracting Irish students. She promised to send her two daughters to Shanagarry if Darina took the plunge. Darina eyed the farm outbuildings and dreamed of converting them into a kitchen and little classrooms. She laid plans for a 12-week curriculum.

She had also been on a week-long cookery course in Italy and felt that there was a real opening for a school in Ireland, particularly with such easy access to high quality fresh ingredients. She went to other famous cookery schools and saw how they ran their businesses. 'I saw what they did and tasted their food and knew what we had was every bit as good,' she reflects. One of the things that put her off opening a school was the fear that students might be bored in the evenings and feel 'buried' in the country. Myrtle suggested they set up a course at the Ballymaloe kitchen. They advertised a 10-week cookery course at Ballymaloe in *The Cork Examiner* and *The Irish Times*. The course was full within three days. There were seven students on the first course in 1982, among them Mark Nolan who went on to manage two of Ireland's most prestigious hotels: first, operations manager at Ashford Castle and then general manager at Dromoland Castle. Although still feeding her fourth child at the time, Darina ended up teaching three days a week. 'By the end of that course I knew two things,' says Darina. 'First, I had a lot more confidence. I felt I could teach because I was so passionate about what I was doing. Second, I knew there was a huge demand because we couldn't take all the people who wanted to come. So, I talked to my husband and mother-in-law and father-in-law about starting a cookery school.' All she needed now was money to make her dream a reality. Although Myrtle had pioneered Irish cooking, the idea that her daughter-in-law could launch an international cookery school in remote Shanagarry was considered fanciful in 1983. At least, the bank manager certainly thought so.

Darina brought him a proposal, explaining that she wanted to start a school in converted farm buildings and it would be as good as any in the world. She outlined the advantages of having their own farm and gardens where they could grow their own produce; they were close to the sea for fresh fish; they could get meat supplies locally. She needed a loan of £18,000. 'The bank manager was very nice and listened to me for ages.' But he turned her down. He said: 'I hate to say this to you but it's just a complete non-runner. You're got carried away with this idea but it won't work in the middle of the country.' Darina felt deflated. She wasn't about to give up, though. 'I never even heard of market research or feasibility studies,' she recalls. 'It was pure gut feeling and I knew I could do it well. I felt that people would be enchanted by what we had to offer. I knew it would work. What's more, I needed it to work. It wasn't a question of just teaching a little class when I felt like it.' Luckily, the Allens came to her rescue. Ivan agreed to guarantee a loan at his bank.

Furthermore, Ivan and Myrtle felt it should be called The Ballymaloe Cookery School. 'That was a huge compliment to me,' she says, 'but also a huge responsibility. I knew I had to operate to the high standards that people would expect from the Ballymaloe name. We worked incredibly hard and tried to deliver more than we promised rather than less.'

The Ballymaloe Cookery School started off in converted farm buildings with nine students in 1983. 'I remember wondering what on earth was ahead of us,' says Darina. There was no need to hire marketing or public relations experts. It quickly built up a reputation for excellence, came to the attention of international food writers, and soon Darina had to turn away students looking for places on her two 12-week courses.

She acknowledges Myrtle's encouragement as the school began to flourish. 'I know it can't have been easy for her in a way,' she says, 'but Myrtle has always been enormously generous in her support. When I started the school, I taught so many of the recipes she had taught me. There was never a problem. Other people would have been much less generous in their attitude and much more protective of their own patch. Instead, she did everything possible to encourage me.' After six years, Darina and Tim converted an old apple building on the courtyard at Kinoith, which now houses the main school kitchen overlooked by a huge ceiling mirror. They increased the intake of students from 18 to 38, with a continuous waiting list. Now there are 44 students who come to Shanagarry from all over the world.

The Allens restored the gardens, which had been created by the Strangmans, to their former glory. 'The gardens are a big passion,' says Darina. 'They are a natural extension of what we do here. My husband says I'll bankrupt him with gardens.' Visitors are in awe of the herb, vegetable and fruit gardens. They require a lot of tender loving care. Three fulltime gardeners tend to the gardens and also to the more exotic ingredients grown on an acre under glass. The gardens are open to the public and attract a steady flow of tourists. Darina's sister, Elizabeth, is the head gardener. Meantime, there is another family connection at Ballymaloe House: her brother, Rory, is head chef and joint manager along with Hazel Allen.

It isn't just a cookery school: students are taught a way of life. For one thing, they're encouraged to pick their own ingredients and also introduced to local fish and meat suppliers and cheesemakers. 'On the first day of the 12-week course,' explains Darina, 'I take students out and introduce them to the gardeners. I tell them these are the people who grow the produce that you're going to cook with. You must never again look at a lettuce or cabbage on a supermarket shelf and just see it as something wrapped in plastic. Remember that somebody has spent five or six months growing this for you and you can make a mess of it in the last couple of seconds by cooking it carelessly. This transforms the way they look at ingredients. The whole thing of living on a farm with gardens is terribly important for the way I operate. And we always cook with the seasons.'

The school is mostly self-sufficient. Meat and fish come from local suppliers. Fresh eggs come from free-range hens who feed on cookery school scraps 'and strut about the place with attitude'. And there are Kerry cows and pigs 'that have happy contented lives'. Lunch is a special time when teachers and students sit down together in the school dining room to taste the fruits of their labours. Practically everybody who completes the course is guaranteed a job afterwards. The greatest tribute to Darina's philosophy-in-action is to see her former students working in the finest restaurants and hotels around the world.

When the school isn't running fulltime courses, there is a programme of 20 short courses covering everything from salads, sandwiches, irresistible breakfasts, pasta to pizzas. One course was even tailored for priests to help them fend for themselves in the kitchen as housekeepers become a relic of the past. There's a lot more besides, with courses in gardening, flower painting, basket weaving, window boxes and hanging baskets and shell decoration. It is, of course, a mini-industry employing 30 people or more depending on the season.

'Have a glass of wine and relax' – that was the advice given to Darina when she went in front of the TV cameras for the first time. It came from another celebrity cook and lover of the grape, Keith Floyd, who turned up in the courtyard one day with a TV crew in tow. It was the first time Darina had seen a television camera. She was about to make her TV debut. Floyd wanted to film a sequence with Darina in the main school kitchen for a programme about Cork as part of his BBC food series. 'I was very tense at the beginning and couldn't do it,' recalls Darina. Floyd reached for a bottle of wine and said: 'Just have a glass of wine and relax.' They did and finished the scene. Then they had another glass of wine 'and got very convivial'. Floyd was very entertaining. He told Timmy later: 'She should do television; she's a natural.' Darina thought the suggestion was hilarious because she says she never had any notions of doing television work.

It was a turning point in her career when RTÉ asked her to do the first television series back in 1989. She was very nervous before filming, but somehow always managed to exude an air of calm and order when the camera started rolling. There was a tiny budget for the first *Simply Delicious* series, shot with a single camera.

Inevitably, there were some disasters: she set the mackerel on fire in the fish series. The cookery school kitchen provided the setting for the programmes. The RTÉ crew filmed each in the eight *Simply Delicious* series during the summertime, when she also had to finish the books that accompanied each series. When the first programmes were screened, she couldn't bear to look at them. 'I wouldn't watch with everybody else,' she says. 'I'd prefer to sneak down later and watch the video.' The first *Simply Delicious* series in March 1989 on RTÉ One clashed with *Coronation Street* on Network Two. 'That will tell you how much confidence RTÉ had in it,' she says. There were rows in living rooms around the country and calls made to Gay Byrne and Gerry Ryan.

Darina had a folksy, downhome no-nonsense style that people liked. She took the snobbery out of cooking. Instead of talking down to viewers like others, she talked to them as friends and brought a sense of fun and adventure into the kitchen. The first *Simply Delicious* series struck the right chord at the right time. The series, which became part of the RTÉ schedules nearly every year into the '90s, was accompanied by books published in association with RTÉ. The publicity also brought spin-off business for her cookery school and her courses booked out quickly. Her own favourite TV cook is Madhur Jaffrey, the international authority on classic Indian cuisine whom she admires enormously. A favourite non-TV cook is Alice Waters, chef proprietor of *Chez Panisse* in Berkeley, California, who is considered to be one of the paramount masters of modern cooking and who shares Darina's passion for top quality produce and real flavour.

Simply Delicious: two words that became music to the ears of publishing house accountants. How many copies of *Simply Delicious* have been sold? Every time a new book appears it gives a boost to the sale of the original book. The publisher had to order 13 reprints of the first book; sales so far are estimated at 185,000, a remarkable achievement for a cookery book. *Simply Delicious* – the TV series and book – touched every culinary soul in the land. Gay Byrne had already given Darina his blessing. Everybody liked her, the country girl-made-good, and wanted to cook like her. She found herself in the glare of national attention. People were queuing at book signings to get Darina's signature on their copy. The books were flying out of the shops. She recalls the buzz: 'Everybody was saying, "isn't it great". But I thought books sold like that normally. I didn't know how many copies were selling but I did know that going into reprint seemed to be a good thing.'

Darina vividly remembers a conversation that took place at the rear entrance to Waterstone's book store in Cork city-centre. She was in the company of a representative from her publisher on a signing tour. They met one of his colleagues from another publishing house who asked: 'How are you getting on?' He replied with delight: 'Oh God, we're having a fantastic year. The *Simply Delicious* book belonging to this woman is selling in telephone numbers.' Darina says she thought to herself at the time, 'that's my book he's talking about.'

A week later, she read a flattering piece by Kevin Myers for the Irishman's Diary in *The Irish Times*. He wrote how people were snapping up this cook book written by a virtually unknown woman who would now become wealthy. Darina said to Timmy, excitedly: 'Kevin Myers says that I'm going to be a wealthy woman!' She asked him: 'Do you think I'm going to make money out of the book?' He replied: 'Of course you'll make money, you twit!' Then she announced: 'Fine, in that case I'm going to build a tennis court.' He said: 'No, we can't afford it'. There were other priorities for the school. But her mind was made up. 'Absolutely no way,' she declared. 'This is money I wasn't expecting to have. I'm building a tennis court.' She immediately picked up the phone and ordered one. 'That tennis court represents the royalties from the first book,' she says. 'Timmy didn't speak to me for about a week, he was so cross. Honestly, I never dreamed of making money from that book.'

The fallout from *Simply Delicious* was good for the Irish publishing industry and retail book trade. RTÉ had found the successful formula for a home-produced cookery programme. RTÉ wanted to make a series every year. Shortly after publication of *A Simply Delicious Christmas*, Darina got a phone call from a woman who'd followed her recipe for plum pudding and ended up with far too much bread crumbs. Darina had decided to include in the book two recipes for plum pudding – each from her mother and mother-in-law. Myrtle Allen's recipe had been taken from her own book. There had been a mix-up in the conversion of measurements for bread crumbs from Myrtle's book. 'So this woman made a plum pudding and the whole thing was practically bread,' explains Darina. 'I checked and nearly died when I saw the mistake. It was coming up to Christmas and I knew people would be ringing me up. The publisher said there was nothing they could do. I told them they could get on to Gay Byrne and Gerry Ryan and get the word out to the papers. It got a lot of publicity and became a huge thing, a bit of a joke.

That actually drove the sales of that book through the roof. People were pouring into book shops asking for the book with the mistake in it.'

Amid all the accolades, the most cherished honour was to have been chosen as Laois Person of the Year in 1993. For once, she was lost for words. 'When I went to collect the award in Portlaoise, I broke down and couldn't speak and couldn't give my little talk. I was so touched that people of my own county were proud of me. All my family and people of the village were there. It was incredibly nice to have been recognised by my own people.'

Simply Delicious became simply unstoppable: it spawned eight TV series' and eight books. The prodigious output in the rise of Darina Allen as a publishing force continued through the '90s, with combined sales of over half a million. To date, she has written 12 books for Irish and UK publishers, including eight in the *Simply Delicious* series. The latest is *A Year At Ballymaloe Cookery School*, and she is doing a TV tie-in with the UK who envisage showing it in New Zealand, Australia and Middle East, while UK and Ireland will see it in Spring '98. And she hasn't put down her pen yet.

Some things get her hot under the collar. Darina and Myrtle were the saviours of traditional Irish cooking and crusading campaigners in the interests of fresh local produce. Both are culinary ambassadors for Ireland who spread the gospel throughout the world. They are members of Euro Toques, the European association of chefs. Darina has been chairman of the international committee of the International Association of Culinary Professionals (IACP). She is also a member of the consumer foods board of Bord Bia and a member of the Food Safety Board of Ireland. Darina wants people to think 'local' and use locally-grown ingredients. 'We work very hard in defence of small producers here,' she says. 'If I know where it's made, how it's made and I'm prepared to buy it from that person, then I think I have a right to buy it and eat it. Many of the people who produce the best quality raw ingredients for us are people who are doing things in a small way, who are passionate about what they're doing and very often not making a lot of money. That kind of food is our life's blood. We can only produce the kind of food we produce if we have that quality of ingredients. Ireland needs these people so badly.' She believes there is great potential for farmers' markets – a concept already in action in Cork – where producers can sell directly to the public. People are now 'desperately craving' real food. And the people who supply it are unsung heroes.

The catering industry has a rotten image. The Allens want to change that, too. For years, youngsters were shamelessly exploited in the award-winning kitchens of Europe. It seemed to be a necessary part of apprenticeship to slave in virtual sweat pits for long hours and little pay and to put up with a lot of abuse. The philosophy was based on survival of the fittest and the very best. Darina doesn't believe it has to be like that. 'Look, I think you can have a happy kitchen and people can cook very well when they're happy. That's always been a factor of the Ballymaloe kitchen. It's a very human kitchen. Nobody yells or curses or throws knives. There are restaurants I won't go to in London and where I won't let my students work. I think it's unbearable for chefs to make youngsters miserable. They got away with that for years. Now there's a huge shortage of staff in the hospitality industry. That's partly because youngsters are simply no longer prepared to take that kind of treatment. The hotel and catering industry is speaking out against this at last, and so they jolly well ought to.'

Darina still gets passionate about tempting the taste buds: her idea of a challenge is someone who insists they can't cook, and she won't let them out of her clutches until they can. She loves the excitement you see in their faces when taking their first loaf of bread out of the oven. Cooking touches people's lives, and in that way she feels privileged to have contributed something and made a difference to them. 'I'm very much against the kind of food which I call a flavour-too-far: overgarnished food, where chefs can't seem to stop, they keep adding extra flavours, and extra flourishes just for the sake of drama and presentation. That kind of food seldom tastes as good as it looks. It's there to create impact. For me the most important thing is the flavour. If it looks good as well as tastes good then that's fantastic. Everywhere I go I find something different and new. There are so many flavours still to explore that you can go on forever experimenting and learning.'

Most people think that fame has given Darina Allen a pot of gold. She says it hasn't. 'I don't want yachts in the Caribbean. That doesn't interest me. I love to put money into the gardens. If somebody hadn't started the gardens in the first place then I wouldn't have all of this. I feel a responsibility to put something back into the gardens; you feel you're passing on something to generations coming behind you. We were fortunate to have inherited this house and to have had something to start off with. Remember, we've continued to reinvest and plough money back into the school and the gardens. I've made some money out of the books but it's all gone back into the place. I wouldn't have it any other way. We've had to educate our children. Now we can take a reasonably good holiday every couple of years. I do travel a bit but most of it is related to my business and part of keeping up-to-date. We've been through difficult financial times. We've been through times when we sailed close to the wind. We've had worries just like everybody else because very few people get off scott free.' Their only indulgence is a small house in Ballycotton, an oasis of tranquillity just five minutes' drive away.

Darina has few regrets apart from not being able to play a musical instrument. If she had her life over again she'd learn to play the guitar. She likes the idea of have-guitar-will-travel, and it would complement her personality. She also thinks it a pity she hasn't done more sporty things like riding, skiing, paragliding and white water rafting. She envies people who can do wonderfully daring things, 'but I'm not brave enough to do it now.'

Inevitably, Darina's national popularity attracted the main political parties who recognised her vote-catching potential. Offers were made. She ruled politics off her menu. If circumstances were different though, she would have gone into politics and championed such causes as rural development, the food industry and the environment and also pressed the need for greater protection for small producers. 'At the moment because of the cookery school and all my responsibilities, I simply can't afford the time to go into politics,' she says. 'If I didn't have ties, I think it's possible I would have found my way into politics. Timmy says I'd be an appalling politician because I'd find it very hard to say the right things. I'd be the bane of the party's life!' Friends say that given her natural determination, she would probably have ended up as Minister for Food, or even running the country.

JIMMY BARRY-MURPHY

THERE IS ONLY ONE JIMMY BARRY

JIMMY Barry-Murphy: the mention of the name anywhere conjures up the excitement and passion of hurling. He was a sporting idol in the true sense, around whom the fans rallied when they needed a saviour. Brazil had Pele, Manchester United had George Best and Northern Ireland had Alex Higgins. For Cork hurling fans, there could never be another Jimmy Barry-Murphy. He had a special charisma, wrapped in the affections of Cork people for quarter of a century. He was the first of the GAA's real superstars; a dual player who first made his name with the all-conquering Cork footballers and, latterly, regarded as one of the truly great hurling forwards, who enriched both games with dignity and magnificent artistry.

His face lights up when he talks of the great victories when he played like a man possessed; you can still feel the heartbreak as he recalls the bad days when the magic deserted him.

It's hard to describe in words the adrenalin rush you experience on the big day when nothing can go wrong and you feel you could scale the highest mountain. The Munster Hurling Final between Cork and their old enemy, Tipperary, at Páirc Uí Chaoimh on 7 July, 1985, was one such day when Jimmy played out of his skin. It's acknowledged that without him they would not have won. Playing at full forward, he scored 1-3. He created two other goals. Three frees that resulted from infringements on him yielded another goal and two points for Cork. Jimmy's point scored out on the left-hand touchline was a gem; it put Cork beyond the range of Tipp.

Christy Ring, the wizard of Cloyne, had been the hero during the epic battles between Cork and Tipp. *The Examiner's* Michael Ellard now pursued the analogy: 'That was the day the memory of Ring lived on in the person of Jimmy Barry-Murphy. Called upon to perform in the manner of the master, he responded with genius. Ring would have whispered from his perch above, "you did me proud boy". When Barry-Murphy raised his arms to his adoring legions of fans, the ground erupted in a frenzy of hero worship.'

Jimmy rates it as his greatest game for Cork. He says he reached a 'high' on the day that would be impossible to repeat. 'It's almost a supernatural feeling. You feel that no-one can stop you. Whatever adrenalin does to you, I felt I couldn't get beaten. I could have done anything that day. I was drained afterwards and thrilled.'

Sport is a cruel business: the darkest days were when he captained Cork hurlers in two successive All-Ireland defeats at the hands of Kilkenny in 1982 and 1983. He failed to score in both finals. He says the greatest heartbreak of his career was the 1982 final when underdogs Kilkenny trounced the hot favourites. The score was 3-18 to 1-13. The red and white tide of Cork fans were leaving the terraces 10 minutes before the end. Kilkenny supporters invaded the pitch minutes before the final whistle; they couldn't believe they had won by such a margin. Jimmy Barry-Murphy was shattered. Looking back, he thinks that the pressure overwhelmed him and he 'froze'. When he left the pitch and sat alone in the dressing room, it felt like the end of the world. 'I made the classic mistake of having said publicly it was my ambition to captain Cork to win an All-Ireland. That probably generated its own pressure. My grand uncle, Dinny, had done it in 1928. A lot of the pressure was self-induced. I couldn't see us losing that 1982 final. I had a litany of successes up to that, and now I couldn't score at all. I just couldn't handle it on the day. In team games sometimes you can get away with it if the team plays well and you're carried along with it. That day we all flopped, and being captain you shoulder the responsibility.'

The cats pounced again in 1983, defeating Cork by two points. For the reds, it was a game of squandered opportunities. Coach Johnny Clifford summed up: 'They threw it away.' Barry-Murphy became the first man to lead Cork to successive All-Ireland defeats, and it hurt. He has always been known for his sportsmanship and as one of the most gracious players in defeat. However, this time he found it hard to hide the bitter disappointment. 'The amazing thing is that they were two of the best years hurling I played up to the finals but I just didn't do it on the day. It was a harsh lesson. After that second defeat, I was gutted, shattered. The All-Ireland final is the showpiece; having failed to score two years running and you haven't played well, naturally you feel you've left yourself down and your colleagues down and haven't delivered. It's something you've got to live with. Coming back to Cork is pathetic, you don't want to meet people. You want to stay on your own and hide away. But you've got to go back to work and face people and be man enough to get on with it. That's the reality of sport: you've got glory days but you've also got days when you play badly and you've got to accept that.' Like the Manchaster United captain Roy Keane, Jimmy Barry-Murphy was once sport's hottest teenage property.

He was born on 22 August, 1954. His father put a hurley in his hand in the back garden one day, and that started him off. The St Finbarr's club had something of a nursery, and as a young boy he played in the Lough parish leagues. He came up through the ranks in the Barr's, playing under 12, 14, 15, 16 and on the minor team. He feels he must have shown promise on the minor team because he was introduced to the St Finbarr's senior championship team at the age of 16. It was his first big game. He was brought on as a substitute in the second half against Muskerry in Bandon in May 1971. He was nearing the end of his schooling at Colaiste An Spriod Naoimh in Bishopstown, and doing the Leaving Certificate a week later, although 'that was way down my list of priorities'.

His 'burning ambition' up to then was to play senior with the Barr's. 'To come in so young was a dream come true,' he recalls. 'It was a great day for me.' They went on to play Blackrock in the county final that year and were beaten.

Christy Ring was the 'icon' who had won eight All-Ireland medals, an idol to all youngsters who regarded him as The Man. 'I saw him playing for Cork once in the Munster Final in Limerick in the early 1960s. He was an extraordinary player to watch; his sheer passion and fanaticism came through. He was a power house around the field.' Years later, Jimmy got to know Ring as a selector when he played with the Cork hurlers in 1976, and remembers 'he had an aura about him even then'.

Jimmy had just turned 17, when he made his first appearance on the hallowed ground of Croke Park in the All-Ireland minor hurling final of 1971; he was a full forward on the team which defeated Kilkenny. The match was memorable for the wrong reasons; he had a poor game and was taken off near the end. 'The whole occasion seemed to pass me by, and I couldn't get to grips with the game,' he says. 'I didn't get a puck of the ball. It was a huge disappointment to be taken off because my ancestors had played here and won All-Irelands. I couldn't believe it had happened. I'd been on a rollercoaster up to that, playing with the Barr's and being on the senior team.'

The youngster was also playing football with St Finbarr's and on the Cork minor football team beaten by Mayo in the All-Ireland of 1971. He was on both minor teams in the finals of 1971 and 1972. Jimmy made his name nationally with the all-conquering Cork footballers in 1973. He was a month short of his 19th birthday when he made his championship debut in senior football, playing a pivotal role in Cork's superb 5-12 to 1-15 victory over Kerry in the Munster final at Páirc Uí Chaoimh. The best was yet to come.

A sunny September Sunday at Croke Park in 1973 stands as the climax of his footballing career when he scored two super goals against Galway that brought the Sam Maguire Cup back to Cork after a gap of 28 years. Those who watched him drive Cork to a famous victory knew someone special had arrived on the scene. Jimmy Barry-Murphy was the talk of the land. His first goal was scored two minutes into the game and the second, a classic, eight minutes from the end. The sharp execution of the second goal, a match winner, was a highlight in his career. Ray Cummins fisted a ball ahead, Barry-Murphy won it, side-stepped an opponent, held the ball momentarily and coolly played it into the corner of the net. The Cup was back Leeside for the first time since 1945, and the fans went wild with delight. 'I'll never forget coming home to Cork on the Monday night,' he recalls. 'The turnout that night was extraordinary; I'd never seen anything like this in my life. We were taken through the city to the Victoria Hotel where the team was presented to the crowd. Patrick Street was mobbed. Looking back I still get goose pimples thinking about it. Coming back to Cork with the Cups, hurling and football, is a great feeling and it's hard to describe. It's a very personal thing; you're playing for your own people.'

It was another two years before he played senior championship hurling, making his debut in the opening game against Waterford at Walsh Park. He played at right half-forward while another newcomer, Denis Allen, played on the other wing. Barry-Murphy made an impressive debut, scoring five points from play. He went on to score a goal and two points in the Munster Final and a goal and a point in the All-Ireland semi-final of 1975 when Cork was beaten by Galway.

Then came the golden era for Cork hurling with three-in-a-row All-Ireland successes in 1976, 1977 and 1978. The Rebels seemed invincible during those late '70s' summers. Some of the best players of all time were on that team, says Jimmy. A new selection committee, which included Ring, took over in late 1975 and brought changes. 'It was a strong, single-minded committee,' he explains. 'New disciplines were imposed on the team. A lot of younger players were brought in. It was a unique collection of great players in one team. Like all great teams, there were different match winners on different days; we didn't have to depend on the same people all the time.' Jimmy was on the half-forward line and didn't play at full-forward until 1981. The full-forward line of Charlie McCarthy, Ray Cummins and Seanie O'Leary was the fulcrum of attack. 'We were a very hard team to beat because we had class players,' he reflects. 'The parties just rolled on every year, and we never thought we'd see a bad day.'

The rousing homecomings and tours of schools and neighbour-hoods with the Cup established him as one of Cork's great personality sportsmen and, of course, a superstar. Although put on a pedestal by the fans, he never swallowed the star trip and kept his feet firmly on the ground. He learned early on that fame was a fickle business: you could be a king today and tossed into the dungeon tomorrow. You're only as good as your last game. He says he quickly learned that 'people have short memories and you wouldn't want to get too big for your boots'. Ray Cummins says his teammate always kept sport in perspective and realised it was only one facet of life.

Off the field of play he was unassuming and modest about his achievements. When you speak to him today about the haul of over 30 medals and all the plaudits heaped upon him over the years he prefers to play down the achievements. The record speaks for itself: 13 All-Ireland medals in different grades of hurling and football; four Railway Cup football medals; one National Football League medal and two National Hurling League medals; 10 Munster senior hurling championship medals and two for senior football; seven All-Star awards, five in hurling and two in football; and a clutch of county championship medals with St Finbarr's, six for hurling and five for football. All the medals are stored at home in a box. Jimmy was a good role model for youngsters and upcoming players. Colleagues say they never once saw him refuse to sign an autograph and never saw him speak disrespectfully to the fans.

Jimmy Barry-Murphy never really regarded the Railway Cup as being competitive enough, yet he electrified Croke Park with a four goal blitz for Munster footballers against Ulster in the 1975 final. His four goals and a point from just five touches of the ball would never be forgotten by the fans who witnessed that breathtaking performance.

Little wonder that the then Kerry County Board chairman, Ger McKenna, remarked afterwards: 'If there was a transfer market in gaelic football on the same scale as soccer we in Kerry would be prepared to pay a million for Jimmy.' Ironically, he was more concerned about winning the All-Ireland club hurling final the day before between St Finbarr's and the Fenians from Johnstown, Co. Kilkenny. 'I honestly had no interest in the Railway Cup final,' he says. 'I was more interested in winning the club final with the Barr's on the Sunday. It was a great game. Once that was over, the pressure was off me. The Barr's went back to Cork. I stayed in Dublin with some friends. It was a long night. To go out on Monday and score four goals was extraordinary.' Barry-Murphy was one of two players – the other was Kerry's Ger Power – who lined out in Munster's four consecutive wins up to 1978.

In 1980, Jimmy Barry-Murphy made history by becoming the first player ever to win National League hurling and football medals. That year he played in the last of eight Munster football finals. He retired from inter-county football but continued on at club level with St Finbarr's up to 1986. He had actually thought of retiring at the start of the 1979-80 season and only stayed on out of loyalty to Billy Morgan who had taken over as coach/trainer to the team. 'I felt I owed him something because of what he had done for Cork football over the years,' he said later. 'The win in the league crowned my football ambitions. We all wanted to win for Billy's sake and we did it with limited resources.'

Looking back, he says he was disillusioned with football because it had become a foul-ridden game. 'There was a lot of pulling and dragging; I wasn't enjoying it and it was hard to express yourself. Even to this day the game hasn't improved much. It was getting harder to play both games because of the time factor. The combination of playing both at the top-level for years was taking a toll. My form wasn't great, so I decided it was either pick hurling or football. I was always going to pick hurling from that time on. Hurling is a more skillful game. There were a lot of regrets, too, leaving the football scene but it was time to move on.' It's arguable whether he was a better footballer or hurler. In the end, football's loss was hurling's gain.

The heartbreak of the All-Ireland defeats in 1982-83 marked the lowest points of his career. The sad thing was that he played his best hurling in those years for club and county, 'but it just didn't happen for me in the finals. The pressure got to me being captain on the big day. I wanted to win too much.' With the team bouncing back, he won a fourth medal in Centenary Year in Thurles.

For the people of Cork there are many moments to savour when Jimmy took a hurley in his hand. He scored fantastic goals at critical times to turn a match in his team's favour. Fans would never forget the Munster championship of 1983 which had Cork and Limerick locked in a marathon battle, first at the Gaelic Grounds and then in the replay at Páirc Uí Chaoimh.

Typically, Jimmy scored the matchwinner. *The Cork Examiner's* Michael Ellard dug deep for superlatives to capture the high drama: 'In a flash of daring Jimmy Barry-Murphy conjured up a goal of magic to sway this titanic duel in Cork's favour. With 10 minutes remaining, the outcome teetered on a knife edge of suspense, with both sides locked in fiery combat and the 38,000 crowd gripped in a palm of passionate anxiety. A first time stroke across the centre, hit with power, by substitute Tomás Mulcahy, seemed to be out of Barry-Murphy's reach. But, with courage, he made the extra precious strides to make contact with a blistering right hand shot which sped with velocity to the Limerick net. That was the goal that turned this delicately balanced, do or die contest in Cork's favour. It shattered Limerick's dream of glory even though they kept battling to the bitter end.' To this day, Jimmy says it was an amazing goal and he doesn't know how the ball flew into the back of the net.

Another incredible moment was Jimmy's goal against Galway in the All-Ireland semi-final of 1983. It happened so fast that few can remember having seen the shot. One second the sliothar was coming through the air towards Barry-Murphy and Galway's Conor Hayes and the next, it was in the net. Jimmy recalls: 'John Fenton hit a ball in and it dipped towards myself and Conor Hayes who was marking me. I think he was slightly in front of me. He was going up to block the ball and I pulled at the same time. I really think it was a freak combination of our hurleys colliding and the ball flying off my hurley. It flew into the roof of the net.' The late Micheal O'Hehir described it as one of the greatest goals he'd ever seen in Croke Park. It was all over in a flash. It was an extraordinary goal. Hayes told *The Cork Examiner's* Jim O'Sullivan some years later: 'I saw John Fenton's shot coming in low and hard and I thought I was slightly ahead of Barry-Murphy. But he pulled on it first. It was an excellent goal, although at the time I thought the ball glanced off my hurley.' The goal happened too fast for the RTÉ cameras to capture, but they accepted their viewers opinion that it was the goal of the year. But Jimmy says he would have 'given it all up' to win the All-Ireland in 1983 because 'flashing goals never meant anything to me'.

Jimmy Barry-Murphy was again crowned the hero in the Munster final of 1985 at Páirc Uí Chaoimh when he powered Cork to a memorable victory over Tipperary, playing what he regards to have been his finest game for the county. His career came to a fitting climax in the 1986 All-Ireland when Cork defeated Galway. He felt it was one of his best finals. He scored a late 'insurance' point which stretched Cork's lead to four points and ensured an unexpected victory. 'Galway were favourites and we hadn't played well during the year,' he says. 'We had a lot of injuries before and during the game. We just rose to the challenge and got dug in that day and won a great All-Ireland. I got the last point, and that was my parting shot in Croke Park.'

That win meant a lot to him because of the previous disappointments of having captained two losing teams in the finals against Kilkenny. Teammates say they had never seen him so overjoyed in the dressing room after a big game. He knew it would be his swansong as a player. His tremendous form over the year was acknowledged in his selection on the Bank of Ireland Allstars team.

On 1 April, 1987, Jimmy Barry-Murphy confirmed his retirement from inter-county and club hurling. At the age of 32 he decided to make a complete break with the lifetime of playing because, in his own words, 'I felt my appetite was gone'. He also wanted to spend more time with his family: wife, Jean, and their three children, Brian, Deirdre and Ann. They have since had another daughter, Orla.

The news of his retirement didn't come as any surprise because of months of speculation. After the All-Ireland final against Galway, he hinted he was going to give up. He had thought about retiring earlier in 1986 but changed his mind after Johnny Clifford was appointed coach. He was always a great admirer of Clifford whom, he said, 'instilled a confidence that we were going to beat Galway'. Before the All-Ireland final, as he was watching the minor game on TV at Jury's Hotel Dublin, Jimmy told teammate Johnny Crowley he was going to bow out. 'Those couple of hours before an All-Ireland final are the worst time,' he recalls. 'You're hanging around waiting to go to the game. I said to Johnny, "I can't take this anymore. If we win today I'm gone". He replied, "get away out of that" I said, "definitely, this is it". I don't know whether he believed me or not.' He now thinks it was a mistake not to have played on for another year or two. He watched Cork being beaten by Tipperary in the Munster final replay in 1987, and he was sorry he wasn't on the team.

The replay at Fitzgerald Stadium in Killarney on 19 July was a day when Cork badly needed the inspiration and scoring prowess of Jimmy Barry-Murphy. It was frustrating for him to watch because Cork had the upper hand for much of the game but were weakened by injuries and demoralised. Tipperary were hugely relieved to take a Munster hurling title after 16 years with a scoreline of 4-22 to 1-22. 'Looking back I feel I should have played on that year and stuck it out with lads. I should have given it another year,' says Jimmy.

As the curtain came down on his playing career, tributes gushed from the GAA world. GAA Director General Liam Mulvihill rated him as a supreme stylist, saying his hurling artistry probably over-shadowed his football skills. Johnny Clifford described him as the last of the personality players. *The Cork Examiner's* Jim O'Sullivan wrote: 'He will be remembered as a player of exceptional skill, admired as much as feared by opponents. The best tribute that I can pay is to say that success never changed him and this was the reason why he was so popular over the years. He was always a player for the big occasion, a fact which explained often indifferent form in winter hurling and, as a sportsman, he never once deviated from the high standards he set himself at the beginning of his career.'

Ray Cummins summed up his teammate and friend: 'He was a very intelligent player, a good reader of the game, quick to seize upon an opponent's weakness and exploit them. He was an extremely good opportunist with, in greyhound racing parlance, a quick early foot. He was an economical player and tended to do just enough to get there which irritated me. I believed that he had the potential to do even greater things which for a player of his standard is quite a compliment. I always considered him to be even more talented as a footballer than a hurler. He was always fair and sporting and enjoyed his game. He liked to win but was quick to congratulate an opponent in defeat. He disliked the dirty player and tended to punish him by whipping in a few goals.' Teammate Tomás Mulcahy reflected: 'When I came on to the team first, in the 1983 Munster final, having a player like Jimmy around made it a lot easier. He was a pure genius on the field. He would never try to score from an impossible angle; he would look around for somebody better placed.'

Jimmy's move to management came with the minors in St Finbarr's within 12 months of retirement. Before accepting the top Cork job, all his work in management had been with minor players: four titles with St Finbarr's; an All-Ireland in September 1995 with the Cork minor team. He says if they hadn't won that All-Ireland with the minors, he wouldn't have had the confidence to go on and manage the seniors. Returning home with the minor champions rekindled memories of the great homecomings; women and children were out on the streets in Blackpool to cheer them.

After three dismal summers in the championship wilderness, a Dream Team was mobilised to restore the fortunes of Cork hurling: Jimmy Barry-Murphy, Tom Cashman and Tony O'Sullivan. Later, after Avondhu won the County Championship, Fred Sheehy took over from O'Sullivan. In spite of high expectations, home truths about the state of Cork hurling began to sink in with the new administration. 'We haven't the players with the skills we had 20 years ago,' reflected Jimmy.

Cork's 1996 All-Ireland campaign ended when they were well beaten by Limerick in the first round on home ground at Páirc Uí Chaoimh. Since Cork last contested an All-Ireland senior hurling final in 1992, they had lost many outstanding players, mainly through retirement. Only five of the starting 15 in the 1992 All-Ireland were in the '96 championship game against Limerick. There was no change in the depressing scenario for Cork in 1997 when they lost their opening game in the Championship to Clare who went on to win the All-Ireland title. 'I think it will turn around for Cork because there's a lot of good young talent coming through,' he says. 'In the past, people tended to take that level of success for granted. Now if we get to the Munster final we'd be thrilled.' Yet, as former Cork team trainer Jim Barry once remarked: 'The Cork hurlers are like mushrooms; they can come up overnight.' But there were also encouraging signs for '97, when the Cork under-21 intermediate hurlers won their All-Ireland titles. The record shows that Cork inter-county hurlers won 101 All-Ireland and 202 provincial titles.

Jimmy's working life has been spent in the world of leasing and financing where he keeps a hectic schedule. Apart from GAA, another passion is greyhound racing, both as a trainer and fan, which he says is a great hobby.

There is no doubt that Jimmy Barry-Murphy would be a millionaire if his skills had been tapped – in a different era – by the cash rich soccer world. He showed potential as a soccer player, with Cork Celtic in the League of Ireland in 1972-73. (Incidentally, his son, Brian, has followed those footsteps breaking into the Cork City League side.) If a fairy godmother could wave a magic wand for the hurling legend, then he would be lining out alongside fellow Corkmen Roy Keane and Denis Irwin on the Irish soccer team. It is his only regret that he never got the chance to represent his country in soccer. 'It's one of the things you're deprived of in the GAA,' says Jimmy. 'I take great pride in Cork sports people representing their city and their country. I'd love to have lined up beside Roy Keane under Jack Charlton or Mick McCarthy. I think he's a magnificent player. And I'd love to have played in the World Cup.' That's the stuff of dreams, of course; one can only imagine the potent combination of Keane and Barry-Murphy. He wouldn't rewrite the script, though, of a career in which he won nearly every honour the GAA had to offer.

And he doesn't regret losing out on the financial spoils that came to Keane and other professionals. 'I wouldn't have changed a minute of it all,' he says.

Jimmy stayed in the GAA world where all the hard work, skill and patience went unrewarded, financially. 'The likes of Roy Keane and Denis Irwin are making a great living and I'm thrilled for them,' he says. 'But when you play GAA you accept that you go a different road. I was rewarded in lots of ways but not in monetary terms. I don't think money could pay me for the days I had with Cork hurlers and footballers and with the Barr's. I got great respect for what I achieved and if I can retain that I'd be happy and wouldn't want anything else. I'd like to be remembered as a sportsman who gave my best for hurling and football.'

There will never be another Jimmy Barry-Murphy.

BARRY GALVIN

LAWMAN WITH A MISSION

ONCE upon a time Barry Galvin was a hero of the criminal underworld – but their legal relationship ended after a train journey home from Dublin to Cork. It was the longest train ride of his life. He had defended a gang of thieves who robbed a business in Cork and now they were cleared of the crime. The gang was caught with a large sum of money, identified as the proceeds of a robbery because the bundles of cash had been folded in a specific way and initialled by the cashier. They were charged but, wisely, refused to make any admissions.

They claimed to have won the money gambling. The State couldn't prove the case when the trial opened in Dublin and it collapsed. Galvin, their solicitor, and his defending criminal counsel, got a direction that there wasn't enough evidence even to go to the jury. What's more, they made an application for the money to be handed back to their clients. It was a job well done, or so the young defence lawyer thought as he left the courtroom.

Then he got a taxi to Heuston station to take the train home, and found himself sharing a carriage with the victims of the robbery whom he knew personally. They were distraught at the outcome of the case. By contrast, the suspects who walked free were downing celebratory beers, and buying drink for everybody they met up and down the train. 'To my mind this was an appalling vista,' he recalls. 'It really soured me. I found it difficult to justify what I was doing, even though I could certainly justify it professionally because the legal system doesn't work unless someone is prepared to offer legal counsel, even for those charged with the worst crimes. When I got off the train, as far as I was concerned it had been a disaster. I felt that the system was wrong. I felt there should be some better way. I made a conscious decision there and then to get out of doing criminal law.'

That train journey was to prove a watershed in his career. In future Galvin would concentrate on putting villains behind bars rather than getting them off, and he would ultimately target the most notorious gangsters in the land.

Barry Galvin is without doubt the bravest lawyer in Ireland. He spoke out fearlessly against international criminals who were using the south-west coast as a major drugs trans-shipment centre, and even went on *The Late Late Show* to spill the beans. He became an outspoken critic of the State's abject failure to deal with the growing drug problem. On his home patch, as State Solicitor in Cork city, he worked closely with the gardaí to fight the new breed of get-rich-quick hoodlums who thrived on the drugs trade and who promoted a myth of being untouchable. Whenever Galvin walked into the Cork District Court to oppose bail applications and in some cases to disclose their properties and produce evidence of hidden bank accounts, they knew he meant business.

Dublin's millionaire crime bosses, who went by nickname in the underworld, crushed anybody who threatened their empires. Gangland murders in the early 1990s made the capital look more like Chicago in the days of mob rule.

When journalist Veronica Guerin swept aside the nicknames and removed the masks for all to see, they shot her dead in her car while stopped at traffic lights on the Naas dual carriageway on 26 June, 1996. The government responded to the public clamour for action by setting up the Criminal Assets Bureau, armed with new powers and better laws to deprive them of their ill-gotten nest eggs, and by appointing Galvin to a pivotal role as its legal officer. He simply took the fight to a wider arena and the wiseguys of Dublin didn't know what hit them. The untouchables weren't untouchable anymore.

He has been compared to Eliot Ness, the prohibition agent who led the squad that brought down Al Capone's $125 million Chicago bootlegging empire in 1931. Galvin eschews that analogy. 'I don't like it,' he says. 'It's quite inaccurate because Ness was an operations man, whereas up to now I wasn't even on the operational side. I was a legal adviser acting for the guards in court.' That advisory role to the bureau expanded in time as Galvin fronted the legal fight in the courts. And it hurts them like hell.

Neither does he like the image of One Man's War Against Drugs, depicted so often by the media. 'All I did was to speak out about drugs and, in my own area of work, to use the law in Cork as best we could. There are examples of things we did that weren't done in other jurisdictions. The guards had to do the work. I gave advice and did the court work where necessary.' He says all the hype about him is unfair to others working hard in the Criminal Assets Bureau.

There are personal risks, of course. That goes with the territory. No big deal. He squared up to people who thought they were above the law in Cork, and then did the same in Dublin. Sure, the risks are discomforting, but these wouldn't stop him doing the job. In the same way, a policeman goes out at night to confront hardened criminals face to face 'without the security measures that I have'. He is part of a team under strict security. The job has meant a huge imposition on his family. 'When a knock comes to the door,' he says, 'you've got to be extra careful.'

The easiest, and safest, option would have been to keep his mouth shut. It was unheard of for a State Solicitor to speak out so publicly about drugs and organised crime, akin to biting the hand that fed him. Cork was awash with drugs, and in danger of becoming the drugs capital of Europe. People with a background of petty crime in the city were now amassing fortunes from drugs, hiding their profits in bank accounts and investing in property. Cork and Kerry were the base for some of the biggest drug dealers in Europe. Cannabis shipments were being landed by the tonne and shipped to international markets. The millionaire smugglers were known to the Gardaí and the Revenue Commissioners and had been untouched for years. These cannabis and amphetamine dealers were living in well-protected mansions amid picture-postcard Irish scenery. The unguarded coastline made us the laughing stock of Europe. And nothing was being done to stop it all. As State Solicitor he had particular knowledge of the crime scene. The paperwork across his desk opened his eyes to the realities. He could list off names and addresses of people who led lavish lifestyles and yet with no visible means of support and were even on the dole in many cases. Galvin watched it all happen, unchecked, from his office on the South Mall. He started talking in 1992, first in Cork, granting interviews this author. At that time, I held the crime brief as Security Correspondent for *The Cork Examiner* and the *Evening Echo*.

Cork fell to the drug culture almost unnoticed. During his years as a defence lawyer in the city, Galvin only once defended a drugs case: a couple of pseudo-hippies from Dublin who were caught smoking hash at Charles Fort in Kinsale. Drink was frequently a factor in crime, but never drugs. Rampant unemployment contributed to the growth of drugs: cannabis in Cork and heroin in Dublin during the early '80s. Cork lost anchor industries like Ford, Dunlop and Sunbeam where sons had followed their fathers into safe jobs.

A couple of years after becoming State Solicitor in 1983, Barry Galvin could see the writing on the wall. 'I began to notice that the pattern of crime was changing and drugs became obvious in the files,' he says. 'It gathered momentum slowly. There was a huge increase in the level of violent crime. The type of crimes being committed were gratuitously violent. People were being badly assaulted in the course of burglaries; there was more viciousness on the streets and criminals being vicious with each other.' Back in the early days of his career, there were few successful criminals and the definition of organised crime was two burglars with a ladder. Things were different now.

There was a ready market for cannabis. The profit margins were attractive. So they took the next logical step to import it directly themselves from Africa and the Middle East. Then the big boys arrived in Ireland.

There were more armed hold-ups and more serious assaults. The Gardaí suspected that certain people were dealing in drugs, and knew they were living beyond their means. The market forces of supply and demand took over. To a large extent, the criminals created a demand for drugs because they were able to bring in regular supplies with impunity. The local gardaí – powerless to act through a combination of weak laws, inadequate resources and little manpower – watched local drug gangs and their leaders get rich almost overnight. Every dog in the street knew their names. Such was the arrogance of one prominent dealer that he arrived in a garda station and boasted to the guards that Cork should be grateful to him because he only sold cannabis and ecstasy and had protected the city from heroin. They were fighting among themselves too, with territorial feuds in the northside and southside and disputes over drug deals.

The Cork boys were on first name terms with Moroccan cannabis suppliers. The Moroccans liked them because they paid cash upfront in advance; there was no messing. They returned home with suntans and waited for the shipment to arrive off West Cork. Galvin tells of two Corkmen who organised early importations of cannabis from Pakistan. 'They were famous in Pakistan because of the trade they gave them,' he says. 'They were welcomed and feted there, brought into the highest levels of society, wined and dined. These fellows were scumbags on the streets of Cork.'

At the same time, information in the files across Galvin's desk showed that the biggest drugs players in Europe were using the south- west as a gateway trans-shipment base for other countries. Some of them were even living here to keep an eye on their operations. Multi-million pound consignments of cannabis, amphetamines and later cocaine were successfully smuggled. Two particularly large shipments of cocaine were never intercepted. 'It's a well-known pattern in a country with no indigenous drug problem, which is used as an importation and trans-shipment point, that an explosion of drug-taking occurs in the country due to the easy availability of drugs,' says Galvin. 'I firmly believe that's what happened in Ireland.' Some of the drugs were sold into the Irish market, but the bulk was passed on elsewhere. Indeed, if the cannabis found in Cork alone over the past decade was all destined for the home-market, then every man, woman and child in Munster would be smoking dope. None of the local dealers would have access to the investment needed to fund large-scale shipments. Among these new residents was the biggest amphetamine dealer in Europe, reputed to make annual profits of £25 million, and also one of the biggest cannabis traders in Europe. 'They came and lived here because there was no perception of danger,' explains Galvin. 'They didn't see any risk of being caught, which turned out to be a fact because none of the big international criminals were caught in Ireland.'

They used others to do their dirty work and took the profits. The Cork City State Solicitor knew the Irish authorities, at a certain level, were aware of their presence and of the smuggling activities. Yet nothing was being done. 'I still reckon that someone has a lot to answer for,' he says. 'In the early '90s there was plenty of information and intelligence and there seemed to be a lack of will to address the problem. If no resources are channelled to guard the coastline, then it's very easy to smuggle drugs. The people who were trying to do the job felt constrained.' Cannabis was being landed by the tonne. In fact, 100s of tonnes were shipped into the country during the '80s and early '90s. Informed estimates were that the authorities managed to seize only a tenth of the £150 million worth of drugs shipped through the country annually. The jagged coastline of the south-west made it a smuggler's paradise. Yachts were chartered in England and elsewhere for the purpose of landing drugs. Ocean-going vessels met smaller craft out of sight of land, and sometimes outside Irish territorial waters, to transfer drugs. Sometimes the drugs were dropped into the sea from a freighter, or 'mother ship', close to the shore and retrieved by smaller vessels later.

Drugs were also dropped into 'dumps' on the sea bed, with buoys and transmitter devices used to help subsequent retrieval. Locals in parts of West Cork remarked that if you stood on a beach there long enough, a bale of cannabis would wash up at your feet.

Galvin's outspoken comments in 1992 about the drugs trade made front page news in Cork, and the story was soon picked up by the Dublin papers. Next he went on *The Late Late Show* to outline the scale of the trade, the presence of international traffickers in Ireland and the inaction to stem the tide. He wanted the establishment of a National Drugs Enforcement Agency to coordinate the State's resources. It was unusual for a State Solicitor to speak so publicly about crime and criticise his masters. 'It wasn't a step I took lightly,' he says, looking back. 'I was speaking out of frustration over nothing being done. Ireland is such a small country that it's very policeable; that's one of the reasons why I was so annoyed that the drug problem had been allowed to get out of hand. If it was addressed earlier, that wouldn't have happened. The guards, if allowed to do their job, are extraordinarily good.'Galvin is not a man who likes being ignored.

The official line from the Department of Justice was that, yes, both the department and the garda authorities were aware of a problem with illegal cannabis in the Cork area, but they were satisfied the problem was on a much smaller scale than that alleged. Critics claimed the Cork solicitor was courting publicity for his own ends and loved the sound of his own voice.

'I suppose it was a shock to think that this was happening in Holy Ireland and being kept under wraps,' he recalls. 'The reaction at the time from the government was, to my mind, most unusual ... they went to great lengths to say that it didn't exist or wasn't as bad as being said.' Two garda officers were despatched to talk to Galvin about his allegations. Those closest to him knew there was no hidden agenda: he wanted nothing out of it for himself and was genuinely motivated to kick up a stink so that the authorities would sit up and take notice. Within 12 months, the seizure of a series of record multi-million pound cannabis shipments off Cork and Kerry vindicated his strong stand and proved that he was right all along.

Forget any notion of a dour, boring solicitor with his head buried in law books. You're more likely to catch Barry Galvin riding motorbikes, driving power boats for water-skiers or sailing his catamaran around the coast than in the library. He is a flamboyant, larger-than-life character who positively bristles with bonhomie.

Law was in the bloodlines. He is a fourth generation solicitor: his father, grandfather and great-grandfather were in the legal profession before him. The family business of Barry C. Galvin can be traced back to his great-grandfather, although it was his grandfather who launched what would become one of the biggest practices in Cork. Both his father, Paddy, and grandfather, Barry C, were solicitors for the city of Cork which meant all the legal work for the local authority went through their office. The story of Barry C. Galvin's pet labrador has been passed down through the generations. The dog had a voracious appetite. Whenever he got the opportunity he liked to devour sausages hung near the door of the local butcher's shop. The prominent Cork solicitor with nine children happened to be one of the butcher's biggest customers, but the losses from missing sausages were mounting. Something had to be done. The butcher knew his valued customer was a gentleman. On the one hand he didn't want to suffer any more losses, yet on the other hand he didn't want to offend him by confronting him directly in his shop. So he decided to approach the problem in a more subtle way by calling to his home one evening. The butcher was invited inside. He broached the subject diplomatically by outlining the facts and pretended to seek legal opinion. He asked the solicitor whether, hypothetically, the owner of an animal would be responsible if his dog stole goods belonging to someone else.

Galvin gave the butcher an impromptu lecture on the law in that regard, explained the complexities and, intrigued, asked: 'Why do you ask?' The butcher finally got to the point: 'Actually, it's your dog I'm talking about.' The solicitor apologised and asked how much the stolen sausages had cost. The bill came to 30 shillings, a considerable amount. Galvin summoned his wife and told her to get the money to pay the butcher. The butcher was relieved to have been paid without any fuss. However, as he left the house, Galvin added: 'By the way, you owe me three guineas for legal advice.'

Frances P. Galvin, better known as Paddy, the youngest of nine, followed his father's footsteps and inherited the legal practice. The family were well respected at a time when Cork was a city ruled by merchant princes who achieved a status unknown anywhere else in the country. They lived in splendour in a big house on Victoria Road, and had a summer home by the sea at Myrtleville. Although only 12 miles away, it was quite an expedition over bad roads and punctures were always expected. There were idyllic summer holidays at Myrtleville where Paddy helped his father to catch crabs and lobsters in the warm pools of sea water. The other children went into the professions; Cecilia, the first woman to qualify as an engineer in Ireland; Wilfred, a doctor in Harley Street, London; Mary, a doctor in Cork; another sister, Nance, ran the Cork Cake Rooms on the South Mall. As a small child, Barry has particularly fond memories of two sisters, Mrs Dorothy Newey and Mrs Kitty Archer, who worked in the Cake Rooms for many years. The sisters had grown up in India under the Raj and hankered after their former privileged lifestyle. As luck would have it, they later inherited quite a bit of money during the mid-'60s. They loved the arts and the theatre. Now it was time to indulge themselves: they bought the finest fur coats in Cork and booked a holiday in London where they planned to see West End shows. Alas, it was not to be. They were among the 61 people who perished onboard a Cork to London Aer Lingus Viscount aircraft, St Phelim, which plunged into the sea off the Tuskar Rock on 24 March, 1968. When their bodies were recovered from the sea, each was said to be wrapped in a fur coat.

Barry's mother, Ann O'Sullivan, was also the youngest of nine, whose father, William, practiced as a doctor in Killarney for many years and was rumoured to have once removed a bullet from Eamon de Valera. Barry Galvin was born on 1 November, 1943, and had a younger brother, James. Barry remembers his father as 'an old fashioned gentleman, a man of great humour and high intelligence'. His mother was a kindhearted woman, well known for her generosity. She couldn't say 'no' to anyone: when beggars came to the door she fed them and even gave them her husband's suits if she thought they were badly clothed.

Barry was closer to the O'Sullivan side of the family. They had a holiday home at Dooks where he spent his summer holidays in the company of his cousins, swimming in the sea and playing golf. 'When we were kids, she'd give us her last penny,' recalls Barry. 'No matter what trouble we got into, and our cousins got into, there was always a welcome at our house and no questions asked. Whatever we did, she'd always forgive us. She was an amazing woman. Although extremely kind, she was strict in the sense that she made us do our homework. It wasn't that we were spoiled: we were reasonably well-off but my mother was the type of woman who made sure we were brought up the right way.' At the age of five, Barry, and his mother were struck down by polio but recovered. Barry has a vague recollection of wearing steel leg braces; he was left with an operational scar.

As a boy, he loved sports and the outdoors. Sport played an important part of his schooldays at Christian Brothers College, off Patrick's Hill, Cork, and then as a boarder at Clongowes Wood. He played rugby at primary school in Christians, which took pride in its rugby tradition. He was a bright student with a hunger for learning. He remembers some of the Brothers being excellent teachers, 'interesting academically and stimulating intellectually'. It was a strict regime in the early '50s. He had little respect for other Brothers, whom he describes as 'thuggish and cruel'. He always felt a strong sense of injustice that if something happened and the Brothers couldn't get anyone to own up, then the whole class got the strap. He spent one year in secondary school at Christians before leaving for Clongowes Wood to complete his second-level education. There were some outstanding teachers, most of them priests, at Clongowes. Again, he indulged his love of sports on the playing fields.

At the age of 16, there were early signs of leadership potential: he was captain of the lower line. He was among a good academic class. He had a strong knowledge of the Irish language, having spent two summers in the Gaeltacht. During fifth year, Barry and his classmates did the Matriculation at the end of the summer, through Irish. He now had the choice of either going back to Clongowes for his final year or going straight into college. He chose the latter and began studying law at the age of 17, in keeping with the family tradition, at University College Cork and later University College Dublin.

His father thought he would make a better barrister than a solicitor. Barry can list off some of the biggest names in the Irish legal world who lectured at UCC and UCD. 'We were very lucky in our time to have immensely interesting lecturers who made it all seem fascinating,' he says. 'Law can be a dry subject, but it can also be hugely interesting.'

His greatest passion though was racing motorbikes. He raced bikes every weekend all over the country. It was a good social scene too: the host club always laid on a meal afterwards that usually consisted of a mixed grill and chips, tea and cake. Then they went around to the pub for the prizegiving. Barry was a teetotaller; he stayed off drink deliberately because 'if you drank while you were racing you could never assume to the best and I was racing internationally at a high level'.

Another big interest was water skiing: at 15 he had won the Irish junior championships; he also liked to drive the boats. By night, he eyed girls at the Arcadia Ballroom on Cork's Lower Glanmire Road where fellow UCC student Robin Power and his friends ran student dances. It was a fairly typical scene of boys on one side of the floor, girls on the other. 'You were practically engaged to the girl if you stayed with her between dances!' he recalls. 'It required a certain degree of moral courage to hold hands as well.' The students' social lives revolved around house parties at Christmas and dances during the rest of the year.

While studying at UCD, he worked as a mechanic in his spare time to earn extra money. Nevertheless, he was a wealthy student by the day's standards. He was given an allowance of five pounds a week by his father. His digs cost three pounds, five shillings, which included breakfast and dinner, and the rest was spending money.

Back on the South Mall, the financial and legal heart of Cork city, Paddy Galvin specialised in banking law: he was famous throughout the country not only for his knowledge of banking law but also his ability to apply it to specific circumstances. The old Munster and Leinster Bank had their head office in Cork, and employed Paddy Galvin as their legal adviser. When Barry took over the banking role some years later, his father advised him: 'Remember, bankers don't want to know what the law is; they want to know the safe road home.' Outside the office, Paddy's passion was horse racing and he loved to watch it on television. When they erected a high aerial at home in Monkstown years later to get English racing on the BBC, 'his cup of happiness was full'.

Apart from legal tasks on behalf of Cork Corporation, the firm of Barry C. Galvin were solicitors to Murphy's Brewery. They were paid a retainer, and then all the work was meticulously itemised on lengthy half-yearly bills to the brewery. The Christmas bill to Murphy's was hugely important: the big money to pay staff and their families. Strict protocol was always observed in handling that half-yearly payment.

Traditionally, the bill was drawn on Christmas Eve. At midday, the office messenger boy was despatched to Murphy's with the bill, together with a letter noting the enclosure of their costs and outlays for the half year and wishing the directors and staff a very happy Christmas. Then, at half past two in the afternoon, the porter from Murphy's came to the South Mall with a cheque, together with a letter from the directors of the brewery wishing the partners and staff of Barry C. Galvin many happy returns and a happy New Year. It was all very civilised.

After graduating with a law degree from UCD, young Galvin studied for the bar at Kings Inns where he mixed with foreign students, some of them from African countries who wanted a qualification so they could return home to top jobs in government: Minister for Justice or Attorney General. The only problem: they couldn't master Irish, which was compulsory. So, Galvin and fellow student Kevin Haugh did a deal to prepare them for the exams: they charged the foreigners 10 shillings each and they all passed. 'We made big money and were rich for months afterwards,' recalls Galvin. He hadn't studied as hard as others during the early college years, but got stuck in for the final lap. He threw himself into the books for 14 and 16 hours a day in the digs. During that last year, it was the only time in his life that he smoked cigarettes. An American student, who was sharing the digs, returned to Dublin from a trip home with a plentiful supply of Camel cigarettes. Galvin puffed on up to 50 Camels a day while studying. He passed the exam and was called to the bar in 1966 and later won first place in the respected Brookes prize.

It can be a lonely existence for a newly-qualified barrister in Dublin. He deviled with Robert Barr, later to become a High Court judge; 'a lovely man who trained me very well in law and we had some great experiences together'. He recalls those early days at the bar: 'The essence of being a barrister is to have some solicitor recognise your skill and give you briefs,' he says. 'It's hard to get started. However, if you come from a family of solicitors you expect that your father's friends will rally around. That didn't happen to me. My father gave me my first brief and then I was launched into waiting. Motor cars were quite faulty at the time. Word got around that I knew about cars. I also got a lot of criminal cases, even though my thing was supposed to be tax, company and bank law. I got a lot of work from local solicitors in Dublin. I was doing well.' Mid-way through his second year at the bar, he even started getting work in Cork.

Fate intervened to put his career on a different course. His father took ill with a serious heart condition. He was being treated at the Mater Hospital in Dublin where doctors gave him three months to live. Father and son had a private conversation at the bedside. 'You're doing fine at the bar,' said Galvin senior. 'Your brother, James, is obviously never going to be a solicitor. It looks as if the firm will pass out of the family. I'd like you to change and become a solicitor and take over my share of the firm.' Galvin junior had great affection and respect for his father, and couldn't refuse him under such circumstances. The agreed volte-face brought a huge upheaval in his life. For one thing, he was engaged to be married. 'In those days you couldn't transfer freely, so I had to disbar myself and become a solicitor's apprentice and head into doing three years of solicitor's exams,' he recalls. 'In fairness, the firm paid me as if I was qualified. I went in to work in the firm. Since I knew law, I was well capable of doing the work. Of course, I didn't do any criminal work while I was an apprentice in the office.' As it turned out, Galvin senior recovered from illness, returned to work and father and son practised together contentedly for the next 14 years.

Fate intervened again, on 10 April, 1969, when Barry Galvin narrowly escaped death in a road accident. He was married at the time and his wife, Eimar, expecting their first child. They now have three children, Barry, David and Ann. They were renting a house at Grange in the Cork southside suburbs. Galvin was driving his car, a Humber Sceptre, on the main road near the house when he collided head-on with another car, driven by a German. His head pushed out the windscreen in the impact. He suffered multiple injuries including a fractured skull, broken ribs, punctured lung, broken right wrist and smashed knee caps and ankle. The doctors weren't sure he was going to survive at all. One long-term effect of the accident was to end his motorcycling career; he continued to ride bikes but could never achieve the same standard.

He returned to work eventually, completed the exams and was enrolled as a solicitor in 1969. His specialities were property and conveyancing, company law and taxation. It was customary at the time for young solicitors to sign on the free legal aid panel. He first made his name as a criminal defender. 'I didn't go out intentionally to get into criminal law,' he says. 'It's just something that happened. Instantly, there was a huge call on my time. Since I was trained as a barrister, they were getting a barrister to do advocacy work. It mushroomed from there; for a long time there were only two of us doing the majority of the free legal aid work in Cork.' His reputation as a criminal defence lawyer spread throughout the land. People came from far and wide to be defended, and he travelled to courts all over Ireland. 'If you weren't caught red-handed, and didn't make a statement, it was almost impossible to convict someone,' he explains. '90% of the people in prison were there because they made a statement. The prosecution has to prove the case root, branch and limb. There is in Irish law an almost untramelled right to silence. In those days if you didn't make a statement it was very difficult to convict somebody. At one stage I noticed that the guards were channelling a lot of work my way. I was a bit suspicious of that because if you were a guard you hardly channelled the work to a lawyer who was reckoned to be a tough nut on the other side. I made inquiries and discovered that the guards were getting statements from fellows saying to them that they'd get Barry Galvin to defend them. So fellows were coming in to me having made statements. For a period of time I refused to take on fellows who'd made a statement. If they'd made a statement admitting the offence, what did they need a lawyer for? But I must say I had great respect for the guards who were working under very difficult circumstances. I enjoyed criminal work because, as a lawyer, criminal defence is probably the epitome of legal science; you're preserving the rights and liberties of your fellow man.'

After that, Galvin specialised in defending drunken drivers. There were some hilarious experiences. He was practising under the old system where drivers were asked to walk a straight line, count matchsticks or touch the tip of their nose with their finger. There was a memorable case where he defended an alcoholic who also happened to be a champion fisherman. The client had spent a beautiful summer's day fishing in West Cork, equipped with two bottles of vodka. While driving home to the city, he was involved in a car smash at Victoria Cross. Although the accident wasn't his fault, he swerved and his car turned upside down. He was taken from the car by the guards. The sergeant decided he was drunk and arrested him under the old Section 49. One of the defences under that section, particularly if there was a crash, was to suggest that the symptoms being outlined by the sergeant were those of shock.

Medically, symptoms of shock were exactly the same as drunken driving: loss of coordination, bloodshot eyes, etc. Galvin takes up the story: 'I can't remember why but it was vital to the case as to precisely when the sergeant had formed an opinion that my client was unfit to drive due to the consumption of intoxicating liquor. There's a rule of advocacy that you should never ask a question unless you know the answer. It's not always easy to follow. If you're in the full flow of advocacy, and you think the sergeant is weakening, then you press on. I was pressing on this sergeant. He was a clever fellow. I insisted, "you must know what caused you to come to the conclusion that my client was under the influence of intoxicating liquor". The sergeant paused for a moment and said, "well, Mr Galvin, I'll tell you. It was when I saw he had his trousers on inside out". We were shot down at that stage.' Galvin discovered later how the strange dress code had come about. While fishing, the client hooked a troublesome fish and he fell into the water. He decided, sensibly, to take off his trousers and hang them on the bushes to dry. Meanwhile, he polished off the other bottle, and put on the trousers inside out.

When Paddy Galvin died in 1982, Barry was already a partner in the family law firm and so family tradition continued. Paddy died unexpectedly in Cork's Mercy Hospital. Barry made a habit of calling to see him on his way home from work and discussed the day's events. He was looking after his father's clients. Galvin senior had been in hospital for about three months but seemed to be getting better. He hated being in hospital, dependent on others. He suffered a variety of ailments but his heart condition put him at most risk. On one particular day, Barry returned from Dublin at lunchtime, worked in the office during the afternoon and called in to the hospital at half-past five. His father was asleep. He was at home when he got the call at seven o'clock. He always mildly regretted afterwards that he hadn't wakened him earlier that day. Barry speaks of his father with great affection and says he can still feel his presence in the firm. 'I opted to work in his office. The wallpaper and furniture were all chosen for him. We furnished the room to his taste when we moved into this office. I will always remember him in that room. I still come across files with his signature on documents.' Today, the firm, which still bears the Galvin name, has five partners and a staff of 19.

Galvin is a former President of the Southern Law Association and also served on the council of the Law Society of Ireland for six years.

The defender turned prosecutor in June 1983 when he was appointed State Solicitor for Cork in succession to Niall Cronin. His knowledge of the criminal underworld as a criminal lawyer proved invaluable. He was now working closely with the Gardaí and knew the names, addresses and track record of every villain in the city. He could even tell their idiosyncrasies and predict their reactions in court. His office on the South Mall was soon bulging with criminal files. He had a charismatic presence in court too where both petty and professional career criminals didn't know what hit them. There were many high profile crimes, murders and, later, major drug busts. That's how it all began. All the time drugs were being smuggled through the south-west, although the Gardaí and customs did enjoy some spectacular successes. Small-time criminals began dealing in cannabis and then in the new trendy drug, Ecstasy. The small number of gangs controlling the drugs trade began to fight with each other over territory in the early '90s. There were shootings at pubs and punishment beatings. It all exploded when a gang member was shot dead in a 'hit' outside a city-centre pub in April 1995. *The Cork Examiner* and *Echo* disturbed the gangland with their coverage of drug-related violence. A number of newsagents were threatened with arson if they continued to stock copies of the papers. Galvin successfully prosecuted those who made the threats.

He says: 'They thought they were above the law and took careful steps to mind their position and to camouflage their wealth by drawing dole. You see, the dole was a great insurance because the taxman took no interest in them.'

Galvin says major criminals did not realise how effective the Criminal Assets Bureau would be in targeting their wealth from its establishment in 1996. It is a multi-agency commission which draws together the expertise and top personnel of the Gardaí, Customs, Revenue Commissioners and Department of Social Welfare. They work in great secrecy and under strict protection. Therefore, the operational side of the bureau involves intelligence-gathering, investigation, following the assets and money through banks, building societies, holes in the ground, anywhere, and then applying in The High Court and ensuring that the legal process takes over. The main legislative weapon is the Proceeds of Crime Act 1996: once the bureau has established that specified property is the proceeds of criminal activity on the civil standard of proof, the burden of proof shifts onto defendants to show that their money or property is not the result of criminal activity. The High Court can freeze and ultimately dispose of property which it is satisfied, on the balance of probabilities, has been the proceeds of crime. Provision was made to appoint a receiver to manage frozen property. The freezing orders can last for up to seven years when disposal orders are made. The fact that serious villains are named in the legal process, and their empires dismantled, is hugely important. It was a real war: hitting criminals where it hurt most. Within eight months, £10 million pounds worth of goods and cash had been seized from villains.

Barry Galvin was uncharacteristically lost for words when honoured as Cork Person of the Year in 1997, chosen from one of 12 monthly award winners. 'I was embarrassed,' he says. 'I wasn't expecting it and felt there were much more deserving people. It was a great honour and, of course, recognition for all the people who worked so hard against crime in Cork and for the Criminal Assets Bureau. In that sense, it was a significant award.' Simply, he would like to be remembered as someone who made a difference in the fight against crime.

He predicts that crime can be brought under control within five years: that is, if the imbalance between the rights of the accused versus the rights of the victim is redressed; if the Gardaí continue to get improved laws and more resources to investigate and solve crime; if the quality of life of the less-well-off improves; and if it becomes unprofitable for people to indulge in crime. 'I've always had the view that if there are no successful criminals, it lessens the attraction for others to take on a life of crime. You're always going to have a hardcore of professional criminals. The only way to reform some guys is to keep them in jail. Time and time again, I've seen offenders coming out after eight to ten year sentences and they've learned their lesson. However, there are others for whom reform is impossible and the protection of the public must be considered.'

For the lawyer who once defended criminals in court, the mission that began after he shared a train journey with the victims of a robbery goes on. It is a constant struggle between good and evil.

NIALL TÓIBÍN

GAME FOR A LAUGH

IT is, of course, the way he tells 'em. Niall Tóibín has a lung-full of well-tuned accents, a prodigious memory and a sharp eye for detail to spin a good yarn.

It takes the quintessential Corkman a long time to tell a funny story: he speaks in colloquialisms, local abbreviations and, as the need arises, four letter words; there is a quest for mischief in every syllable; the accent can rise like the hills of Montenotte or fall flat like the Midlands; he goes up alleys and down streets, digressing to recall memorable characters of his childhood until, finally, he gets to the punchline and you collapse into laughter. Cork may have given Murphy's to the world, but Niall Tóibín will always rate as the city's most popular export to stage and film. He's done it all: in his own words everything except striptease, ballet and the circus since he started acting over four decades ago.

There is an endless store of Cork yarns, each brought to life by the sights and sounds of his home town. Like the night the Swans ended up in the North Infirmary. *The Swans Of The Lee* shows at the Opera House were a theatrical institution in Cork, billed as a 'riot of laughter, song and dance'. The company celebrated on the closing night after setting a box office record; they were brimful of the joys but one of the lads, Tommy Dynes, fell on the street and cut his forehead. The others took him to the Accident and Emergency department at the 'North Infir'. As a nurse examined the wound, Tommy, still elated after the show, told her with pride: 'I'm a swan, you know.' The nurse took a doctor on duty aside and explained that the patient seemed 'badly concussed'. The doctor decided to approach the group of friends. 'I understand this man says he's a swan,' he said. 'That's right doctor,' they chorused, 'we're all feckin' swans!'

Don't say so out loud, but Tóibín isn't actually a northsider, even though he's long been adopted as one of their own. He was born in 1929 in the southside, Friars Walk, 'the one skeleton in my cupboard'. He was one of seven children – four boys and three girls – in an Irish speaking family. They were reared in the northside under the shadow of the Bishop's Palace in the Bishop's Field at Redemption Road, between North Monastery CBS and St Finbarr's diocesan seminary, Farranferris. His father, Seán, a Gaelic scholar, was deeply committed to Gaelic Ireland, and it hurt to hear him described as a 'fuckin old madman' because he preferred to speak in Irish. He was a teacher and also a keen botanist who wrote two nature books in Irish. Niall's mother, Siobhan, came from Beaufort, near Killarney, and had a natural sense of humour. He thinks he inherited her humour and quirky way of looking at life.

It was a happy childhood. Hurling was a religion on the northside, which housed Glen Rovers. Every youngster had a hurley in his hand after school. The Glen's Jack Lynch was their idol. Lynch played football too, with their sister club, St Nicks, although he once said he never knew what to do with his hands on the football field. Young Tóibín knew all the Lynchs who lived down near Shandon. He and Jack were lifelong friends, 'though I wouldn't have been on the same side politically'. Drag-hunting and bowl-playing were popular too during his childhood, 'though tennis and golf were curious affectations of people in the pages of *The Cork Examiner*'.

Young Tóibín was nearly 10 when the war broke out; there are memories of the American Liberty ships and British mine-sweepers coming up the harbour and the city streets filled with uniforms. 'Since the British were just in sailors' uniforms nobody paid the slightest attention to them,' he recalls. 'In the same way you'd seen RAF men home to Cork on holidays and they'd be going around in nice greyish-blue uniforms and nobody bothered them. But the funny thing was that if a British soldier had walked down the street in an army uniform he'd have been thrown into the river.' The American GIs, also in uniform, brought glamour. Patrick Street was unusually colourful. 'On a summer's evening you'd go down and see the girls chasing the Yanks and the Yanks chasing the girls. That activity was very new and strange to Cork.'

Another indelible memory is of going to matches down in the 'old' Park. Once, coming out of a Cork and Kerry match, he saw Paddy Bawn Brosnan, wearing only a jacket over his gear and in his boots, climb over a barbed wire fence and join a group of Kerry supporters leaving the grounds. 'We followed him all the way down the Boggy Road and saw him go into the first pub in the Victoria Road area. He still had the boots and togs on. I don't think you'd see many fellows doing that today.'

Early school years were spent with the nuns at St Vincent's Convent before moving to the Christian Brothers at the North Monastery. The 'Mon' was the country's greatest nursery for hurlers and had produced Jack Lynch of Glen Rovers: he would make history as the only player ever to win six senior All-Ireland medals in a row for hurling and football between 1941 and 1946. Tóibín played hurling through his teenage years until he had to wear glasses.

Another hurling hero during the '40s was Alan Lotty of Sarsfields and, of course, the Glen's Christy Ring of Cloyne. Ring captured the souls of every youngster who knew the shape of a hurley. Years later, Tóibín got the chance to meet the maestro who, in spite of his achievements in winning eight All-Ireland medals, was always a man of few words. 'I'm not much good at speeches,' he once told thousands who welcomed him and the McCarthy Cup home to Cloyne in 1946, and promptly shut up after four sentences. The Tóibín-Ring encounter took place during the '70s at an All-Ireland victory celebration dinner for the Cork team at the Spa Hotel in Lucan. 'I was usually invited to these to tell a few yarns,' he says. 'Christy was always invited but rarely turned up; he didn't go in for that kind of thing. The MC was in the middle of a speech at the dinner when Christy made an unexpected appearance. He stopped and told guests, "My God, here I am talking about hurling and the greatest hurler in history has just walked in the door."

'Christy got a standing ovation and prolonged applause. After a while Christy began to applaud himself. There was a hasty re-arrangement of seats at the top table and a place cleared for him. He was seated opposite me. He just looked across at me and said, "You're Tóibín, aren't ya?" I said, "Yes." And then he said: "I like you." I felt that I could relax. He had sort of given me permission to stay.'

Tóibín's favourite Ring story concerns the great man's carefully-chosen and brief words to the media after Cork's All-Ireland victory in 1966. The Rebel County had not won an All-Ireland since 1954. Asked how he rated the present team, he replied: 'They achieved one thing no team that I played on for Cork ever did: they won an All-Ireland after twelve years.' Then he shut up.

Liking or disliking school all depended on whether or not you liked your teacher, 'and for the most part I liked my teachers'. Tóibín was a bright student who managed to avoid most of the corporal punishment.

He witnessed some appalling hidings, though. 'The worst beating I saw was given to a fellow who had run away from home,' he recalls. Pupils were held up to ridicule in front of the class and, in one case, a boy with a stutter was mocked by a lay teacher. 'In fairness, I think the regime looks much crueller and harder in retrospect than it actually was,' he says. 'Remember, at that time it was perfectly acceptable for a father to give his son a clip across the ear or a boot up the arse. It was called putting manners on you.'

Boys crossed the river from Sullivan's Quay CBS to attend the North Mon secondary school. It took them at least a year to be accepted; 'they were regarded as southside fellows and, therefore, slightly inferior!'

There was little drama at school, but Tóibín did make his first stage appearance at the Mon. At the age of eight, he was chosen to play the 'Bloody Child' in the school version of *Macbeth*. It was produced by Brother Byrne, nicknamed 'H₂S O'Broin' because he taught Chemistry as well as English, Irish, Latin, History and Geography. A number of future members of the Abbey took part in the play including Edward Golden, who was then a teacher and played Macbeth, his brother Geoff, and Chris Curran, who lived next to the North Infirmary and who was one of the witches. Years later, when Tóibín was in a play in Dublin, Brother Byrne came to see him 'and pointed out that I had come a long way since my first dress rehearsal when I was crying that it was 10 o'clock and I hadn't yet had my tea'.

Like Dublin, the streets of Cork were home to wonderful characters; the best known were Klondyke, Jerry Bruton and the Rancher. Klondyke – real name, Jeremiah Healy – was an ex-British Serviceman and a likeable eccentric. He was nominated by the UCC students to contest the local elections and made it to the city council, much to the disgust of the then City Manager, Philip Monahan. On the campaign trail, he promised voters: 'I stand before you to be behind you.' The students 'conferred' the degree of Doctor at Law on him during Rag Week in a ceremony conducted at the corner of the Coal Quay and Cornmarket Street. He campaigned for a ladies public toilet; the first such loo on Lavitt's Quay stood as a memorial to him later on. Klondyke demanded that his portrait should hang in the foyer of this public convenience; instead, the City Manager offered to put his face on the toilet paper.

Tóibín's favourite character was Jerry Bruton, who liked to raise his voice on street corners, at queues and particularly down at GAA matches in the old Park. 'Jerry had great charm, with a real twinkle in his eye. He was an absolute rogue. He always wore a grey jacket and grey shirt with a cravat or scarf tucked in under his shirt and a pork-pie hat.' He had two familiar songs. The first began ...

> We'll all go down the Marina,
> it's a beautiful place for a hike.
> You can sit on the seat there,
> and rest your old feet there,
> or walk to Blackrock if you like.

The second song was composed by Jerry in honour of the new Shannon Airport, known at the time as *Rineanna*. Bruton the ballad singer was also adopted by the UCC students, although he never made it to City Hall. 'The Healy campaign started off as a joke that became serious, but Jerry Bruton's bid started off as a joke. The one who enjoyed the joke most of all was himself. He saw this as a nice way of getting a few pints. This was just an extension of his professional activity as an entertainer towards a wider audience. His speeches were hilarious. I remember one where he attacked the City Manager for importing cement from Japan to build houses in Cork when there was plenty of limestone and sandstone locally. Yet, the City Manager was going around blowing his horn about his achievements. Jerry said, "I won't be blowing me horn. I haven't had a horn for twenty-five years". That was the kind of speech that went down well, and he might have up to a hundred people listening to him. The respectable citizens of Cork thought he was a disgrace, bringing the city into disrepute. It was just a bit of fun.'

Another familiar character on the northside was the Rancher, Jerry McCarthy, who used to push a box car around town. He boasted of his exploits as an armyman and liked to drop on his knees to fire an invisible rifle, complete with sound effects. Tóibín got early inspiration from these characters although, occasionally, inspiration for a good story came from the political utterances inside City Hall. He tells of a certain city councillor who challenged the City Manager about a large financial allocation for overheads in the spending estimates. 'That's all very well, Manager,' said the councillor. 'The overheads are entitled to their rights. But what about the ordinary worker?'

Tóibín was a bright student. He went as far as the Leaving Certificate but didn't do the exam because he had passed the civil service clerical officers' exam in 1946. He wasn't disappointed to leave school. 'I had lost interest in studies at that stage.' He left home for Dublin at the age of 17 to join the public service. His parents were delighted that he had got a job.

'In those days in our strata of society, if you became a civil servant, a garda, a teacher, a bank clerk or a priest, you were doing well and were regarded as a success,' he reflects. He started off in the Statistics Office and did spells in the Department of Industry and Department of External Affairs. He met great people who introduced him to the art of drinking porter. During this period he became involved in amateur dramatics, initially with the Gaelic League at Parnell Square, and acting in amateur plays with Compantas Amharclainne na Gaeilge, a bilingual theatre company that ran shows in the Olympia. He was also doing semi-professional work with the Abbey Theatre.

At the age of 18, a future President of the United States bought him a bottle of Guinness at a pub in Abbey Street. Movie stars Ronald Reagan and Joan Caulfield came to Dublin for a charity premiere at the Adelphi Cinema. They called to the old Abbey Theatre and wanted to look around. Tóibín, at the time writing scripts for the pantomime, was with stage manager Sean Mooney and Walter Macken. They showed the American visitors around the theatre. Afterwards, the future President asked: 'Can I buy you guys a drink?' They went over to The Flowing Tide in Abbey Street where Reagan bought the Corkman a bottle of stout. 'It was an unremarkable incident,' he says. Many years later, he regarded Reagan as a great 'pro' playing the President.

After nearly six years in the civil service, the big break came when Tóibín did an audition for RTÉ and landed a job with the Radio Éireann Repertory Company in July 1953. He met his wife, Judy Kenny, in a lodging house off the South Circular Road, and they were married in 1957. He spent 14 years with the Radio Éireann players, doing everything from Shakespeare to sports reports. A childhood neighbour from Cork's northside, Joe Lynch, had earlier served his apprenticeship with 'the Rep.' Joe was a great showman. In his autobiography, *Smile and be a villain*, Tóibín says it would be a great pity if his fellow Corkman was to be judged solely on the strength of *Glenroe* by people who never saw him in serious theatre or in top-class variety where he was very good.

At the Rep, Tóibín met Micheal MacLiammóir and was awestruck. MacLiammóir once claimed to have come from Blackrock in Cork – a kind of 'baptism by desire'. He had a wicked sense of humour. Tóibín recalls that when someone read from a newspaper, 'I see that woman who was raped got £50,000'. 'As well?' asked MacLiammóir. He also almost invented the one-man show with *The Importance of Being Oscar*. Cyril Cusack was a 'totally theatrical being, in every way.' Tóibín tells of an incident involving Cusack and Rod Taylor during the filming of *Cry of the Innocent*, directed by Michael O'Herlihy in 1980. Taylor is burying his wife and child, killed in a sabotaged plane crash as they holidayed in Ireland. Cusack played a policeman investigating the case. During the burial scene, Taylor is overcome with grief. In mid-scene, he snapped: 'Will someone tell Cusack to stop crying. I'm the one crying – he's just fucking watching.'

Tóibín cut loose from the Rep in 1967; he felt like a nun who had vaulted the convent wall, 'a well-paid nun, fat and alcoholic'. That year he played in the first production of Brian Friel's *Lovers* at the Gate Theatre and had a huge hit playing Brendan Behan in *Borstal Boy* at the Abbey. The opening night of *Borstal Boy* was the greatest moment of his career. 'I had only left Radio Éireann six months before and gone freelance,' he recalls. 'I couldn't have known that the play would have made such impact. The first night was just astonishing. I was stunned by the reaction.' Behan would cast a long shadow over his career. *Borstal Boy* was the role that made him famous: the 1970 Tony award winning Broadway show, and reprised in about nine different productions over 29 years. *Borstal Boy* made Tóibín a star in Broadway; New York was his kind of town. He was joined by Judy and their five children, then ranging in age from eleven to two. There were rave reviews 'and I didn't have to pay for a drink for donkey's ages'. When Tóibín was mugged on the way home one night the story made the front page of the *New York Daily News*. The Tony Award for Best Play was 'the equivalent of first prize at the Feis'. Simply, Niall Tóibín was the stage personification of Brendan Behan. The Behan link was reinforced by his work in three productions of *The Hostage*. In 1974 he performed 'The Bells of Hell' at the Gaiety; an anecdotal and musical portrait of Behan, together with Ronnie Drew.

Tóibín first met Behan at a party in Stamer Street, off the South Circular Road, in May 1952. The moment is recalled in his autobiography: 'In the middle of this party, a man arrived wearing only trousers and singlet. The shirt had been discarded somewhere. He was grossly overweight, reeking of porter, streaming sweat, with black, tousled curly hair, and he was roaring his head off singing. He went from one song to the next, pausing only to grab a swig of porter and hurl a tirade of political abuse at all his nearest and dearest – because he would have been very close to all these people, politically.' They got drunk together and were firm friends by the end of the night.

Behan was once refused drink when he walked into Joe Dwyer's pub in Leeson Street. He was drunk and carried a cooked chicken in a tinfoil bag under his arm. In a fit of temper as he walked out the door, Behan threw the chicken across the pub and it landed among bottles on the shelves. Not surprisingly, he was barred.

Tóibín's favourite Behan story, though, comes from his New York days. Behan was drinking with two acclaimed artists at a pub in Greenwich Village after attending an art exhibition. A woman approached them and raved about their paintings. She turned to the Irishman and asked: 'And what exciting thing do you do?' Behan replied: 'I mix Calvados with brandy.'

Looking back, he says his association with *Borstal Boy* was a good and bad thing. 'It was part of my entire professional life. I was involved with the same play for 29 years, and you can't expect much more than that. I've been accused of milking it and making more money out of Brendan Behan than he made out of himself. I take that kind of comment as sour grapes. But it's true that if you're associated with one part for a long time, people expect you to play every part in the same way. I was very lucky in that I was able to divide my approach between straight acting and doing my one-man show, which is purely comedy. Originally, *Borstal Boy* had a huge success because I looked like Brendan Behan and sounded like him. People who remembered him found it very exciting and a bit unnerving. When another generation came along who didn't remember him at all, it took on a different life of its own. Then it developed and meant different things to different generations.'

Above all, Tóibín believes in the business of showbusiness; actors play for a paying audience and their success in measured by box office appeal. He's a born realist and knows that you can't argue with commercial success. Audiences never tired of *Borstal Boy*, so they got what they wanted. It's unlikely he'll have another outing as Brendan Behan because he's too old. But that's what he said 10 years ago. He says it stretches the credibility, though, even with a wig, to pretend to be only 41.

Tóibín has done a lot of 'swerving about madly' in a versatile career on stage and screen that took him all over the world. There was a lot of boozing too, during those decades of swerving; he was blessed and cursed by the demon. Someone once asked him if he ever had a problem with drink. He said he was fine; other people were having the problems.

Professionally, Tóibín has done everything from *Hamlet* to *Coronation Street*. Most of the swerving was 'accidental' – 'you set out to do one thing and end up doing another'. Everybody has their favourite image of him: whether giving a powerful performance as Bull McCabe in John B. Keane's *The Field*, the mischief-maker in William Trevor's *Ballroom of Romance* or frustrated husband in Eugene McCabe's award-winning *King of the Castle*. For many, he is the master of the one-man comedy show who knows how to reduce an audience to a heap of laughter.

Others prefer the TV image, ever since two early comedy series on RTÉ during the '70s, *If The Cap Fits* and *Time Now, Mr T*, which poked fun at the establishment and generated controversy. The send-up of Holy Ireland brought a lot of flak. Whenever *The Cork Examiner's* Robert O'Donoghue walked through the English Market in Cork, he was regularly mistaken for the late Larry Lyons, his colleague and TV critic, by one stallholder who always offered an opinion. After Larry wrote an unfavourable review of *Time Now, Mr T*, O'Donoghue was intercepted by the stallholder. 'Good morning, Mr Lyons,' she began, 'I see where that boy Tóibín is disgracing us again. But you didn't let him away with it. And you're quite right, Mr Lyons. Slam the bastard.'

Tóibín's screen roguery became known to wider TV audiences in Ireland and England as Slipper in *The Irish RM*, and other series including *Dempsey and Makepiece*, *The Detective* and *Stay Lucky*. Cork people remember him for his portrayal of one of their own, the late Tony Murphy, in *Murphy's Stroke* in May, 1980. Among the cast was Irish actor Pierce Brosnan, later to become secret agent 007. It was based on the true story of how Murphy and some pals stung bookies in England by pulling off a remarkable betting coup. That was dubbed the Gay Future affair, after the name of a horse they entered in a race at Cartmel in Cumbria. Murphy, who stood trial in England and got off with a fine, was chuffed by Tóibín's portrayal of him in 1980. 'I liked it. Enjoyable like,' he told the actor. 'You flattered me. You've a fine head of hair, God bless you. I'm gone as bald as an egg.' Larry Lyons, easily Cork's most flamboyant journalist at the time, who first broke the story in *The Cork Examiner*, wrote a book about the Gay Future affair. It also gave the inspiration for a theme bar at the former Victoria Hotel run by the late Dominic O'Keeffe.

Tóibín is still a familiar face on British television; work-in-progress is the hugely successful BBC drama series, *Ballykissangel*, shot in Avoca, Co. Wicklow, which surpassed all expectations reaching weekly audiences of 13 million. 'It's the most successful TV series I've ever been involved in,' he says. 'I have a very nice part. It's an enormous hit and looks like continuing for quite a while yet.'

The big screen gave him a platform with some legendary figures of the cinema, most notably the late Robert Mitchum and the late Richard Burton. During the filming of *Ryan's Daughter* on the boreens above Dingle, Tóibín shared a set with some of the biggest names in the industry and, inevitably, spawned a lot of pub talk. One myth was that he told Mitchum to 'fuck off' in a pub one night. Not so. That would have been a very foolish thing to do. It was true that John Mills – who won an Oscar for his supporting role as the local idiot – nearly drowned in the sea at

Coumeenoole during filming. After he had been hauled out, he remarked to the director, in typically British stiff-upper-lip style: 'Sorry, Guv, ruined the shot I'm afraid.' The British crew were impressed, but the Irish thought: 'Fuckin' eejit. Why doesn't he sue the bastard?'

Tóibín rates Mitchum as the greatest film actor he's ever worked with. 'Remember, he started off as a cowboy extra and learned how to be an actor in films and through films. He was part of the history of filmmaking and outlasted everybody in that genre. He was there before John Wayne and after him. He was superb in gangster movies too. He had a lovely underplaying style.'

Whenever Tóibín tells his favourite *Ryan's Daughter* stories the accent changes, words are summoned carefully and a familiar look of mischief lights up his face to set the scene. Mitchum, who played the schoolteacher in Robert Bolt's screenplay, had been ordered off the booze by director David Lean. Mitchum didn't like Lean, the filmmaker who is forever remembered for *Dr Zhivago* and *Lawrence of Arabia*. Asked by a local journalist to describe Lean as a director, Mitchum replied, laconically: 'He's a tall director.'

Lean imposed a strict daily routine on the set to keep Mitchum sober. As a kind of discipline, Mitchum was sometimes called at 8 a.m. but not used until 5 p.m. The actor demanded Florida orange juice: supplies were flown in specially and kept aside for him. A set dresser, Liam Pyke, spotted him sitting alone outside his caravan above Coumeenoole beach during filming one day, drinking orange juice. Liam helped himself to a glass, took a gulp 'and nearly went on fire'. It was 90% brandy. 'Jesus, that's beautiful orange juice,' remarked Liam. Mitchum caught him by the shoulder, sat him down and said: 'Now, you know that it's not orange juice; I know that it's not orange juice. But if that bastard down on the beach ever finds out that it's not orange juice, it won't be me that told him, and I'll knock your fucking head off.' Tóibín says Mitchum's performances were always flawless. Asked once how long he'd been an actor, Mitchum replied: 'I'm not an actor. I'm a movie star.' Tóibín would return to the Dingle Peninsula in 1991 for the making of *Far and Away*, a romantic tale of emigration to the United States starring Tom Cruise and Nicole Kidman.

Tóibín established a close relationship with Richard Burton. They worked together on two movies. They spent seven enjoyable weeks on location in Munster and in the West shooting *Tristan and Isolt* which was never released. Tóibín played Sir Andred to Burton's King Mark. Off set, Burton talked a lot about the theatre, poetry and Elizabeth Taylor. 'He had a really hypnotic voice, a wonderful conversationalist,' recalls Tóibín. 'We spent days and nights together. He was on the dry. We talked about everything under the sun. He was one of the most interesting people I ever met because he seemed to have read everything; he could quote reams of poetry. He also loved Ireland and the people.' Later, Tóibín and Burton worked together throughout Europe on *Wagner* which also starred Laurence Olivier, John Gielgud and Vanessa Redgrave. It was regarded as an uninspired biography of the composer, monotonously acted by Burton. 'He wasn't well by that time,' says Tóibín, 'and physically not up to it. He was under medical supervision and getting physiotherapy during filming. It was sad.'

Tóibín delivered a powerful portrayal of an IRA leader in *The Outsider*, directed by Tony Luraschi in 1980. He rates it as his best film performance. American actor Craig Wasson played a GI who returns from Vietnam and is coaxed into joining the IRA by his grandfather, played by Sterling Hayden. The movie was critically acclaimed for its no-frills, authentic narrative. Apart from *The Coal Miner's Daughter*, *The Daily News* said it was the best film of the year. Inevitably, the theme stirred up controversy. 'Unfortunately for me it fell foul of the authorities in Britain and it was never widely distributed there. It got the same treatment in the States. Political pressure was brought to bear to suppress the distribution because it seemed to them to be a pro-IRA film which it was not at all. But then even the very mention of the IRA seemed to be taken by certain elements of the press in Britain as meaning that you support them.'

Some things are best forgotten. Take two notable duds, for example, both musicals. Tóibín got the call to play Frank Harris in David Black's production, *Fearless Frank*, at the Princess Theatre on Broadway. He knew the writing was on the wall early on. The stage doorman, a Cuban immigrant called Pepe, knew the score. During rehearsals, Pepe could tell him precisely when the show was going to close, even before it had opened. The first night reviews lambasted the production. The word was out at the first night party in Sardi's restaurant. Frank Rich of *The New York Times* gave Tóibín a good notice, but otherwise *Fearless Frank* was dumped upon. 'It was billed as a musical, which was a dreadful mistake. It should have been billed as a play. Having been billed as a musical, because there were some musical items in it, it was reviewed by the people who review musicals as distinct from the people who review plays. They came along, took one look and said "this is shit". They re-worded the criticism so that it was printable. They said the music trickled horribly over the entire production like cold porridge. They said the dancers couldn't dance and the singers couldn't sing.' Rich gave Tóibín one of the best reviews of his career. It was, unfortunately, worthless. 'It's better to get a bad review in a successful play, than a good review in a flop,' he explains. 'You could be terrible in a play that happens to run for two years. All that anybody will ever remember is that the play ran for two years. Therefore, you must be good because you were in it. On the other hand, if you're outstanding in a play that everybody agrees is shit and is going to close in a week, then the notice isn't worth a damn.'

The other big flop was *Crock*, billed as a rock musical based on *The Crock of Gold* by James Stephens. This time it was a 'home game', directed by Alan Simpson at the Gaiety Theatre. The Dublin critics were unanimous: it was lousy.

It has been an enjoyable spin on the merry-go-round. There are few, if any, regrets. Sure, he'd love to have been the big classical actor. It was not to be. 'I think I've been lucky,' he says. 'I didn't do exactly what I wanted to do. I wanted to be a straight actor. I thought I was going to be the new Olivier, which would have been the ambition in my time. That's not what happened. Who knows, maybe there's some young fellow down in Blackpool who wants to be the new Niall Tóibín.'

Off stage, he'd love to have played hurling for Cork in an All-Ireland team, 'even a losing one'. How would he like to be remembered? 'With affection, if at all.' And his epitaph? The Irish are great for heaping praise on the dead, he notes. That familiar mischievous smile creases his face again. He quotes the words of a fellow mourner at a mutual friend's funeral. 'Say what you like,' remarked the other mourner to him as they left the church together, 'but he never gave a bollocks.' Tóibín adds: 'That'll do for me. You can quote me on that.' He's still smiling.

PROFESSOR
JOHN A. MURPHY

HOLDING FORTH

'WHAT about all the dead Protestants?' The question was shouted in anger at a packed match in Páirc Uí Chaoimh one Sunday. Thousands had risen to their feet to observe a minute's silence for four IRA and INLA hunger strikers who died in the Maze Prison H-Blocks. The silence fell in waves. Senator Professor John A. Murphy made his own protest by remaining in his seat while crowds rose around him. His shouting about the Protestants punctuated the silence. It was a gesture against the tide in the long summer of 1981. The minute's silence had been called ostensibly for GAA workers who died in an accident. The dead hunger strikers were included in the request to crowds across the loudspeaker.

'I thought that was sheer opportunism tacking these people onto this innocuous local tragedy,' he says. 'I just sat down. I was furious. My larger concern there was that the GAA should not be involved in politics. Part of my political philosophy was that bodies like the GAA could become a bridge in a divided Ireland; they could become part of a shared and common heritage rather than being identified with one tribe. So the very worst thing in my view was that the GAA should be lined up alongside the Provos. That's what was behind my protest that day.'

John A. Murphy has strong views about most things: predictably, his public stance against the hunger strike provoked extreme reactions amid the highly charged political atmosphere. It was a battle of wills between Republican prisoners in the Maze H-Blocks – so called because of their shape – and the British government. Bobby Sands, elected MP for Fermanagh-South Tyrone, was the first hunger striker to die on 5 May after 66 days without food. Nine more would die up to 20 August in pursuit of special concessions. The deaths landed the Irish and British governments with an enormous political crisis and caused controversy worldwide. The Cork historian regarded the hunger strike and its aims as an IRA political propaganda exercise, and said so. In a lunchtime speech to members of the Cork Rotary Club, he said the H-Block committees' campaign was reminiscent of the fascists' rise to power, 'undermining the normal process of law, putting up black flags everywhere and ordering people to shut their doors'. He warned of the dangers of caving in psychologically to their demands.

John A got hate mail during the seven-month hunger strike campaign – including bullets, mock bombs and documents smeared with excreta. Fake devices assembled with small Hermesetas sweetener tins, batteries and wires were sent to him at UCC and Leinster House. He didn't take the threats seriously. The only physical assault happened after a verbal exchange at a pub in the Lough suburb of Cork. He was incensed to see someone selling copies of *An Phoblacht* to customers. 'I made no secret of my attitude to selling this terrorist rag.' A man thumped him out in the car park later and ran away. 'I suppose he was probably just annoyed with me,' says John A. 'I don't think he gave me a black eye out of any great ideological motives.' Although it was a worrying time for his family, he regarded the threats as 'daft'. A cousin once 'cruelly' told his wife, Cita: 'Don't be worried about John at all, he's not important enough. They wouldn't be bothered with him!' When he was invited to deliver the commemoration address at Beal na mBláth on the 60th anniversary of the death of Michael Collins, a detective from Union Quay called to see him at UCC. There were threats that he would be 'got' at Beal na mBláth. Professor Murphy laughed 'because I thought this was slightly hilarious'. The Gardaí wanted to give him protection. They'd be discreet. He wasn't enthusiastic. The detective insisted on an escort, saying 'you never know what lunatics are around'. Still, he demurred. The detective said, quite crossly: 'Listen, professor, you have to have an escort because if anything happens to you on Sunday the sergeant in Bandon will be in big trouble.' Looking back, he laughs heartily at the garda's reaction and says: 'I thought that was great!'

'John Aah' – as he is affectionately known in Cork – has a lot to say about religion and politics. The whiff of controversy is usually in the air. A gifted and straight talker who isn't afraid to stand up – or sit down – and be a lone voice. He is the doyen of Irish historians; a public figure well respected in education and politics and widely regarded as a profound contributor to national debate. The accent is unmistakable; the use of language colourful; words chosen with surgical precision, and the perfect barb summoned to dismiss a fool or critic. He's a good man for a song, too.

John Augustine Murphy is a native of Macroom, born in 'the town that never reared a fool' on 17 January, 1927. His father, Timothy, was a carpenter and came from small farming stock. He was skilled with his hands and built their house in Macroom with the help of local labourers. He was also an accomplished gaelic footballer, playing on the Cork team which won the All-Ireland in 1911. When Cork won the All-Ireland in 1973 after a gap of 28 years, the players brought the Sam Maguire Cup to show him and he was over the moon.

John A's mother, Nellie O'Shea, came from a middle-class background; her father was a prosperous draper and she had the rare benefit of second-level education. John A's parents shared strong patriotic views and a common interest in Irish language and music. They were both de Valera and Fianna Fáil supporters. It was a strong nationalistic home environment: a simple philosophy of faith and fatherland.

John A was the youngest of four – two boys and two girls. Although there was no poverty in the house, they depended on their father's pay packet 'and there was little to spare'. His mother played the piano and taught him a lot about singing. He enjoyed an extraordinary range of musical experiences. At the age of eight or nine, he was introduced to Verdi and Schubert as well as nationalist songs in Irish. Macroom had a strong Irish language hinterland: as a schoolboy he recalls people coming to town on fair days who spoke Irish, and also Irish-speaking cousins calling to see his mother. 'All that struck me as quite exotic and fascinating,' he says. He was 'bookish in the extreme': by the age of ten or eleven, he was 'devouring' Dickens.

He liked to talk a lot, even then. There were early signs of the future senator: making speeches at the age of seven or eight to the applause of neighbours. His sister used to be ashamed of her life 'because I would occasionally express these oratorical talents on the town hall balcony'. It was a happy childhood, 'apart from the usual terrors induced by taking religion too seriously; the imaginative powers of religious preaching and terrors of the confessional.' He was an altar boy at St Colman's parish church and much taken with the colour and excitement of liturgy. On one hand, there was great comfort and conviction in the certitudes of dogma. On the other hand, he recalls the terror of lenten retreats and the fears of retribution. 'Maybe I was particularly sensitive,' he says, 'but I would develop all kinds of mad scruples which troubled me a great deal about religion and which would be inconceivable to a modern adolescent.' One tended to think of women as either belonging to the saintly, chaste category or else lurid and sensual. Falling in love was a romantic, nonsexual business. 'In this artificial division,' he says, 'the boundaries would sometimes crumble and you'd get quite mad fantasies.'

He was schooled by the De La Salle Brothers in Macroom. He was a bright student, though wouldn't have made much progress without scholarships. It was gaelic football territory, though he 'only very reluctantly and under pressure togged out for school matches and performed dreadfully'. He preferred to watch from the sidelines and got into the habit of following the Macroom and county football teams. As a small boy, he was exposed to political fervour during the '30s; the colour of elections when Fianna Fáil came to power for the first time; the days of the blueshirts and street fights. He grew up in a political house. People called to talk politics. Civil war passions were still bubbling.

The Emergency cast a shadow on his childhood: the feeling of being a nation at risk defending itself, 'which was a lot of baloney but that's the way it seemed then'. He says it's a mistake to think that the period 1939-45 was a boring, dull and suffocatingly insular time. The local reality was that most people would not have missed being part of the outside world. 'It would be a mistake,' he insists, 'to exaggerate the claustrophobia and repressiveness because youth can make its own of any culture. The feelings attributed to that generation of being depressed and isolated are frequently retrospective attributions by intellectuals rather than what people actually felt at the time. It was still possible, despite all that insularity, and undoubted sexual repressiveness, to have a good youth.'

He packed his bags for UCC in 1945 on a university scholarship. But life could have taken a different turn. Young Murphy had done the civil service exam 'which was the only outlet for most bookish minded kids'. He reflects: 'It was inconceivable to me that I would do anything else with my life other than do something with my pen, whether that meant going in to the civil service or becoming a teacher.' For a while he thought of becoming an army officer, until his mother put her foot down. 'Despite the nationalist feelings and pride in the national army, the soldier had a very poor image. It was totally out of the question for any genteel person to be a soldier.' Oddly enough, in spite of all the piety, he never had any interest in becoming a priest. During his first week at UCC, he was offered a job in the civil service. It was a dilemma for the 18-year-old: taking an arts degree with no guarantees of a teaching job afterwards or else money in his pocket immediately. His older brother was already working as a civil servant in Dublin and about to move to Foynes. John A was tempted to abandon college and go for the money. One of his teachers from school, Sean Sweeney, told him: 'Stay where you are; this is what you should be doing.'

As a first year student, he was now among a population of over 800 students. The late Alfred O'Rahilly was College President. Former students have since described UCC in those days as being parochial and inward looking, 'full of restrictions and paternalism and authoritarian rule by college chaplains and presidents'. That picture is true in a way, says John A. It was a place for the privileged, though no longer alien to the wider community. There were social grades within the student body. He remembers students 'who walked around as if they'd inherited the place, a lot of them in the medical profession'. As a scholarship boy, he was required to live on base in the Honan Hostel during his three undergraduate years. 'If it was a privilege to go to college,' he says, 'it was a special privilege to be part of that particular community. It was a real university community: residential, cross faculty and brilliant. There was a great air of debate and excitement. There were intellectually scintillating conversations. The people staying in the hostel were by definition an élite. It was a great place to be. In many ways, you didn't have to bother about the irritating snobbery in the rest of the college if you stayed in the hostel.' As a hostel resident, he continued to be an altar boy and served Mass in the nearby Honan Chapel. There are warm memories of being in the chapel on early Spring mornings. 'The eye was filled by the beauty of the altar cloths and vestments, the gold plate and sanctuary lamps,' he recalls. 'It was a satisfaction of the artistic sense as well.'

He was a serious-minded student; with strong convictions about religion and about Ireland moving towards an age when church and state were fulfilling a grand, divine mission. He buried his head in books and worked hard. He certainly didn't think that student life was about letting your hair down and running wild. Rags had been banned by the time he came to UCC, 'because of the excesses down town where money collected for charity was never seen again. Little shop assistant girls took grave exception to being mauled in the name of high spirits; even before the days of sexual harassment they got tired of this kind of behaviour'. John A was never part of those high-jinks, though he liked the idea of 'hard men'. Anyway, he wouldn't dream of doing anything that might imperil his immortal soul, imperil his place in the Honan Hostel or, indeed, offend his parents 'for whom being in college was a big thing'. There was a wave of bright students in his class, among them journalist Con Houlihan 'who liked to put on the rustic intellectual act quite a lot'. Con gave the impression that he never opened a book, yet always managed to get first-class honours. John A and Con went down to the railway station to welcome Sean MacBride after he founded Clann na Poblachta in 1946 and had been 'hailed as the new charismatic leader'. Con turned to John and remarked in his unmistakable tones: 'There's a revolution, Murphy boy.'

He launched into a teaching career at St Finbarr's Seminary, Farranferris, after graduating with an arts degree in 1948. There were close links between UCC and Farranferris, part of the clerical intellectual élite which was inter-connected throughout the city. There were few career choices anyway: those who left college with an arts degree either went teaching or else sat the exam that brought them into the civil service at a higher administrative level. A lay teacher at Farranferris had retired, and he got the job. He taught History, Latin and English. He had studied Shakespeare passionately while in college, and now relished the opportunity to declaim *Julius Caesar* and *Hamlet* in front of the class.

He was the only lay teacher among a staff of 12 priests. He had married Cita McCarthy in 1952, who lived off College Road, and settled into his teaching job at Farranferris. She lived in the shadow of UCC. They would have five children. 'I was accepted generously and totally into the priests' company,' he recalls. 'For 10 years I got all my meals there, even after I got married. I was invited to all their parties. It was marvellous to participate in their company – I remember we had great table talk.' The priests were, of course, 'totally intolerant' in those days before Vatican Two. 'They regarded the Protestant Bishop and all the Church of Ireland with total contempt and as heretics, which was worse than pagans. To some extent I participated in that as well. That was the world I knew.'

At the same time, he was feeling his way towards an independent liberal view. The Farranferris priests thought they could afford one liberal layman. He subscribed to *The New Statesman*, which they viewed as a mild eccentricity. When controversy broke over the Mother-and-Child scheme put forward by the Minister for Health, the late Dr Noel Browne, in 1951, he took an independent line and challenged the clerical establishment at Farranferris in arguments about the rights and wrongs. It was a bold move by the 23-year-old teacher, particularly since the scheme had been condemned by the Catholic Bishops. He regarded Browne as a great hero and considered his expulsion from politics to be the result of a 'tyrannical alliance'.

It was a different world for the students of Farranferris. Life in a boarding school in '50s Ireland was 'pretty horrible'. He says: 'They had a rough time of it in terms of poor food and discipline.'

He closed the book on Farranferris after a decade in 1960. He had kept up scholarly research and published original work with the encouragement of Professor James Hogan, a strong influence in his career, who offered him a job in the History Department of UCC. He hadn't intended to stay in Farranferris, partly because he resented the 'chronically inferior status' of the lay secondary teacher at the time. He became assistant lecturer in history. The earlier experience in teaching techniques at a secondary school gave him an enormous advantage in the history department. 'You taught everything,' he recalls. 'I taught European and Irish history. I remember teaching with great interest the Crusades, the Renaissance and the Reformation. It was hard work because you were aware you had to teach it at a particular level.' Then the first of many controversies broke around him.

The spilling of Irish blood in the Congo on 8 November, 1960, provoked a national outcry. For the first time the nation was jolted into the reality that soldiering for international peace carried a deadly price. Nine Irish soldiers serving with the United Nations forces in the Congo's Katanga province were slaughtered by the Balubas when their patrol was ambushed at Niemba. 'The question in the Congo crisis,' he recalls, 'was whether we would take the pro-United Nations line; on their side trying to make a fist of this emerging Africa, or else beat the Catholic drum.' John A took a pro-UN stance and gave lectures arguing their cause. His line went against the college establishment. The UN was associated in the minds of many people with secularism and anti-Catholicism. Professor Hogan was a conservative, Cold War anti-Communist. It was rumoured that Murphy would get the boot. He regards the controversy as his baptism of fire.

The debate over Humanae Vitae in 1968 exploded in Ireland when Bishop Cornelius Lucey of Cork and Ross censured one of his priests, Jim Good, a respected theologian, for his public opposition to the papal encyclical on birth control. He was the only Irish priest to make a clear statement of rejection. He was suspended from his priestly faculties by the bishop: forbidden to preach and hear confessions in the diocese. It was the ultimate sanction. John A was incensed that Good, one of his teaching colleagues, should be silenced by the bishop.

He explains the background: 'Good was lecturing in General Philosophy. That was his university position, where he got his bread and butter. He was also Professor of Theology. That was an experiment the bishops were making, consistent with the rules of the National University. At that time you couldn't have a chair of theology endowed by public funds. But you could have a privately-endowed chair. The Bishops appointed Good as Professor of Theology. What they didn't know was that Jim Good had his own mind. He had been to places like Innsbruck and realised there was an entirely independent intellectual theological tradition out there; that you didn't have to parrot what your bishop was saying. In the end because of the whole controversy they folded up the professorship of theology and never tried to appoint anyone again.'

John A says he didn't defend Good in the name of secular liberal freedom of speech. He defended him 'in the interests of harmony between the college and the church; because he was a priest and member of the college community and greatly valued who had fallen out with his bishop and we should do something about him.' To have his priestly faculties suspended was a terrible reproach 'because it implied that he wasn't a fit priest to serve the community which was very wrong'. The students saw Good as a champion: because he had opposed Humanae Vitae 'he was the bee's knees altogether'. Hundreds of students signed a petition requesting Bishop Lucey to allow him continue his college activities. They thought he was the liberal secular champion. He wasn't. He was a conservative priest with a solid and orthodox base. Good would never have wanted to be seen as a trendy, radical priest. He asked the students not to hold any protests on his behalf.

John A and others went to meet Bishop Lucey. 'We spent a fruitless two or three hours talking to the man,' he recalls. 'We tried to persuade him in the interests of good college-church relations to restore Good. It became evident talking to him that he wasn't much interested in Humanae Vitae or whether or not it was moral or otherwise to use contraceptives. Bishop Lucey was interested in all of this because it was a matter of discipline. He refused to back off.'

Fr Good remained in Cork for two more years but the suspension in his priestly faculties stayed in force. He later moved to the Redemptorist monastery at Mount St Alphonsus in Limerick city, and then went on the missions with the Kiltegan Fathers in the Turkana Desert, Kenya. But the controversy that divided both men would have an extraordinary sequel: they became reconciled and corresponded with each other over the years. Shortly after his retirement from the Bishopric of Cork and Ross, Lucey left the city at the age of 78 on 26 January, 1981, to work in harsh conditions alongside his old adversary in Turkana. Lucey stayed for 15 months until struck down by malaria and returned home to Cork where he died on 24 September, 1982. On reflection, John A thinks he was totally wrong to have become involved in the Good affair. 'Now I would see that as a purely ecclesiastical quarrel and none of my business.'

He began to see the hypocrisy of the Catholic Church in Ireland, particularly after Humanae Vitae, and became more anti-clerical during the early '70s.

'Everybody was supposed to have a limitless family,' he explains. 'I remember days when the term family planning was thundered off the pulpit in Turner's Cross when I was a young married man. Family planning meant either contraception or using the laughingly so-called safe period without good reason. You were supposed to bang away in the name of God. That struck me as total hypocrisy. I think I went on from there to see the shortcomings of the church and the divisive role of religion in Irish history and particularly then in the context of the northern troubles.'

He stopped practising, something he didn't conceal 'though to be honest at the same time I didn't parade it from the housetops or put an announcement in *The Cork Examiner'*. He believes that God is a necessary part of man's vanity; he doesn't believe in the living God. He thinks that the notion of heaven and hell is only a 'superior form of fairytale'. He doesn't believe in the after life, 'though there is the intriguing possibility that a particular personality may be implanted in some body in the future at conception. How do I know that my consciousness won't survive again in some other form?'

He saw other inconsistencies in church positions. To enter a place of Protestant worship was regarded as sinful. When a retired professor of civil engineering died and his remains were received into St Fin Barre's Cathedral during the mid-'60s, 'only four or five of us went in to participate in the Protestant prayers while the other members of the college community, including the President and Secretary, stood with their backs to the wall outside. They were totally wrong at that stage. They were uncharitable. There was certainly no Holy Spirit informing their actions.'

Yet, he never lost an academic interest in the Roman Catholic Church: in the scholarly sense, he was always intrigued by the social history of Catholicism in Ireland. He regards it as 'an extraordinary dividing line' in his life that up to his early forties he was a committed and practising Catholic, holding strong views about the role of the Church. Later, he took the secular, liberal line, 'very much aware of the evils of Church influence in Irish society, both historically and in the day's politics. I detect nothing in me that would make me think of going back; in fact, it's probably one of the liberations in my life'.

The former scholarship boy was appointed Professor of Irish History when a vacancy arose in 1971. He set about building up the department by appointing those with their own specialities, while he began almost immediately to specialise in modern Irish history. He lectured at undergraduate level and also administered the department. The students liked his style. Since he always voiced his opposition to fee increases and never refused to take part in student debates he was seen to be on their side. Students never really changed over the years: they have an illusion of perennial youth, and the model has survived immortal since 1960. He loved the 'detective work' of history. Back in the '60s, the kind of history books used by students were no more than extended nationalist tracts. He feels privileged to have lived through a great revolution in Irish historiography. One of the most satisfying parts of his professional life has been directing postgraduate research, a one-to-one relationship, and then to see the fruits of that supervision.

America gave him a taste of adventure in the early '70s. He built up a strong reputation by doing terms as visiting professor in prestigious American colleges, delivering lectures and attending conferences. He spent terms at Loyola University in Chicago, James Madison University in Virginia, Boston College and Colby College in Maine. Those American experiences enriched his life, professionally and personally, over a 25-year period. America was a great liberation. There was, of course, an initial culture shock. An old Jesuit took him aside to give a valuable piece of advice when he arrived at Creighton University in Omaha, Nebraska. 'I discovered we had to leave the door ajar if any student was consulting with us,' he recalls. 'This was a precaution in case of false accusations of sexual harrassment or sexual assault. There was a danger you could be set up by someone.'

Inevitably, Professor Murphy made an impact on Irish-American debate. 'I operated as an historian, teaching classes, but at another level I was quickly drawn into the controversial dimension in places like Chicago and Boston. When I went there first there was a wall of Irish-American ignorance. Any real understanding of the complexity of Ireland was simply absent at that stage. I hope I helped to inform people in that regard.' But he says it's too easy and facile to be condescending about Irish-Americans and to sneer at their greenery. 'What we might regard as a kind of inferior culture for Irish- Americans held them together in their bad years,' he says. 'Their songs and stories and their admittedly exaggerated visions of the old sod gave them great solidarity and cohesion. We have no right to sneer at them.' Professor Murphy fostered contacts which opened up the American dimension for UCC. He helped to establish exchange programmes with colleges. On a personal level, he made lasting friendships with notable academics of Irish historical research, particularly Emmet Larkin, Larry McCaffrey and James Donnelly who have all lectured at UCC. He regards the building of bridges between UCC and American institutions to have been one of his most important contributions to UCC.

By the late '70s, the Cork professor was also national figure: a senator, broadcaster and writer who helped to shape public opinion. He was rarely out of the headlines, and could always be counted on to stir up debate on many issues. His mailbag testified to the reaction. Religion provoked most mail, even more than nationalism. He was first elected to the Senate in the NUI constituency in 1977, and topped the poll. He felt a great sense of achievement. 'It showed that in a sophisticated, élitist election there were enough people out there to vote for me,' he says. 'It was the climax of a most enjoyable summer campaign.' He served terms from 1977-1983 and from 1987-1992. It was a great privilege, as an Irish historian, to be elected to an Irish parliament.

It was very fulfilling to be in the Senate for 11 years. 'It's too easy to talk about the frustrations and limitations of the Upper House,' he says. 'Of course, the Senate cries out for reform. Being independent gave you a particular advantage you wouldn't have in the Dáil. I got great satisfaction at two levels: first, putting down and developing debates on controversial issues; second, participating in the legislative process, contributing to Bills like the Environmental Protection Agency. Some Bills were tacitly left to the Senate. The Dáil likes to assert itself as a superior House and won't leave the Senate take the initiative in too many things. As regards education and culture we were given a fair bit of the limelight.'

Not everybody shared his commitment and conviction in the Senate. In hindsight, he reckons that only about one third of the House were serious about the job at any given time. There were some splendid parliamentarians. He liked the idea of being a member of Leinster House. 'One has the sense of belonging to a very privileged club,' he says.'Even though you weren't privy to what was going on at the highest level, nonetheless you were on the sidelines.' To be a member of the Senate not alone gave him access to the national debate, but also to take platforms elsewhere.

He also got the chance to travel as a member of the Oireachtas. Some of the trips were 'total junkets'. Trips to the European institutions was 'routine stuff'. Yet, he never saw Leinster House as his main activity: UCC would always be the most important part of his professional life. His contribution to public life was seen as good for the college. He lost his seat in 1983 to Michael D. Higgins, a 'sore thing'. Oddly, many people didn't even realise he was out of the Senate during those intervening years and still called him Senator. He was 'enormously gratified' to be re-elected in 1987 with comparative ease.

When he retired from the Senate in 1992, colleagues there praised his colourful and outstanding contributions, particularly on Church and State, and the economy. He was described as a non-conformist who could be cranky at times. Senator Joe O'Toole said he did his best to talk him out of leaving the Senate but failed. However, it was on the question of Northern Ireland that he made his most memorable and controversial speeches. 'I was saying things back in '77 about the need for good relations between north and south and the need for constitutional adjustment that became commonplace some years later. I would say one of the best contributions I made in the House was when Garret FitzGerald came in to talk about his constitutional crusade, one of his first missions as Taoiseach.'

The Professor and Senator began his life as a United Irelander: he won an essay competition once for his vision of the day when a United Ireland would dawn, with the tricolour fluttering over Belfast City Hall. He shared the national outrage over Bloody Sunday in 1972 and led a protest in Cork. The IRA campaign helped to change his mind. They were claiming to act in the name of the people of Ireland. This raised questions about the nature of Irish republicanism and what justification the IRA could have.

What particularly enraged him about the IRA was the assassination on 7 December, 1983 of unionist Edgar Graham, a barrister and lecturer in law at Queen's University Belfast. It was very traumatic for Professor Murphy because he had dined with him in Cork three weeks before the killing. He admired Graham because he resisted moves among other unionists to get an agreement with the loyalist paramilitaries in the event of a doomsday situation. Graham would have nothing to do with that because he was totally opposed to violence. But John A had already taken a hardline stance against the Provos since the hunger strike campaign of 1981. He explains his thinking: 'I began to ask questions like, "are the Provos simply people who have the courage of our half-hearted convictions?" and "are they doing what we all would do if we had the guts to do it?"

'In my view, the least important priority now is a united Ireland. In fact, rhetoric about a united Ireland – and with that I would include the idea of cross- border political institutions – is only aggravating the situation. I am in favour of the status quo, territorially, for all kinds of reasons, not least internationally. Articles Two and Three have no international force; we haven't a leg to stand on. There are legal reasons why Articles Two and Three are total rubbish. They run counter to all our professed intentions of abiding by the consent of the northern majority. I'm all for the maximum traffic between north and south. I think if I was Taoiseach I would revive the constitutional crusade; I would tell people these Articles are a hindrance ultimately to peace and understanding and we have to adjust them. I think it was a mistake now to have gotten involved in the Anglo-Irish Agreement. It seems to me that we're able to meddle in northern affairs but when the chips are down we're not able to do anything about it. The Agreement managed to provoke the unionists without satisfying the nationalists. I think it would be much closer to our historical development were we to maintain an even and equitable attitude to unionists and nationalists. I don't see that northern nationalists are really temperamentally or historically a part of this State. I think the gulf has grown enormously between north and south. Furthermore, I don't believe that this state could handle a united Ireland if we got it on the plate tomorrow morning, in terms of security to say the least.'

In May 1990, John A retired after nearly 20 years as head of the Irish History Department. After his last lecture, when he walked out into the sunlight and found he still had a piece of chalk in his hands, he threw it across the Quad. It was his symbolic farewell to the class hall. It meant that he could become a full-time politician, 'with a clear conscience', for the next few years.

Then the President of UCC, Michael Mortell, asked him to write a book on the history of the college in time for the 150th anniversary in 1995. He promised to take on the task. 'I wasn't getting anywhere, so when the election was called in 1992, I decided this was the moment of truth and I wouldn't go again.' He spent the next three years 'quite happily and very industriously' researching and writing the book. 'That has been the great achievement of my retirement really,' he reflects. 'I got a great kick out of doing that book: because I did it and it was based on a lot of research and I wanted people to be entertained by the book as well as informed.' He also enjoyed bracing 10-15 mile walks in his native countryside with Seán Teegan, a close friend. It was a great physically and psychologically liberating exercise.

Since John A was a bookish person all his life, he often fantasised about being a sports star, either hurling in Croke Park or scoring goals for the Irish soccer squad during the Jack Charlton era. 'I'd like to be getting all the adulation,' he says. 'That would be very important for me; to be achieving such esteem and respect that people would have to listen to me singing whether they liked it or not.' Another fantasy was to have been the Archbishop of Cashel. 'I couldn't imagine a more desirable status. For one thing, you wouldn't have to be hassling fellows for two tickets for the Munster final.'

ALICE TAYLOR

ALICE IN BESTSELLER LAND

IT was the night Alice Taylor sent her suitor home sweatin'. The romeo was a young Kerryman with red hair who shared the back seat with her on a car journey to and from a dance outside Killarney. A girl who worked with Alice at the telephone exchange had asked her to come along with herself and her boyfriend. She didn't know it was going to be a foursome. When they picked her up, Alice was landed in the back seat beside the stranger. He was quiet as a mouse all the way to the dance; no words were exchanged between them. He wasn't to be seen again until all four met up afterwards for the drive home to Killarney. 'I knew why he wasn't at the dance because I could smell the porter from him,' recalls Alice. She had been dancing to the showband beat all night and, exhausted, fell asleep on the back seat on the way home. Romeo made his move, brimful of dutch courage. 'I woke up and this guy had a grip on me and his arms were around me,' she says. 'I thought to myself, "My God, what am I going to do now?"' It was time for quick thinking. She slipped off one of her stiletto heels 'and hit him a crack on top of his knee'. She remembers that his reflexes were instantaneous and he retreated to the other side of the seat. She warned him: 'If you move out of your corner again I'll give you another belt of it.' He didn't. Alice had just learned an unwritten female rule of the ballroom days: never trust the quiet fellows.

Dancing was a religion in 1958. Alice loved the Clipper Carlton, the original showband who started it all and lit the fuse for the explosion of bands in the '60s. The Clippers were magic. Alice and her girlfriends thought nothing of travelling 20 miles to see them at the Star Ballroom in Millstreet. Dancing was the only social outlet for young people. Along with a group of friends from work, Alice danced at the International Hotel and the Town Hall in Killarney. By today's standards, the dancehalls were the platform for a bizarre mating ritual: men on one side, women on the other. Separating the sexes was 'No Man's Land'. Young men crossed the floor and asked the girls of their choice up to dance. It was impolite to refuse. Drink was frowned upon: those were the days before women frequented pubs. Pioneer pins were worn with pride. All the dancehalls were 'dry'; only minerals were available to quench the thirst. The air was heavy with the smell of sweat, after-shave and Sweet Afton cigarettes. For Alice, the Star in Millstreet was the place to be, especially if the Clippers were in town. The ballroom was a thriving regional dance venue that packed in 2,000 on a big night; a hall where many love stories began since being opened by the Chick Smith orchestra on 1 November, 1953.

Proprietor Denis McSweeney, who also ran a cinema in the town, realised the pulling power of the Clippers in '58. When he wanted to book the band, in those pre-fax days, he had to drive to their home base of Strabane, Co. Tyrone. He left Millstreet in the early hours of the morning and made it back in time to open the cinema at 8 p.m. that night. Alice says that the northern band were superstars in the late '50s, the U2 of their generation.

Alice, the working girl, had spent a year learning domestic science at Drishane Convent and now liked the independence of being on her own for the first time and having her own money. She trained as a telephonist in Killarney and worked with nine girls in the exchange during the winter of 1957 and spring of 1958. She loved Killarney, especially the friary with its wooden panels, and stayed in digs at Molly Horgan's house on St Anne's Road. 'There was a crowd of us working together and we used to have a great time,' she recalls.

Romance blossomed when she met a young man who worked in the bank. They went out together for about five months. During the courtship Alice accompanied him to her first dress dance. One of her sisters, who was nursing in Cork, sent down a dress. 'It was my first long dress,' recalls Alice. 'I thought I was the bee's knees.' Alas, the relationship was cut short: he was transferred to Dublin; she was moved to Bandon. They remained friends and met up again many years later in 1996 when US Ambassador Jean Kennedy Smith launched her books at the National Library in Dublin.

Alice Taylor was born on 28 February, 1938, the sixth child of a family of seven. Since her little brother, Connie, died from meningitis at the age of four when she was just over a year older, she was the youngest for most of her life. She loved being part of a big family and, with four older sisters and a brother, tended to get her own way a lot of the time. She liked being on her own too, and growing up on a farm meant it was easy to find your own space.

She made her own little den in the attic. They were reared on a 100-acre mixed farm, Lisdangan, near Newmarket in North Cork, surrounded by animals; cattle, pigs and all forms of poultry from hens and chickens to ducks and geese. The animals were part of the family; the children saw them being born and dying and their burial ground was at the bottom of the orchard. Death was part of the cycle of nature – whether people or animals. Farm families in the '40s were virtually self-sufficient. They had to be. The girls helped out: making hay or bringing in calves or whatever needed to be done. 'I often think that if we were cut off for six months we could have survived,' she says. 'We had no electricity. All we needed was a gallon of paraffin oil. Today, if the electricity breaks down, everything comes to a standstill. The wheat went to the mill and flour came back. My mother baked. We killed two pigs every year. All the vegetables were grown on the farm. It was probably organic farming but we had no name for it. Everything was recycled. There was no waste.'

Alice and her sisters and brother walked to school through the fields: actually, through 10 fields to Dromanarigle National School, located between Newmarket and Boherbue. They'd meet up with their friends, and the journey took about half-an-hour in the morning. There was no rush home after school in the afternoon, mainly because they had so much do: check on the water hens, look at birds' nests, etc. The only danger was when they strayed into a field and disturbed a cross bull. 'You might see a bull making for the bottom of the field,' she recalls, 'so you'd always have to be one step ahead. We'd heard of people killed by bulls, so we were very cagey.' Those walks to and from school gave them a great appreciation of nature and the changing seasons. From May, they usually went barefoot; the feel of the grass under their feet on a sunny June morning was something special, as long as there were no thorns. It was an idyllic lifestyle, full of the sounds and smells of the country.

But there were also uncomfortable realities to be found behind this picture-postcard image of rural childhood. Winter was a different story. When the children reached school on a rainy morning, their shoes were wet and these had to be kept on all day long. Conditions at the school were atrocious, bad enough to provoke a strike today. There were three teachers but only two classrooms. An old range was insufficient to heat the building. 'The place was freezing,' recalls Alice. 'The windows were always rattling. You could see out under the door. There were holes in the floor. I often saw a rat looking up at me through a hole in the floor. We didn't really take any notice of the cold and got warmed up playing during the breaks.'

Alice thinks she unconsciously absorbed a lot from her parents, Lena and Denis, who seem to have had contrasting personalities. Both lived into their nineties. Her mother was a practical woman, a realist, and deeply religious. She worked hard and lived for her children. She had a Christian outlook and liked to think the best of people. It was typical of her to be non-judgemental if told about some terrible deed in the community, with sayings like: 'Sure, nobody would do that if they knew any better' or 'They couldn't have been in their right mind when they did that.' Her faith was rock solid. Alice has an image of her lighting candles. 'She always lit a candle if we were doing exams or if there was any problem. She knelt us all down every night to say the Rosary. My father would kneel down too but if my mother had too many bits or pieces at the end, he'd say: "Lena, we'll be here all night".'

Denis Taylor didn't share that religious commitment; for him there was no divide between God and nature. For him, God was an outdoor man. He advocated conservation too, long before protection of the environment became a popular cause. He hated to see people chopping trees for no particular reason. He used to say it took 40 or 50 years to grow a tree 'but a fool could cut it down in five minutes'.

He was tolerant of other religions long before it became acceptable. Every Sunday morning he switched on the Church of England service on the radio. He told the children: 'Remember, there's no great difference between what they're saying and what you'll be listening to in our own church. We're all the same, only going different roads.' He was cynical about certain Catholic rituals that were taken very seriously at the time. 'When we'd be doing the rounds for the Holy Souls on the first of November, he might say: "I've never heard such nonsense". His God was a lot more tolerant than the God of the time.' As a father, he was impatient and had a quick temper. 'It was just that he talked fast and moved fast and expected others to move fast as well,' she says. He gave the children a clip on the ear if provoked.

Alice got her secondary schooling at St Mary's in Newmarket. She particularly liked English, History and Latin. She read anything she could get her hands on. *Oliver Twist* was the first hardback she read as a child. She also read the Bröntes and Biggles. She studied Commerce up to the Inter Cert, which came in useful many years later when she did the accounts for their shop at Innishannon. She always liked to write, carrying a notebook and pencil around in case a thought or a poem might strike her. Writing was a way of making things clearer; of putting feelings into poetry if she was upset about something.

After completing the Leaving Cert in 1956, she spent a year with the nuns at Drishane Convent, learning domestic science. When her mother told her about Drishane, Alice snapped: 'What would I want to go there for?' Drishane wasn't so bad after all. She remembers the nuns with great affection. 'Having done the Leaving Cert, we thought of ourselves as adults and they treated us as such,' she recalls. 'I wasn't very domesticated because, being the youngest of the family, I didn't have to do very much. Now I was learning about cooking, laundry and general housecraft. The nuns instilled in us a desire to improve the quality of our lives, to do things well, to be able to lay out a nice table for instance. Why shouldn't making a nice home be important? What I learned at Drishane was of infinite value later on when I opened a guest house in 1966.'

Alice still wasn't sure of the path ahead, although she had thought about teaching or studying interior design. She had already done one of the civil service exams and got the call up while at Drishane. In the winter of '57, she landed a job with the Department of Posts and Telegraphs and packed her bags for Killarney to train there as a telephonist, later moving to work in Bandon.

The Bandon switchboard connected Alice to her future husband: Gabriel Ó'Murchú, whose family ran the Post Office at Innishannon, a village four miles away on the main road to Cork. She got to know his voice first. They met at a Sunday night dance in the Innishannon hall where he played the records. She came regularly with a group of girls from Bandon. A friend introduced them, and they fell in love. They were going out for some time when Alice went home to tell her mother she was thinking of getting engaged. She was 20 at the time. 'My God, you're too young,' ruled her mother, putting brakes on the plans. They were married two-and-a-half years later in 1961.

Alice loved Innishannon and worked alongside Gabriel in the Post Office and their next door shop with his relatives, Uncle Jack and Auntie Peg. The shop and Post Office had been in the family for four generations. Unconsciously, she was soaking up the atmosphere of village life and developing the writer's eye for characters who would fill her pages one day. She had swopped farm life for village life and also joined a community of mixed religions. 'If you want to get to know a village and parish, then the shop is a good place to start,' she says. 'The shop was open until 10 o'clock at night. From seven onwards, people came in for a chat. I'd be with Uncle Jack and I'd come out for a chat. We'd talk for hours. It was like a social occasion.'

Villagers 'had the measure' of one another: they looked out for each other. That was a good thing. She didn't find village life claustrophobic; instead, she enjoyed the intimacy. When that closeness disappears in rural Ireland today, she says it is replaced by Community Alert.

Gabriel was involved in a lot of local organisations, so she had space to develop her own personality and stand on their own two feet. The first couple of years of marriage are crucial: 'You are like two stones in a bucket and as the years go on you run the corners off each other and blend together.' They have four sons and a daughter: Mike, Gearoid, Sean, Diarmuid and the youngest, Lena.

Alice and Gabriel opened a 17-bedroom guest house when they bought the building next door in 1966, expanding their business operations from a shop and Post Office. Running a big guest house was a mighty undertaking, 'although I didn't know enough to be frightened by the thought of it'. Her Drishane training now proved to be an invaluable asset. They wrote to Bord Fáilte about getting a grant and, after a lot of sweat, their door was opened. Tourism was booming: GB cars poured into Innishannon every morning on their way to West Cork. 'We were up to our eyes in debt in the bank,' she says, 'but you could make money fast in a guest house at that time and it paid for itself after a while.'

All kinds of people passed through the door; nothing really surprised them after a while. Most came and went without any fuss, while some left their mark. Rows between husbands and wives were fairly typical. While working in the garden one evening, she heard a husband screaming in anger. Later, his wife explained that he couldn't stand their own child crying and had lost his temper. Then there was the honeymoon couple who kept the house awake with their frolics on a creaky bed.

During the late '70s, Alice and Gabriel were run off their feet, working day and night to keep the businesses ticking over. The guest house had regular callers, although tourists were becoming an extinct species as the Northern troubles ended the '60s boom and the GB cars no longer poured into West Cork. Uncle Jack, who was running the shop with Gabriel, suffered a heart attack and his health was deteriorating. 'One day we sat down and decided we'd too much on hand trying to bring up children, look after Uncle Jack and run the shop, Post Office and guest house. Something had to go. We decided to close the guest house and open self-catering apartments. It was still busy, but there wasn't the same pressure. I did the accounts in the shop with Uncle Jack and helped out.'

Uncle Jack died in 1977, followed by Auntie Peg in 1978. Next came a pleasant surprise in 1979: the birth of Alice's only daughter, Lena, after a gap of eight years. They moved into the former guest house and extended the shop into a supermarket. 'We always seemed to be building and doing things,' she says. 'Every time we do something, I say, "this is the last time, never again." Gabriel says, "I've heard that before". There were fierce long hours running a supermarket and the work didn't finish when we closed the doors.'

By the early '80s, their eldest son, Mike, who studied accountancy and was changing jobs, came home to take over the supermarket which has since joined the big Centra chain. 'That was the best thing we ever did,' she says. 'Gabriel was still doing the Post Office but the responsibility of the supermarket was gone.'

Then Alice found herself with more time and could concentrate on her first loves, writing and painting. 'I'd always been writing for my own sake but there was never enough time,' she says. 'I was always writing poetry and bits and pieces as a hobby. That's what's great about this time of life. You finally get around to doing things you've always wanted to do.' She thinks a lot of people can write, but they have a kind of mental block about it. By 1983, she felt that local events and stories should be recorded for posterity; she approached the people of Innishannon and asked them to write for *Candlelight*, a booklet published locally at Christmas time. Alice settled down to write the tale of her own childhood on the family farm in Newmarket, thinking some of the stories might be useful as fillers for *Candlelight*. Alice sharpened her pencil: she was about to embark on an amazing adventure in bestseller-land.

To School Through The Fields came from the soul of rural Ireland. Alice felt that she was standing at an historical crossroads, part of a generation that stepped from the old Ireland into the new; a child of the '40s who became the young parent of the '60s and '70s. Her generation had taken the mindboggling leap from rural electrification to computers. She wanted to record a way of life in danger of being forgotten. The source of inspiration was the Taylor family home on a farm at Newmarket where eight generations had lived. She told her own sons, who liked to go on holiday there, about growing up without bathrooms, phones, electricity or cars. The tide of emigration had taken people from the area and new generations returned to learn about their ancestors who had lived in that house.

Alice regretted that nobody had recorded how her grandmother and great-grandmother lived. Indeed, she knew that when her own grandchildren would visit the house one day, there'd still be no record of the way things were. So she took pen to paper. Of course, she had always been writing, stories and poems, but it was all done in 'snatches' because she was too busy raising a family and running a shop and Post Office in her adopted village of Innishannon with her husband, Gabriel. By the mid-'80s, Mike, her eldest son, stepped in to run the business and her other four children were grown up. Her day had come.

So she submitted her stories to a publisher. She received an acknowledgement 'and I thought that's it now, I've cast my bread upon the waters'.

Alice, Gabriel and two of their sons went on a trip to England. When they returned Mike said a letter had arrived, addressed to Alice Taylor. He put it aside somewhere but now they couldn't find it. A few days later Alice was having a cup of tea with a friend in the kitchen when one of the boys rushed in and said: 'Mam, there's a fellow with a fierce posh accent on the phone.' It was her publisher. He wondered why she hadn't answered the letter, saying he liked the script 'but there wasn't enough of it.' She remarked: 'It musn't have been so bad if you want more.' They met for lunch at the Metropole Hotel in Cork in April. 'He didn't exactly spell it out but I knew he thought my writing was good. He said I had a distinctive style. To me, that was a confirmation about something I had been doing for a long time by myself. He said I only had about a third of a book so far, so needed to do more. I drove home thinking "I can do that, no bother at all". I was on top of the world.'

To School Through The Fields was written 'in a small room at the end of the corridor and also in bed'. She wrote early in the morning and late at night. When one of the children had to stay overnight at the Bon Secours Hospital in Cork, she wrote at the bedside. The story was all in her head: when she sat down it was like turning over page after page and the memories came flooding back. A friend, Maureen Bowen, typed up the finished work and Alice despatched it to the publisher in September. There were some points that needed to be developed. Finally, it was all over. The publisher called to her home at Innishannon on Sunday and they went for a walk. He asked if she would go along with their publicity plans for the book. 'I remember saying, "what have you in mind, like?" I was thinking of *The Southern Star* and, at a fierce stretch of the imagination, *The Cork Examiner*. He said there might be radio and television. *The Late Late Show* might pick up on it. I thought, "Mother of God, sure that won't happen at all".'

Every household in Ireland would soon know her name. The publisher rang to say that a researcher from *The Late Late*, Brigid Ruane, was coming to Innishannon to meet her. 'I answered the phone out in the hall and I really clung to the ground with fright,' she says. 'This couldn't be happening to me. Brigid was a grand girl, very professional. After she left, I said to myself, "how am I going to face it?"'

When *To School Through The Fields* was published in May 1988, *The Late Late* had finished for the season, so her date with Gay was transferred to his morning radio show. It was a weight off her shoulders. Radio seemed to be a relief compared to the prospect of TV cameras. Alice declined their offer of overnight accommodation in Dublin before the radio interview. She preferred to leave from home with Gabriel that morning. Murphy's Law intervened. First, their car wouldn't start, so they had to take Mike's car instead. Second, they ran out of petrol near Portlaoise. 'I thought, "We'll never get there on time."' They managed to find a petrol station. 'Then we were caught in the early morning rush coming into Dublin,' she says. 'I was a bundle of nerves. I had a map trying to find RTÉ. We were looking out for the pylons. I'll never forget it. I remember running up the steps. Somebody said, "It's okay. You're on time. You won't be on for another 20 minutes." I sat down to relax. Then there was a change and somebody else shouted: "Come on, you're on". It was my first time in a broadcasting studio. Gay sat there with all these things sticking out of his head. Gay was very good, always listening, and the next question followed on as a result of what he heard. That's probably the secret of his success. I found other interviewers afterwards were only thinking about their next questions and weren't really listening. Gay was excellent. I didn't think the radio thing made any difference. When we came back to Innishannon, Mike said to me: "All hell is after breaking loose here. The phone hasn't stopped. *The Cork Examiner* were on and they came out looking for photographs."'

Later that week, Alice got the first inkling that her life would never be the same again when she went to sign books at Easons in Cork. Her thoughts were on the Eucharistic Procession at Innishannon that Sunday, an important event in the life of the village. She'd sign a few books on Saturday morning 'and come home and get the place ready'. She was surprised to find Easons so busy, until someone told her that everybody had come to meet her. 'I was signing all that day until five that evening,' she recalls. 'I couldn't get over it.' People queued for as long as an hour and a half, most with just one copy but many with five or six copies to send abroad to friends and relatives. One man was almost at the top of the queue when he realised he should have taken a book off the shelf first. By the time he realised his error, it was too late and the books were sold out. So he went to another bookshop and returned to wait in the queue at Easons for another hour and a half. Alice was flattered.

She finally went on *The Late Late Show* in October to talk about her simple book of childhood memories. Of course she was nervous. There was no need to worry. Alice was a natural in front of the cameras, and the audience and viewers at home lapped up her wholesome fireside chat. The commonsensical wit and anecdotes of a different time in rural Ireland struck a chord with the whole country that night. 'Television wasn't so bad after all, and I got used to it after a few minutes,' she says. 'The studio seemed very intimate really. The lights were down and you could cod yourself into thinking there was nothing beyond that small circle.'

Alice Taylor was now a national figure, wrapped up in the affections of everyone who could empathise with her richly evocative portrait of childhood. And they went out and bought her book. 'I didn't realise the effect *The Late Late* would have until afterwards,' she says. 'People could quote back to me things I'd said, even months later.' She was recognised everywhere she went. It was a strange feeling to be a celebrity.

To School Through The Fields was a publisher's dream come true. The publishers liked the book but could not have foreseen that it would hit the jackpot. They knew they had discovered a little gem which would be more than just a local book. The first print run was for 5,000 and they reckoned they might double that. While the second edition was being printed, booksellers around the country were dealing with hourly requests from people desperate to get their hands on it. The publisher was inundated with orders. There were 13 reprints. When the publisher told Alice that she was top of the bestsellers list, she wasn't sure what that meant 'but I knew it was taking off at a fierce rate.' The book made publishing history in Ireland.

Alice Taylor became an export commodity, too. The appeal of her story-telling spread to England, Europe, America and even Asia. There are Japanese, German and Polish translations. It is the biggest selling book ever published in Ireland. The sales blitzkrieg left many established authors slobbering with jealousy at their word processors. The figures pyramid into a crazy crystal that throws off light from any angle: *To School Through The Fields* (1988), 310,000; *Quench The Lamp* (1990), 140,000; *The Village* (1992), 110,000. Apart from these international bestsellers, the prodigious output includes: *An Irish Country Diary* (1988), 8,000; *Close To The Earth* (1989), 8,300; *Secrets of the Oak* (1991), 8,000; *Country Days* (1993), 60,000; and *The Night Before Christmas* (1994), 75,000. The American editions of the most popular titles – published by St Martin's Press in New York – have sold well. *A Child's Book of Irish Verse* was added to the shelf collection at Christmas 1996. And it all started with a simple story of childhood written on sheets of A4 paper with a pencil and a rubber on standby.

It became clear that she had made the world of her village universal. People everywhere who either grew up in the country, or else wished they had, from Tipperary to Tokyo, yearned for the simple, uncomplicated lifestyle that could never be recaptured. *The Mail on Sunday* said her book reminded people 'of a time when the only fertiliser spread on the earth came out of the rear ends of animals and when it was still possible to swim in the rivers and call on one another without invitation.' The Japanese, an island people also close to the earth, recognised and respected her philosophy. After the Japanese rights were sold, the translator, Toyoko Takahashi, a pleasant woman, came to Innishannon to get a feel for the landscape that Alice had written about. On the way to Cork airport to return home, she told Alice: 'I have seen everything, but I haven't seen a tumbling paddy.' The Japanese edition appears quite strange: printed sideways, read from back to front, 'and looks a bit like algebra'.

There is, of course, no magic formula for publishing success. If it was easy to put the right ingredients together then everybody would be doing it. One thing is for sure: success seems to happen to those who least expect it. Just ask Roddy Doyle or Frank McCourt. Alice Taylor used simplicity of method, thought and language to produce a book that everyone could identify with. No one was more surprised with the runaway success than Alice herself. Her method was far removed from the technological world of word processors, software, electronic typewriters and tape recorders.

Why did the book capture the imagination of so many people? One clue to the answer can be found with a farmer's wife who spent her life on the land in Sligo. Her daughter had emigrated to work in London where she met Alice before a radio interview. The young woman explained to the author that her mother never read books. Yet, when she came home to Sligo for Christmas she found Alice's book in the pocket of her mother's apron. She asked her mother why she was reading it, and she replied: 'My life is inside in that book.' Another clue was to be found at a signing session at Eason's bookshop in Limerick. 'This elderly farmer wearing a cap sized me up for a while. Then he came over and said, "when I saw the cover of that book, I knew that was my book".' Similarly, at a signing session in London, an emigrant from the West of Ireland told her he didn't normally read books but he kept hers under his pillow, read a chapter every night in bed 'and it took me home'. Somebody else told Alice she'd slapped a great face of respectability 'on what we all thought was fierce hardship'.

Ordinary people made *To School Through The Fields* a bestseller. Many of her readers wouldn't normally buy a book: be it the farmers on their way to the creamery or their wives going to town for the messages. Alice touched a nerve in a whole generation. 'You see, there was a certain amount of dignity attached to people who lived that life,' she says. 'They were honest, decent people who worked very hard and lived frugally. I think they needed to be saluted and acknowledged. There was something noble about them. I'm glad I wrote it for that reason. And it was important that somebody who lived through it should write about it, not somebody doing a thesis or study in years to come. That way of life had slipped away unnoticed, like having a visitor who slips out the door without saying goodbye.'

Her portrait of that lifestyle struck a chord too with the Protestant farming stock; her story transcended borders, not only around the world but within Ireland itself. Alice thinks it was probably the right book at the right time. 'I fell into it,' she says. John B. Keane once told her: 'Don't think you're the first to try it. People tried before but didn't get it right.'

One of the last children of the '40s, Alice Taylor dug deep into a personal reservoir of memories and experiences to chronicle an era of oil lamps, horse ploughs and milking by hand. *Quench The Lamp* told the story of change, when people stepped from the old Ireland into the new; 'a time when rural Ireland quenched the oil lamp, removed the po from under the bed and threw the black pots and iron kettles under the hedge ... rural electrification flooded our homes with light, clearing away old ghosts and beliefs and sending fairies scurrying underground. Modern plumbing replaced the bucket of spring water from the well and the timber rain-barrel at the gable end ...'

The next bestsellers – *Quench The Lamp* in 1990 and *The Village* in 1992 – confirmed her status as the biggest success story in Irish publishing. Of all the books, *The Village* is still her favourite. It recorded a way of life in the village she'd experienced and captured the character of wonderful people who lived and died there. Her first novel, *The Woman of the House*, has just been published.

The idea of turning the books, especially *To School Through The Fields* and *Quench The Lamp*, into a film seems appealing, provided the moviemakers tell the story accurately, without any stage-Irish approach but with a real feel for rural Ireland. It's not a burning ambition, though. 'I'd rather it wouldn't be done at all if it's not done properly,' she says. 'I'm not so sure about it.'

As a consummate realist and pragmatist, she wasn't about to lose the run of herself amid all the attention. There was initial surprise among the villagers. 'God, we never knew you were writing a book,' was a typical remark. Now the literary success is accepted and respected among the community. Locals are well accustomed to greeting visitors who make the pilgrimage to Innishannon to see her. A group of Americans once asked one of her neighbours if Alice would mind if they called on her. 'In the name of God,' he replied in lilting Cork tones. 'Why would she mind?'

The newfound wealth was certainly unexpected, but didn't dramatically alter her lifestyle. She wasn't about to buy a Merc or a villa in the South of France. That would be 'pure daft'. In her own words, she'd prefer 'to be digging a hole in the garden'. She would be the first to admit she's not a big spender.

A friend asked: 'Do you still intend to live in Innishannon?' Alice laughed off the question, saying: 'Sure, where would I be going for God's sake.' Alice loves the village and its people. Nevertheless, the money has brought freedom to travel to places she'd always wanted to see 'and help out in different things'. When the commercial success dawned on the family, her son, Mike said: 'For years you were slaving in the shop trying to make money. If you gave that up long ago and went writing you'd have made a lot more money.'

Apart from her writing career, Alice's secret ambition is to have a beautiful garden. She's working on that, too.

The gospel of Alice Taylor has a lot to do with respect for rural Ireland and the people of the land. Scratch beneath the surface and there is a complete philosophy to be found in her books. She says that emigration and the population drift to Dublin has drained the country; there are parts of West Cork where 'you wouldn't be able to field a football team'. Yet, while upcoming generations turn their backs on rural life, the Germans and French are moving in to live blissfully in places 'where we'd die of the hunger'.

Alice is saddened by the over-population of Dublin: families living on top of each other in high-rise flats and trying to raise children in confined spaces with nothing for them to do. 'I think we've got it wrong,' she says. 'There's a fierce imbalance in the country. It seems to me that we're going through a rejection phase in rural Ireland. People are leaving economically viable farms. Love of the land needs to become a passion again. And to close down schools, Post Offices and garda stations in rural Ireland might make economic sense but doesn't make any sense in the long term. All the money is pouring into Dublin. That's wrong.'

Our values need to change too, she says. 'There's a lack of internal peace in people today. They're looking for things outside of themselves instead of looking within. They want more and more and are never satisfied. We're living at such a fast pace these days that people don't have time to stop and think anymore. It's very sad.'

Alice Taylor would like to be remembered as someone who made a difference to the way people think about rural Ireland; someone who returned a sense of pride to country people and who made the farmer's wife from Sligo, and thousands more like her, hold their heads high.

BILLY MORGAN

REBEL WITH A CAUSE

IT reads like the script of a Dodge City high noon shoot-out between the new sheriff and his enemies who want him on the next stage out of town. The sheriff, Cork football coach Billy Morgan, and his enemies on the Cork County GAA Board, had previously exchanged fire, but now they squared up for a final showdown. Morgan was outgunned and outnumbered. First to draw was the county board gang. The bullets were flying, but the sheriff could not be downed; the support of the townsfolk gave him the best protective shield. It's hard to avoid the wild west analogy in the skirmishes between the former Cork coach and some members of the local GAA hierarchy which exploded into the biggest controversy of his career and a national headline story. This drama was real; the pain hurt deeply because Morgan had given his heart and soul to Cork football. It was the worst moment of his life.

The rebel-with-a-cause tag fits him neatly. Football was a lifelong passion; the dedication to his sport was unquestionably on a level with Christy Ring. As an outstanding goalkeeper for 16 years and coach for 10, he consistently fought to improve the status of players and never shied away from taking a stand against the GAA establishment. There were many notable brushes. Then came the so-called Morgan Affair when the local board tried to dump him.

Morgan, a former schoolteacher, had led Cork footballers to two All-Ireland titles and four Munster championship victories in a row within five years, reigning supreme over old rivals Kerry. He considered quitting after achieving a personal ambition to beat Meath, in the second All-Ireland victory of 1990, yet stayed on in the hope of winning three-in-a-row. Kerry crushed those hopes when they toppled the champions in the first round of the 1991 Munster championship. Now the knives were out for him. He says he was oblivious of the moves afoot to oust him in October 1991. The bombshell was dropped when the executive of the county board did not put his name forward for re-election as a selector, a position he had held since 1987 along with being coach to the team. There was uproar in the board. It was decided at the next meeting to add his name to four nominees originally recommended by the executive for a new selection committee. In a subsequent vote, he came last out of the five candidates for the four positions. The controversy over Morgan's rejection heightened when the county board executive put forward 10 allegations which they felt prevented him continuing as the team manager. He says these were 'drummed up' and intended to shaft him. 'I had a stormy relationship with the county board for a long time prior to that,' he reflects. 'There was a lot of factors. Certain members of the board were consumed by jealousy and out to get me. From day one I always stood up to them. I didn't like the way they ran things at times and said so. As a player and coach I had put a huge amount of effort into the game and nobody could contradict that. I had worked very hard for the players. That's why I was so disappointed that people could come along and throw allegations that they knew were just pie in the sky.'

The county board came under fierce pressure to reinstate Morgan. The controversy was brought to a head by the resignation of three selectors – Ray Cummins, Dave Loughman and Bob Honohan. Former Taoiseach Jack Lynch added his influential voice to those clamouring for Morgan's recall. The Cork players backed their coach and even considered a boycott of inter-county matches unless he was reinstated. Billy Morgan, his wife, Mary, and their children were under siege throughout October '91. The family anguish was such that one of their sons was being teased at school over all the publicity; he came home crying because other pupils were saying that his dad had been sacked. The man under the spotlight could not sleep at night. 'It was a very traumatic time for us, and there were reporters and photographers at my house,' he says. 'There were cameras outside my door and pointed at the windows. The players stood by me and that was important to me. Only for them I would have told the board to shove it.' In the end, the pressure on the board to reinstate Morgan as a selector was irresistible. Ray Cummins and Dave Loughman persuaded him to go back. Dave told him: 'In any war there are casualties. We are the casualties, but if you stay on then we've all won the war.'

To this day, Morgan will not shake hands with his county board enemies who tried to oust him – with one exception. 'I have no time for them. There is only one of them I have spoken to since because he explained that at the time he was led to believe there was a breakdown in discipline where the Cork team was concerned. He now knows this wasn't true and he was led by people who didn't have the right reasons for trying to remove me. ' Six years on, he believes as fervently as ever that the cobwebs need to be brushed away in the GAA and in the Cork county board. The rebel still has a cause.

The politics of the GAA boardroom, with all its intrigue, had no place in his agenda. Billy Morgan was always a 'player's player' and 'player's manager' in the best sense. For one thing, he felt the players deserved more respect. 'I felt that they were exploited quite a lot,' he says. 'Cork teams were not being given the confidence they should have had. They were afraid to make a mistake. ' During his 16 years as player, he noted that whenever any of his teammates made a mistake the first thing he did was to look apprehensively at the dug out. When Morgan took over as coach, he told them at their first meeting to 'go out and play football and I will look after things on the sideline'. His relationship with the players was critical to his success. He regarded them as his friends. In the words of Larry Tompkins, the last man to captain Cork to All-Ireland success in 1990 and who succeeded him as coach in 1996, 'the players knew he had given his life's blood for Cork football.' His skills as a team motivator were beyond question. The players would have scaled the highest mountain for him.

Football was everything to Morgan; those closest to him say he was probably more comfortable with football people than with anybody else. His heart was in the right place; it sometimes ruled his head. From the sidelines he was a troubled spectator, agonising with emotions that could not be contained. During his first year as coach in 1987 he was suspended from GAA activities for four months for an impulsive incursion on to the field during the All-Ireland final when Cork lost to Meath. The referee intervened in a scuffle and sent him off. He missed most of the National League as a result of the suspension.

For most supporters, two images of Morgan will linger on. When he captained Cork to the famous All-Ireland victory over Galway in 1973, Jimmy Barry-Murphy's second goal eight minutes from the end brought him to his knees in thanksgiving. Fourteen years later, when Kerry captain Mikey Sheehy scored a goal with his team two points down in the 1987 Munster final, the Cork manager fell to the ground in frustration.

The collection of medals with his club, Nemo Rangers, and with the Cork team is the perfect answer to criticisms levelled against Billy Morgan over the years. He presided over Cork's successful period at provincial and national level. As a county player, he won one All-Ireland, one National League, five Munster championships, four Railway Cups, one All-Star; with Nemo there were seven county titles, five Munster club, and two All-Ireland club medals. As a manager, he led the Cork senior team to seven Munster championships, two All-Irelands and two National League titles.

The family roots are in East Galway where hurling is a religion. Billy's father, Tom, who came from Mullagh outside Loughrea, played junior hurling with Galway and his brothers were on the senior team. Tom Morgan joined the guards and was sent to Cork. Billy was born on 2 February, 1945, and grew up in Tonyville Terrace, off High Street. Hurling was his first love, but football soon took over. He was educated at Colaiste Chriost Rí in Turner's Cross where he won Dr Rodgers, Frewen Cup and Simcox Cup medals. The first person to notice Billy's football ability as a small boy was George McCarthy, goalkeeper for the St Finbarr's team which won the county senior football championship for the first time in 1956. McCarthy told him he'd play for the 'Barrs when he got older. Young Morgan wanted to play for the 'Barrs, even though Nemo Rangers were his parish club. He joined Nemo at the age of 11 and played under-age. In order to transfer from Nemo to the 'Barrs he had to stay on the line for 48 weeks. He lasted three weeks and was back playing with Nemo again. At the age of 16, Nemo moved him back to goal in the second half of a minor championship match with St Finbarr's. After playing with the Cork minors as a half-forward in the Munster final of 1963 when they were beaten by Kerry after a replay, Morgan enrolled at UCC for a BA and H Dip Ed.

Morgan gave up gaelic football temporarily to join Munster Senior League soccer club Tramore Athletic, for one season. The GAA ban was in operation. Tramore Athletic played him in goal because of his practice of handling the ball. The UCC gaelic football club were gearing up for the 1964 season. A trial was arranged but one of the college sides was without a goalkeeper. Dr Dave Geaney, the force behind the club, asked Morgan to play in goal. Morgan kept goal for four years, and never again played anywhere else but between the posts in gaelic football. He won two Sigerson Cup medals at UCC in 1965 and 1966. His goalkeeping prowess caught the eye of the Cork under-21 selectors: he kept goal for the side that was beaten in the All-Ireland final of 1965. He was brought into the senior panel a month later and made his senior inter-county debut on Easter Sunday 1966 in a challenge game against Offaly in Tullamore. He graduated from UCC in 1968 and returned to play with Nemo. Now he was on the side to face UCC in the Cork county championship semi-final of 1969. 'I had a disastrous match,' recalls Morgan. 'I left in two terrible goals.' One came about as a result of a misdirected short clearance by him straight to college full-forward Ray Cummins, a lifelong friend who is also his brother-in-law. Worst of all was the fact that Nemo full-back

Denis McDonnell broke his leg while trying to avert danger. 'Not only did I make a mistake and give away a goal but I was responsible for my full-back getting his leg broken,' he says.

Had circumstances been different Billy Morgan might have become a professional soccer player and won a European Cup medal with Glasgow Celtic.

After a terrific performance against Kerry in the Munster final of 1969, he was offered a month's trial with Celtic. He went to Parkhead secretly because the ban on foreign games was still operating and he stayed for a week. Celtic was managed at the time by the legendary Jock Stein. Celtic coach Sean Fallon took Morgan under his wing. 'It was a very tempting offer,' he recalls.

'Celtic goalkeeper at that time, Ronnie Simpson, was out of the side with injury and his deputy was also on the injured list. The snag was that I had been offered a teaching job in Cork as well, so if I stayed with Celtic for a month the teaching job would have been gone. In the end they signed Evan Williams from Wolves as cover for Ronnie Simpson.' At home, Morgan was disappointed he never got to play in the League of Ireland after signing forms for three clubs – Waterford, Cork Celtic and Cork United.

Billy Morgan revolutionised gaelic football training in the 1970s. In 1970-71, he took a diploma in physical education at Strawberry Hill in London and returned with valuable technical skills to take over the coaching of Nemo. Training sessions at the time involved running and hours of lapping the pitch before ending with a brief match. Morgan brought in a policy of training with many footballs, virtually one for each player. He captained Nemo to achieve their first county senior success in 1972. They defeated UCC, which 'erased the bad memories of '69'. A few months later they proved themselves the best in the land when they beat Vincents, Dublin. Morgan was to become the leading light in all of Nemo's county championship triumphs after the first win in '72.

But a dream came true a year later when he captained Cork to All-Ireland victory over Galway and brought home the Sam Maguire Cup for the first time since 1945, the day when Jimmy Barry-Murphy scored two goals and became the new golden boy of gaelic football. When he scored the second goal that clinched the game, Morgan dropped to his knees. 'I suppose it was a spontaneous reaction,' he says. 'I remember saying to myself, "we have it now, we're not going to loose it". I realised we were going to win an All-Ireland.'

The team was managed by Donie O'Donovan, 'the type of coach you'd go out and die for and yet he hardly ever raised his voice'. After all the excitement in Croke Park, the winning captain and a couple of the players were locked out of a team reception at the Green Isle Hotel in Dublin on that Sunday night. 'There were bouncers on the door,' he recalls. 'I told them who I was but they still wouldn't let me in without a ticket. Eventually, Frank Murphy of the county board had to come out to the door and let us in.'

The homecoming brought Cork to a standstill. 'I will always remember coming up MacCurtain Street, around Barry's corner and seeing this sea of people before us down in Patrick Street. It was a unique experience.'

Morgan has no doubt that the mighty '73 combination squandered the opportunity of winning more All-Ireland titles. That year Cork had a sensational Munster final victory over Kerry, and kept their rivals at bay in '74 to retain the provincial title. However, the Cork conquerors were shocked by Dublin in the All-Ireland semi-final of '74. He says of the team: 'They had great natural ability. We let the whole thing go to our heads and we took Dublin for granted in '74. If we had got over that semi-final with Dublin we would have beaten Galway again in the final. We never got back to the form of '73. That team should have captured at least three titles in four or five years. That they succeeded in winning only one All-Ireland was a waste of talent. I blame myself and the players and nobody else; they went from one celebration to another after the '73 success and refused to heed any warnings. I remember Donie O'Donovan warning us "uneasy lies the head that wears the crown". Donie might as well have been talking to the wind. For natural talent and spontaneous movements of play Cork were probably better than the subsequent Dublin side and Kerry's four-in-a-row team. Just look at the forward line alone. Gold would not buy players like Declan Barron, Jimmy Barry-Murphy, Ray Cummins, Dave McCarthy and Jimmy Barrett. They were all brilliant individual footballers but their innate ability linked them into a marvellous attacking unit.'

1973 had been Morgan's year: he led Nemo to the Munster and All-Ireland club championships, led Cork to All-Ireland victory, won his only All-Star award and was voted Texaco gaelic footballer of the year. It was also the year when circumstances robbed him of the chance to play top-level soccer. Waterford had reached the League Cup final. On the morning of the match, Morgan was telephoned by Waterford manager Shay Brennan who offered him a place on the team because Peter Thomas was out due to injury. Brennan told him to get a taxi to Dublin. But

Morgan was delayed in a traffic jam in Patrick Street. They wouldn't have reached Tolka Park in time, and turned back at Watergrasshill. The Waterford side went on to create history by winning the League of Ireland championship on six successive occasions. Due to Nemo's success, he never got the chance to play with Cork Celtic after being signed as Alex Ludzic's understudy. He signed with Cork United at a later stage; torrential rain spoiled a chance to play in a Munster cup final that had to be called off.

Morgan revolutionised gaelic football goalkeeping by countering attack with attack with astute short passes to his defenders. 'I always believed in possession football,' he explains. 'I could not understand a goalkeeper saving a ball and then punting it downfield between one of his own players and a rival. He was giving the opposing player a 50-50 opportunity of gaining possession and I felt this was wrong. So with Nemo first and then with my Cork defensive colleagues I worked on and developed the short pass to an unmarked teammate.' This brought a new dimension to gaelic football goalkeeping. It wasn't all plain sailing, though. There was heartbreak when the college he coached, Colaiste Iognaid Rís, lost the Munster final to St Brendan's in '74. Iognaid Rís were heading for their first Munster title, leading by four points with eight minutes to go. But three goals within five minutes gave St Brendan's victory.

Morgan and the Cork players were in the wars with the Cork county board when they wore the Three Stripes gear in the 1977 Munster championship. He was seen as a ringleader in that affair. Adidas had offered in February to supply the players with jerseys, shorts, boots and tracksuits. 'The offer was made to me, so I put it to the selectors and they said they would put it to the county board,' he says. 'It was going on for months and there was no news from the county board. We found out later that the selectors didn't put it to the board because they felt it wouldn't be passed. They were right. When you played for Cork at that time and went out for a game, all they handed you was a jersey; you brought your own shorts, socks, boots and tracksuit if necessary. After a couple of months we went back to Adidas and said we couldn't make any decision on a jersey but we'd take the rest of the stuff. They agreed and the only proviso was that we'd stand for a photograph in the Adidas gear. We played in the first round of the championship against Clare in Limerick and stood for photographs in the gear. We beat Clare, four weeks before we played Kerry in the Munster final. I was called in by the executive of the county board because they claimed I was the go-between with Adidas and the team. I said that all we were doing was what nearly every team in the country was doing at the time. I said that we weren't looking for confrontation. Our idea was to win. The board said they didn't want any confrontation and hoped it could be settled amicably. There was no more communication until the Thursday before we played that Munster final. We got a letter from the board saying that if we used the Three Stripes gear on the Sunday we would be suspended. We had a training session on the Saturday and a team meeting afterwards. The feeling was going towards that we would comply with the county board when a selector came in and there was uproar in the dressing room. We decided to use the Three Stripes gear and we got suspended indefinitely. Two players, Jimmy Barry-Murphy and Brian Murphy, were also in the hurling team and due to play in the All-Ireland hurling semi-final a couple of weeks later. Quite conveniently, the board said we were only suspended from football. Negotiations went on to resolve the situation, and it was resolved just before we started the National Football League.'

America beckoned in 1982: Billy, his wife, Mary, and their two children left for New York where he took a Master's degree in physical education, after getting leave of absence from his teaching job in Cork. He also worked behind the counter at Rosie O'Grady's bar in New York. 'I loved it there,' he says. 'I was very tempted to stay and would have stayed longer but my leave of absence ran out and I had to come home to keep my job.' The family returned to Cork in August 1985.

It was always his ambition to coach the senior football team after his playing days with the county. He was certainly well qualified. He got the call in October 1986. So began the Morgan Years when he led Cork to seven Munster Championship titles out of ten and played in four All-Ireland finals in a row, winning two of them. Larry Tompkins and Shea Fahy made their debut for Cork against Limerick in the first round of the Munster Championship. Morgan always regarded these as the two most influential signings made during his 10-year term as coach. Cork were underdogs going into the Munster final against Kerry but eventually beat them after a replay, taking the title for the first time since 1983. It was a great start for the new coach because Cork had only notched up one Munster final victory over Kerry since 1976. Killarney on Munster Final day was Morgan's favourite ground. Players could sense his mood changes as big games approached. Cork would keep the upper hand over Kerry until 1991.

The late '80s marked a period of epic battles with the hard boys of Meath. Morgan thought his team had a great chance of beating Meath in the 1987 All-Ireland final, but they were well-beaten in the end. Meath overran Cork. Morgan was sent off by the referee after running into the pitch and later suspended for four months. Cork and Meath battled for the All-Ireland again in 1988. On this occasion, Cork players decided before the match they were not going to 'lie down' before the Meath onslaught. 'We beat them off the park but the referee's decisions went against us, particularly the one which led to the Meath equaliser,' recalls Morgan. Before the replay, the Cork side heard that Meath players were saying they were going to do it their way 'and sort us out'. Cork adopted the motto of The Three Musketeers – all for one, one for all. It was the only way to stand up to Meath. The replay was a tough physical encounter. When Niall Cahalane was struck by a Meath player, the other Cork players joined in the fight. Morgan instructed them to concentrate on playing football and not to retaliate, and repeated that instruction at half-time. He now thinks it was a huge mistake. 'I should have said, "next time it happens get stuck in".' He claims Meath were allowed 'to do what they liked in the second half'. Cork again went down to Meath. 'I was shattered after that All-Ireland because I knew in my heart and soul that we should have won,' says Morgan.

In 1989, Cork tasted All-Ireland glory after beating Mayo in the final, 'one of the best seen in the modern era'. The captain, Denis Allen, now back playing inter-county football, had already led Cork to a National League triumph over Dublin. Cork again beat Kerry to retain the Munster title. By the end of the year, Morgan considered leaving the job, but desperately wanted to beat Meath first. Cork faced Meath in the National League semi-final of 1990, and again it was a physical affair. Dave Barry was 'stretched' about 60m away from where the ball was at the time. Meath won the game. 'I remember going into the dressing room afterwards and saying, "look, never again are we going to be beaten physically by Meath".' That advice sowed the seeds of the 1990 All-Ireland success when Cork finally toppled Meath. The win completed the famous double. Morgan says Meath's reputation for toughness was well justified. 'I played against Meath in an All-Ireland final in 1967 and they were the same then as they are now. They're a very hard crowd to beat, very resilient. They will tell you they're not dirty. Other people will say they are. In fairness, they have this attitude of refusing to be beaten. I often said to the lads, "if we have what they have it would be very hard to beat us too".'

Morgan felt that now was the time to go. 'When I started off as coach to the Cork team, I gave myself three years. We had won the All-Ireland in 1989. I continued on because we had not beaten Meath. We beat Meath in 1990 at the end of my fourth year. We had beaten Kerry four years in a row. I had achieved everything I set out to do.' A few days after arriving back in Cork with the Sam Maguire Cup for the second successive occasion, Morgan met Dave Barry on the South Mall and told him his intentions. 'You can't go now,' replied Barry. 'We're going for three in a row.' But it was not to be. When Cork travelled to Killarney to face Kerry in the first round of the 1991 Munster Championship, Morgan sensed that the old hunger was missing. Kerry knocked out the champions by two points. Morgan again thought of quitting; in fact, he would definitely have resigned that year if the county board had kept its mouth shut.

Next the Morgan affair broke, and he faced the biggest crisis of his career. After being re-instated, he was fired up and raring to go. But 1992 proved to be a season of disasters. Kerry again spoiled the party for Cork, beating them in the Munster semi-final. Cork fielded players who were not fully fit and were punished as a result.

The tide turned a year later when Morgan brought in new players and built a young team. Kerry were seen off in the Munster semi-final, Tipperary beaten in the final and then faced a showdown with Derry in the All-Ireland final. Morgan believes they would have won that All-Ireland but for the sending off of Anthony Davis 'which shattered us. Never in all my times were so many tears shed in a dressing room.'

During the train journey back to Cork next day Morgan told Frank Murphy of the county board he intended to resign. Murphy told him to think carefully before taking any decision. Morgan was persuaded to stay on for another year. Cork beat Tipperary in the Munster final for a second successive year in 1994 and defeated Kerry to make it three-in-a-row in 1995. However, there was bitter disappointment when Cork lost the All-Ireland semi-finals of 1994 and 1995, at the hands of Down and Dublin. After the 1995 Munster Championship victory, Morgan was convinced they were going to win the All-Ireland. But the team 'fell apart' in the semi-final against Dublin after a goal from Jason Sherlock. In the dressing room afterwards the coach told his players he was finally stepping down. After talks with the county board and the players he was again persuaded to stay on. He made up his mind it would be his last year.

Cork lost to Kerry in the Munster final of 1996 – the last game under his stewardship. Critics claimed he was showing too much loyalty to some older players who could not deliver on the big occasion. Morgan never got to take his new team to an All-Ireland title.

The end of the Morgan Years came on 20 August, 1996, when the coach tendered his resignation at a county board meeting. Larry Tompkins was unanimously chosen as his successor. Morgan knew Tompkins was willing to take up the reins and recommended him to the county board. Once he knew that Tompkins was confirmed, he was happy. 'I didn't want to leave somebody else take up the job who might allow Cork to slip back. I felt that the one fellow who had the enthusiasm and driving force to keep it going was Larry Tompkins. He is 1000% dedicated.' Tompkins was re-appointed coach by the county board on 20 August, 1997, after a dissapointing year when Cork lost to Clare in the Munster Championship semi-final.

Inevitably, Morgan had mixed emotions: the sense of relief was tinged with nostalgia for a man who had given his life for football. When the team played their first game without him, away to Donegal in the League, Morgan was eating Sunday lunch with his family in Cork. His eldest son asked: 'Well, dad, do you miss it?' Sometime later he went to see the team play against Kildare at Páirc Uí Rinn. 'It was a strange feeling,' he reflects. 'I had to pay going in the gate and sit in the stand. It felt strange to be sitting down watching them and not being part of it. In one sense it's a great relief, but in another sense I do miss the close involvement with them.'

It was a career marked by highs and lows and more than a little controversy. He looks back on his record as a player and as one of Ireland's top football coaches with justifiable pride. His contribution to Cork football was enormous. 'When I was playing I always believed we had teams as good as anybody in the country,' he says. 'What I brought to them was organisation and a sense of belief in themselves and then trusted them. Before that, good players used to come and go on the Cork team but they were never given a chance to settle down. They might play one game poorly and then they were gone. I guaranteed that everybody would be given a fair chance and the first mistake they'd make they wouldn't be looking at the sideline. What I brought to the Cork team was a level of organisation and a level of commitment to them that they probably hadn't seen before.'

There were some regrets, of course. 'As a player I regret that we didn't win more All-Irelands with the team of 1973. My two greatest regrets as coach would be the All-Ireland finals of 1988 and 1993 which I thought we deserved to win.' Not surprisingly, Morgan often wondered over the years about what might have been if he had accepted the Glasgow Celtic offer of 1969 and opted for top-level soccer. Yet, he says no amount of money could have bought those glory years with Cork when he made great friends, had great times and saw the world. Still, if he was a youngster today he would definitely aim for a career in professional soccer, play at the highest level and, hopefully, in the World Cup. The former Cork football coach is a keen Liverpool supporter.

Apart from sport, the former schoolteacher is an insurance broker; his wife, Mary, runs Billy Morgan's pub, a thriving business, in the heart of Cork city. They have two sons – Brian (22) and Alan (17) – who have inherited an interest in sport. Both are playing with Nemo and also enjoy soccer. 'I'm not going to put them under any pressure,' he says. 'Once they're happy, that's all that matters. They can play tiddley winks if that keeps them happy. If they said they wanted to concentrate on soccer, I'd say "fair enough, off you go".'

Fifteen years ago, before he left for America, Billy Morgan said the winds of change needed to blow through the GAA and the Cork county board. He feels the county board is still not in touch with the grassroots: it needs the active involvement of former players who competed at inter-county level. Morgan believes it is only a matter of time before the GAA turns professional. 'With the time and effort being put into the games now, it's professional in everything except in practice,' he says. 'If you look at the club scene, not to mention inter-county, the level of commitment is enormous and there are experts in fitness, nutrition and psychology. Professionalism is inevitable.' The GAA should have a fixed playing season like soccer and rugby; at inter-county level teams could assemble on the weekend of a big match, just like soccer and rugby internationals, and with set fixtures. Morgan would give the manager full control to pick his own backroom team as happens in some other counties. The referees should be paid and graded to make for a better game.

The ban on soccer in top GAA grounds will have to go, says Morgan. It can't be justified any longer. Croke Park and Páirc Uí Chaoimh have hosted pop concerts and American football. Yet, soccer internationals are kept out. 'It's crazy,' says Morgan. 'I mean, how can they say that Oasis, U2, Michael Jackson and Prince uphold the principles of the GAA? Anyway, most of the playing population of the GAA play soccer these days. Take Dave Barry, who won an All-Ireland with Cork and now manages Cork City. I'd love to see him playing European Championships in Páirc Uí Chaoimh but they won't let him in. There's no consistency in that position. I think the GAA were mad not to put forward Croke Park as a national stadium. They could have dictated terms to the government because they only need Croke Park free on 10 or 12 Sundays in a year.'

The GAA is at a crossroads; it needs to raise its head from the sand. The former Cork coach thinks it's time for a commission to examine the structure, operation and rules of the games. Bluntly, if he was a youngster today he wouldn't play gaelic football. 'To be honest, it wouldn't attract me with all the pulling and dragging and fouling,' he says. 'Everybody knows it's happening and nothing is being done about it. Gaelic football could be the best ball game of all because it has the best of handling and foot skills. But it's being ruined at the moment. Look at the way the rugby scene has become professional. Shea Fahy was a school's rugby international and also a very good gaelic footballer. He chose to play gaelic football. I wonder what he would choose if he was coming out of school today?' And the GAA is competing with soccer for the youth of the nation. Morgan says he knows parts of Kerry and the West of Ireland, traditionally GAA strongholds, where the youngsters are now playing soccer. The glamour of the Charlton World Cup era and success of Irish players like Manchester United's Roy Keane in the UK Premier League made a huge impact on the youth culture.

Billy Morgan says he would like to be remembered as an honest, straight-talker who did his best for everyone who came into contact with him and that there were no half measures, 'no bluffing or bullshit'.

The Sheriff who couldn't be silenced deserves nothing less.

FERGAL KEANE

ON THE FRONTLINE

SOUTH African President Nelson Mandela got irritated if his morning porridge wasn't the correct temperature; F. W. de Klerk, the former President and leader of the National Party who had freed Mandela from jail, was happiest with a cigarette and glass of whiskey in his hand; and Chris Patten, Britain's last Governor of Hong Kong, loved to chat late into the night about films, food, music and books and anything except politics.

Fergal Keane, the BBC's most celebrated foreign correspondent, knows a lot about the idiosyncrasies of the world's best known newsmakers. Like the morning he had breakfast with Mandela at the Carlton Hotel in Johannesburg and discovered one of his little known secrets: he won't eat porridge unless it's heated to suit his sensitive palate. Mandela sent back his bowl three times until they got it right. 'He was always very pernickety about food,' recalls Keane. 'That trait probably came from prison life where he got used to an extremely rigid routine and everything was just so. He didn't like any deviations.' By contrast, de Klerk, with whom Mandela shared the world stage and also a Nobel Peace Prize, wasn't so fussy about food. Whenever Keane met the then NP leader privately, he smoked cigarettes and drank good whiskey.

There were other more obvious differences: Mandela was an imposing, dignified character who measured his words carefully; de Klerk came across as a real political street fighter who liked to gossip and 'who'd have done well in Ireland because he was that kind of constituency hustler politician'.

Patten was a 'highly intelligent, very empathic human being.' He relished a lively argument in lively company 'and he didn't get defensive or paranoid but took it on the chin'. The Irish journalist spent many hours with the outgoing Hong Kong governor, and they became pals before he sailed out of the harbour for the last time on the royal yacht, *Britannia*, on 30 June, 1997. Keane has unique insights into the newsmakers of Africa and Asia, some of whom he now considers to be personal friends. 'It's often away from the cameras and when the microphones are switched off and you have a drink with someone or dinner with them that you get the greatest sense of what this person is really like,' he says.

Keane, the former Cork 'Pres' boy made good, has been on the sidelines of the world stage for well over a decade, with a notebook or microphone in his hand, and in that time he took a ringside seat reporting on civil unrest, wars, genocide, famine and defining moments in history in the two continents. It is no empty cliché to say that if journalism is the first, rough draft of history, then Keane is one of its authors. He has told the story better than most, and his outstanding reporting earned a clutch of awards and an OBE from the Queen of England.

The talent is undeniable. But there is much more to Fergal Keane's journalism than someone who has a clever way with words. For a start, he didn't just win the confidence of big newsmakers. He has always felt more at home with the voiceless, oppressed and dispossessed, whether in Soweto, Rwanda, Afghanistan or Northern Ireland. That's because he recognises the innate decency in others, and the human dignity that someone else wants to strip away. This makes his reporting all the more powerful. He fervently believes you've got to show respect if you're reporting on people's lives and the tragedies that tear them apart.

Decency is the adjective that others most often apply to him, too. Keane's canvas has broadened since his days as a cub reporter on the *Limerick Leader*. 'But, the fundamental principles are the same wherever you are!' he says. 'It's a story about the denial of people's legitimate right to live in a secure and peaceful environment and with proper facilities. The scale of it may be different in Soweto, of course, but the underlying principle doesn't change; that people have a right to human dignity.'

Keane hasn't always chased the Big Story. It is the small stories that frequently make his reporting special: his ability to see the indomitable spirit of ordinary people caught in extraordinary situations. Great events can inspire great journalism, but so can small events. For example, he told the story of a mother who lived in a squatter camp outside Johannesburg. The residents of the camp slept under plastic sheets at night. When dawn broke, they dug holes in the ground to bury the plastic because they feared their shelters would be levelled by the local authority. The camp disappeared during the day and reappeared after dark. He met a woman who had to rear four children there under awful conditions. Yet, she managed to turn them out in clean school uniforms every day. 'It meant she had to go to the river and wash their uniforms and then dry them under the sun so that her children could have that dignity,' he explains. 'I think that says a hell of a lot about the human spirit. For me, it was humbling to see that.'

A lot of water has passed under Patrick's Bridge since young Keane packed his bags and left Cork for his first newspaper job in Limerick. It has been an amazing odyssey: one adventure after another for nearly 20 years. Yet Keane is no gung-ho globetrotting newsman with a cold heart. He's a sensitive soul who tends to absorb the suffering, or the elation, he witnesses. His work is illuminated by a deep sense of humanity. If you suspend your feelings as a journalist, he says, then you stop being a human being. He tells it straight. Superb reporting is still the most basic and often the most underrated skill of any journalist. Yet this is one of the main reasons Keane's stories remain so memorable.

Keane's memory banks are filled with striking images collected along the journey from Cork to Limerick, Dublin to Belfast, London to Johannesburg and then to Hong Kong. The early images are personal, drawn from his own experiences of a traumatic childhood and which are told in a book he wrote for his own son, *Letter to Daniel*. Other images are drawn from people and places: victims of war such as Sharja, a 12-year-old girl orphaned after the deaths of her parents in Afghanistan who guided him through the ruins of her home; or places of death such as the churchyard in Rwanda where, in a ransacked classroom, he found the battered bodies of a mother and her three young children who died huddled together. There are images of great joy, too: the wave of euphoria among the black majority of South Africa after the election that swept Mandela to power after the bitter years of apartheid. It hasn't all been a river of tears for Keane.

The pride of the BBC is an adopted Corkman, and mightily proud of it. His affection for the city and its people runs deep. Cork wrapped him in a warm blanket of security during a difficult childhood. It still has a soothing effect in adulthood; his sanctuary from the troubled spots of the world. His voice – calm, articulate and incisive – is known to millions of BBC radio listeners around the world. Occasionally, in mid-flow, the accent rises and falls with tell-tale signs of his roots. The years of overseas service have not quite eradicated those unmistakable local tones. And he wouldn't have it any other way.

The creative side of his personality was undoubtedly passed on from his parents. A love of the stage united Maura Hassett and Eamon Keane, amid a vibrant theatre scene in Cork during the late '50s. Eamon, a brother of playwright John B. Keane, came from Listowel, Co. Kerry. Maura grew up on Upper Doyle Road at Turner's Cross on the outskirts of Cork, then part of the countryside, where her father, Paddy, had built a house before the Second World War. Maura was academically bright, artistic and impulsive by nature. She once worked as an au pair in France and hitchhiked around the country, a daring exploit for an Irishwoman in the mid-50s. She loved languages and graduated in English, French and Latin with a H Dip at University College Cork.

While qualifying as a teacher, she was involved in the college drama society and later acted in local theatres. The Group Theatre on South Main Street, now Sir Henry's, set the scene for her first romance with the Kerryman. It was a poky, intimate theatre that had played host to some well-known names, among them the late Sarah Churchill, the British actress and daughter of Sir Winston. Maura met Keane, a visiting actor, and they worked on stage together in the Theatre of the South's production of John B's *Sharon's Grave*. Keane felt at home in Cork's artistic environment; a big fan of the work of Frank O'Connor and Seán Ó Faoláin. It was a whirlwind romance. They toured Ireland together with the play. She fell head over heels in love with Keane, who was older than her. They were married in 1960.

There was little acting work in Cork, so the newly-weds took the plunge and moved to London. They lived near Regent's Park. Their early years of marriage were not easy. Keane was a gifted actor but had a drink problem. Acting was a precarious existence, even without personal problems. They were often penniless, and frequently any money Keane earned went to pay for his alcohol habit. Still, they were in love and enjoyed both happy and sad times.

Fergal, the first of their three children, was born in London on 6 January, 1961. The circumstances of his arrival made a striking image, which he conveyed in his *Letter to Daniel*. Maura went into labour on a bitterly cold winter's morning. There was no money for a taxi, so she had to walk on snow-carpeted streets to University College Hospital. A taxi-driver saw her sitting in a doorway and brought her to hospital for free. She was ecstatic at the birth of her first child, 'a most beautiful son'. Her husband wept with joy when he held him for the first time.

They returned to Ireland where Keane joined the RTÉ Players, known as the Rep, acting and writing for the radio company. He also worked as an Abbey actor. The Keanes lived at Casement Green in Finglas, Dublin, a tough area with 'wonderful neighbours'. Maura had to take up a teaching job to help support the family. Breda Thunder, their next-door neighbour who became a lifelong friend, looked after Fergal and his brother, Eamon, and sister, Niamh, while their mother worked every day. Fergal describes Breda as a 'remarkable woman and a true Dub'.

An early memory is of his mother leaving home shortly after 6 a.m. to cross the city to her teaching job at Kostka College, at the junction of Seafield Road and Vernon Avenue in Clontarf. There are other scattered memories of early childhood: his mother and father rehearsing lines of poetry together; singing along with his mother to the Beatles' *Strawberry Fields Forever* on the radio.

As a small boy Fergal loved the radio and liked to read and be read to. Going to school for the first time was a shock to the system. He was scared out of his wits, but a kind teacher promised to buy him a marmalade cat if he came every day. As the eldest of three, Fergal shouldered a lot of responsibility early on. He was a naturally caring and compassionate child. After making his Holy Communion, he collected money from his cousins and neighbours but instead of spending it on himself he went down to the local chemist and bought his mother a lipstick and perfume.

There were dark days, when a small boy lost himself in a world of books to escape the dramas at home. Alcoholism gradually engulfed Eamon Keane, with all the inevitable consequences for his young family. Fergal describes his father as a man of many dimensions and alcoholism was just one of them; the one which ultimately destroyed his life. Although only a small child, Fergal knew what was happening. He thinks children are much more aware than their parents realise.

He loved visiting his grandmother, May Hassett, who had a huge early influence on his life. He remembers the train journeys from Dublin to Cork: counting down the stations along the way and his excitement rising as they entered the tunnel on the final approach to the city. Next, the familiar image of a billboard opposite Kent Station, advertising the Dixies showband. The Keane children were always greeted by their grandmother and her housekeeper and loyal friend, Minnie, who swept them up in their arms.

The Hassett home, St Declan's on Upper Doyle Road, conjures up blissful memories, 'a place I always associate with warmth and laughter and the good things in life'. There were magnificent apple trees in the garden: by the end of the summer, sweet smells filled the air. There were apple tarts galore and crab apple jelly.

Young Keane remembers his grandmother as being 'incredibly sensible and wise'. She had a liberal streak too: what he describes as 'that great Cork, sort of sang-froid, of being able to take things in her stride'. She wasn't easily shocked, and didn't bat an eyelid when Fergal experimented with his first cigarette in an old shed at the back of the garden. He went into convulsions of coughing 'and nearly died'. He recalls: 'She could see the smoke coming out of the shed. She was bursting her sides laughing up in the kitchen. She knew that we would poison ourselves with the cigarettes. We came out vomiting. She didn't need to say anything; the point was made.' Later, when the Keanes moved to Cork, Fergal knew her door was always open on rare occasions when he went on the hop from school. When he got his first job in Limerick and learned that her Pekingese had died, he bought a new puppy for her and hitched a lift to Cork with the new pet.

The Keane children spent their childhood summers in Cork, and holidayed in Ardmore every August. Fergal was only a few months old when his grandmother first took him to the Waterford resort. He retains a sentimental attachment for Ardmore and bought a cottage there a few years ago.

The marital split in 1970 threw the family into turmoil. He says of the break up: 'Of course it was a huge upheaval. Of course I knew what was happening. But nothing I say now can undo it. What I've tried to do is look back on those days and, while accepting the pain of it, also try to have compassion for both of them. People never set out to get into these situations. These things happen. You spend a long time trying to understand why and to deal with it. Paradoxically, I think it was more difficult to deal with as one got older than it was at the time.

'When the whole thing happens you're into coping and you develop various mechanisms to survive at the time. The older you get the more you become aware that those survival mechanisms aren't necessarily appropriate to your later life and you have to unlearn a lot of behaviour patterns that are rooted in the past.'

Maura took her children home to Cork, continued teaching to support the family and started a new life. Although it was a traumatic time in their lives, Fergal regarded Cork as a deliverance. They moved in with their grandmother for a while before setting up home at Skehard Road in Blackrock and, some years later, settled in Montenotte.

Young Keane enrolled in a new national school, St Joseph's at the Mardyke, which was run by the Presentation Brothers. It was a culture shock. He'd been used to the 'bourgeois environs' of Terenure College in Dublin where the students played 'rugger' and wore school uniforms. It had a refined Prep school atmosphere. St Joseph's wasn't so refined and attracted a tougher lot. On the first day at his new school, a big country boy called Larkin asked him: 'Are you handy?' Keane didn't have a clue what he meant but said 'yes', foolishly. 'In Cork parlance handy meant tough,' he explains, 'I spent the next few weeks trying to fend off requests for fights.' That was an era in Irish education when kids were walloped if they stepped out of line. Keane thinks that approach was wrong. He has always regarded the idea of somebody big hitting somebody small as an 'obscenity' and clings to this view passionately. He was a sensitive boy who kept to himself and read voraciously. At lunchtime, he watched the other lads outside in the rain, thumping a ball or thumping each other, and he decided that he was different and would make something of his life.

His happiest school days were spent at second-level attending 'Pres' on the Western Road. That was where the seeds of his journalistic career were sown. He has 'universally positive memories' of the place. Brother Jerome, the principal of Presentation Brothers College, had the earliest and greatest influence on his life. Bluntly, the world would never have discovered his talents were it not for the early guidance of Brother Jerome. He was an innovative educator: he passed on a disciplined yet liberal education where the students were encouraged to question and challenge.

'We got a perspective on education that extended beyond the narrow academic view,' he recalls. 'Brother Jerome believed in building people: finding out what each person's talent was and working on it. I wouldn't be where I am today were not for his singular influence.' The principal was impressed by Keane's sincerity and later described him as a person of great character, even as a teenager. He was struck by Keane's great authenticity, his tremendous capacity to be real and reach out to his peers.

Keane says his favourite subjects were English and History. He was 'desperate' at Maths. He was a member of the school debating team, which gave him a platform to express his opinions about everything under the sun. He loved words: books could transport him to another world, 'beyond the mundane, the grey skies and the cold winds of an Irish winter'. He read Alan Paton's *Cry The Beloved Country*, a stark account of the apartheid regime in South Africa. The book left a deep impression. Keane was happiest in the school library rather than on the rugby fields. No doubt conscious of the school's reputation for rugby, his mother bought him three sets of kit, but he hated it.

There were fun-filled days, too. Keane was a teenage rock'n'roller. He formed a band in the '70s with his brother, Eamon, and some schoolpals. They called themselves The Streets, a combination of The Beatles and The Rolling Stones wrapped into one outfit. Keane played the guitar 'extremely badly' and fronted as lead singer. He thinks he fancied himself in a big way. He did a mean Mick Jagger routine. The Streets played their first gig at the Pres Rag Dance, in aid of Conquer Cancer. Keane has always been a rocker, when he lets his hair down away from the cameras and microphones. During his posting to South Africa, he formed a band called Total Onslaught, the phrase used by the then South African government to whip up fear of Communism. Later, in Hong Kong, he planned to set up another band with his friend Mark Austin of ITN but it never got off the ground. Rock'n'roll was an antidote to the harsher realities of life as a foreign correspondent.

Keane discovered girls, too, in his early teens, although he was 'hopelessly inept' at the dating game. He was terribly shy. He experienced his first slow dance at a hop in Ashton School, Blackrock, where his mother taught class. The smooching song that brought couples closer on the floor was Elton John's *Candle In The Wind*. The long hot summer of '76 stands out in his memory 'because there was an air of great freedom and the whiff of awakening hormones'. Keane and his pals targeted the midweek dances that attracted visiting Spanish students to the old Stardust Ballroom on the Grand Parade. The introduction of jumbo seats to the Capitol Cinema brought a new dimension to courting in Cork. 'I'll never forget my first jumbo seat excursion,' he recalls. 'There was the dreadful business of inching your arm slowly along the seat around the shoulder of your target: utterly mortifying, not knowing what the reaction would be and always sure of rejection.'

The teenage culture had not yet been swamped by drugs. It was a time when the word 'ecstasy' had an entirely different meaning. The greatest temptations were sneaking an under-age pint somewhere or working up the courage to ask girls out.

Keane was bitten by the journalism bug at Pres. 'On the most basic level, I wanted people to take notice of me,' he explains. 'I had a reasonably strong social conscience, thanks to my parents. I thought that journalism would be a very good vehicle to give expression to that; a good way of giving witness to the concerns and lives of other people. Both of my parents identified with the voiceless and the oppressed and encouraged me to do the same. Also, when you grow up feeling a lot of the time that people don't really hear you or see you this must have fed into the whole psychology.'

Keane was in his element when Brother Jerome set up a media training centre at Pres, comprising a small television studio complete with cameras and an editing suite. Pres was the first school in Ireland to put a premium on media studies and provide such infrastructure. It was run at different stages by teachers Dan Collins and Pat Casey, who both went on to establish successful media careers. 'We were taken right through the whole business of production,' he says. 'It was great training. Once you get used to the camera and the microphone you never let go of it and it never lets go of you.' Business and civic leaders were invited into the school to participate in those early broadcasting experiments. Keane was among bright students who were very interested in current affairs and who voiced strong opinions on social issues.

Casey remembers him as a 'reflective and perceptive' young man who stood apart from the others to make incisive contributions on socio-economic matters of the day. 'One could see the beginning of the empathy he has since shown with people who are marginalised and disadvantaged and also his great humanity,' says his former teacher. 'I rejoice in his success.' At the same time, Keane was devouring the newspapers because if you want to be a journalist then you've got to know what's going on.

The budding journalist knew what he wanted and longed for his first break during Leaving Cert year: to walk out of school for the last time and straight into a newsroom. Keane got good results, with the notable exception of Maths. On the day of that dreaded exam, he walked down to Pres, paused at the door and asked himself: 'Why am I fooling myself and fooling them?' He recalls the moment of truth: 'I knew I was going in there to spend two hours twiddling my thumbs. So I turned around and walked away. I didn't bother my arse sitting Maths. It would have been an absolute waste of time.'

Equipped with a good Leaving Cert, shorthand and boundless enthusiasm, he went job hunting. All he wanted was a start. It didn't come easy. Keane applied for a job on *The Cork Examiner*, but they told him he'd have to wait for a vacancy to arise in their Reading Room. He looked elsewhere. If he had joined *The Cork Examiner* then, he reckons that he would never have left Cork because he loves the place so much. Around the same time, his uncle John B. Keane helped to open doors to a job on the *Limerick Leader*. John B introduced him to the Buckleys, proprietors of the newspaper, over drinks in Ballybunion. An interview was arranged with the editor, Brendan Halligan. He went to the *Leader* editorial offices on O'Connell Street and made his pitch. Halligan recalls that Keane wasn't an outstanding candidate. He was shy, slightly nervous and not a bit streetwise. But his obvious enthusiasm impressed the editor who decided to take him on. After the

Leaving Cert results came out, Keane got the call to start on 17 September, 1979.

Like all mothers, Maura had mixed emotions: she was broken-hearted to see her son leave home, yet realised he had to make his own way in the world. She helped him pack his new suit, shirts and socks and wished him luck. Like all sons who leave home for the first time, he was soon back with a bag full of dirty clothes. Keane moved into digs in Ballinacurra, on the outskirts of Limerick, and returned home on the train every weekend. The fare was £5. He has vivid memories of waiting to change trains at Limerick Junction, a miserable place on winter Monday mornings.

Keane recalls his first assignment on the *Leader*: he was despatched along with colleagues Billy Kelly and Cormac Liddy to cover the annual meeting of the Limerick Harbour Commissioners, who hosted a press lunch afterwards. 'On my first day in journalism,' recalls Keane, 'I was treated to a choice of fillet steak or duck à l'orange. I said to myself, "this is the job for me". I knew I had arrived.' He made it into print for the first time with a report on a press conference given by the Federation of Musicians, who attacked dancehall owners. He was walking on a cloud after the presses spewed out his printed work. He cut out his first story and sent it home to Cork.

The *Leader* gave Keane a solid apprenticeship: covering news and sport and diverse assignments from courts to greyhound racing 'although I didn't know one end of a greyhound from another'. He worked hard and wised up quickly. He speaks affectionately of the journalistic characters who showed him the ropes. 'To be honest, we laughed ourselves silly a lot of the time,' he reflects. Cormac Liddy, a seasoned hand, had an acerbic tongue but also a heart of gold. Liddy had a strong influence on the new recruit. Jimmy Woulfe, a top-class reporter, helped to cultivate a strong news sense. Bernard Carey, his first news editor, went by the nickname Chum.

Keane's talents soon surfaced, and he was rarely off the *Leader's* front page. When he sniffed a good story, he went after it 'like a dog with a bone and he wouldn't let go', according to editor Halligan. When Keane started writing about blacks in Limerick, he created an almighty stink. Four black Nigerian students had been refused admission to the Savoy disco bar and club at Bedford Row, allegedly on racial grounds. Keane was appalled and believed the story should be told. He accompanied the Nigerians in another failed bid to gain entry: this time he recorded the conversations and got photographs taken.

The editor knew that the story would rock the boat, but he backed his reporter. 'Brendan came under a lot of pressure,' recalls Keane. 'He was steadfast and we ran the story.' The inevitable public backlash forced to Savoy to relent, particularly after the Minister for Foreign Affairs and the Nigerian Ambassador became embroiled in the controversy.

Halligan was sorry to lose a gifted reporter when the chance of a job on the *Irish Press* in Dublin came Keane's way. Halligan's lasting memory of Keane is of his 'decency and goodness' that always shone through. He packed his bags and headed for the big smoke in 1982, 'after three happy years of good groundwork and hard labour'.

A vivid report from the field always sets the pulse of a newsroom racing. Keane's eye for detail and colour illuminated several big stories while working on the *Irish Press:* including the freeing in December 1983 of supermarket executive Don Tidey from IRA kidnappers in a wood near Ballinamore, Co Leitrim; and the heartbreaking deaths of schoolgirl Ann Lovett and her newly-born baby son in late January 1984 at a grotto in church grounds at Granard, Co. Longford.

Keane reported on the big political stories, most notably the heaves against Charlie Haughey's leadership of Fianna Fáil in the early '80s. He didn't like the 'vicious, violent streak' evident among Haughey supporters that was aimed at the media. He recalls the venomous atmosphere outside the gates of Leinster House after one of the most famous leadership challenges in 1982. 'They'd jostle you and punch you, if they got the chance,' he says. 'You were perceived to be the media enemy. That was nasty stuff, although I've had a hell of a lot worse since. The fact that it was being encouraged and directed by people who should have known better made it infinitely less pleasant.'

After the scandals of the so-called *gubu* years of Haughey-led governments, Keane says he didn't sign up to the Haughey hating bandwagon driven by some sections of the media. 'One could see that there were things very wrong about his style of government,' he reflects. 'Make no mistake about it: they were bad and shady times. But there was also a lot of pious, sanctimonious claptrap talked as well. An attempt was made to portray Haughey as the single baddie: a sense that he was the problem and if only he went away everything would be okay. Life is more complicated than that, and a lot of the journalists signed up to that bandwagon in a very unhealthy way. Their personal animosity towards Haughey was far too apparent in journalism of the time. That was unhealthy for both sides. Haughey was the kind of man who provoked those extreme reactions in people, good and bad. I just don't think it was our job as journalists to become involved in a massive campaign of antagonism. Irish society at that time was in a great period of ferment and change. Haughey was only one symptom of that. I think that Garret FitzGerald, by contrast, was given an incredibly easy ride a lot of the time. People were too polite and reverential with him. It was terribly dull and tedious.'

Haughey was the great survivor, and critics who predicted his demise were confounded. Keane pokes fun at the 'most unglorious episode' of his career when he and newsroom colleague Stephen Collins were asked by *Irish Press* editor, Tim Pat Coogan, to write Haughey's political obituary.

Keane always had a 'soft spot' for Haughey and got on well with him back then. Things were certainly never boring when Charlie was around. Years later, Keane followed reports of Haughey's public humiliation at the McCracken Payments To Politicians Tribunal in July 1997 from his BBC base in Hong Kong. He sums up: 'I thought it was all so sad and unnecessary, for him and for Ireland, because there's no doubt that he's an incredibly talented man, a gifted politician and a natural leader. To finish his career in such a way was pretty ignominious. But in the end, he had nobody to blame but himself.'

The *Irish Press* was a marvellous institution, and housed some of the best journalists in the country. There were colourful characters, too: among them Gerry O'Hare, who had a Republican background and held the brief as tourism correspondent, and Corkman T. P. O'Mahony, who wrote racy novels in his spare time and was responsible for religious affairs coverage. Keane reckons that modern journalism suffers from the absence of laughter, and modern journalists take themselves far too seriously.

He says he was privileged to have worked with two particularly outstanding journalists: chief news editor Mick O'Kane and *Evening Press* news editor Paul Dunne. O'Kane was competent, cool and clever. Dunne could see all the angles in a story. 'I've worked in many organisations but the *Irish Press* newsdesk was the best and most efficient that I've ever come across,' says Keane. 'They were brilliant. They would have risen to the top in any news organisation in the world. They were very sharp. They had a wonderful way of organising people and thinking of all the angles. I learned so much from them: a news sense, identifying the key issues of a story and going straight to the heart of it.'

The *Press* was special for other reasons: he fell in love with a colleague, Clare girl Anne Flaherty, during a long hot summer when they were on strike together. They got married in 1986. Keane was reporting from Hong Kong when the Press group of newspapers closed down in May 1995. The death of his old newspaper hurt him deeply. His verdict is that the *Irish Press* was a great newspaper, but the management had a dreadful lack of vision. 'The great strength of the Press was that although it did take a Fianna Fáil line, it was also a radical paper with some excellent writers and played a very important role. Ireland needed that voice. To see it end that way was terribly sad.'

Keane began a broadcasting career that would take him around the world when he landed a job with RTÉ in 1984. 'I've always felt I knew when it was the right time to move,' he says. 'There was no grand plan. You work hard at trying to make your breaks and give it everything you have. There's also a bit of luck. There was a long tradition of people going from the *Irish Press* into RTÉ, again because Press reporters had a very good name.' Keane went through an interview and screen test and accepted a job offer. He did not adapt easily to broadcasting at the start, and found the medium 'terribly intimidating'. If anyone listened to his tapes from the early days, they wouldn't recognise him.

After a spell in general reporting he moved into the news features department on radio where Shane Kenny led an accomplished team of broadcasters including David Davin-Power, Fintan Drury, David Hanly, Michael Ronayne, Shane Mc Elhatton and Michael Good. His talents as a broadcaster were cultivated in news features. He had found his niche. 'They were all great broadcasters and great guys to learn from,' he recalls. 'It was a small team of people. There was a priority on excellence and journalistic inquiry. It was a fantastic place to work. You did everything: produced and presented programmes, and reported.'

Keane developed good interview skills, and went head to head with top politicians on RTÉ's *This Week* programme on Sundays. Kenny says that his dedication to journalism was 'truly marked, beyond the norm'. He went 'live' with Haughey for the best part of 40 minutes. He recalls their epic encounters: 'Haughey was tough. He didn't like you getting stuck into him. But when you did go for it, you got the best out of him. I remember once pressing him on how things were going to be funded. At the end of three or four questions where I kept at him, there was an audible growl at the microphone.' On another occasion, Keane recalls that when he put the microphone too close to Haughey's face during a street interview, he was told: 'If you don't take that away, I'll shove it down your fucking throat.' Then Haughey smiled at the reporter.

Keane was despatched to the field whenever the big story broke. He was woken by Kenny in the middle of the night after the riot and burning of Fort Mitchell prison at Spike Island in Cork Harbour on 31 August, 1985. But the intrepid reporter was lucky to make it to Cork at all. He and Anne took off in their car, an old Renault 5, which was 'a heap of junk'. The car broke down on the Dublin-Cork road. 'We had no choice but to thumb a lift and put ourselves through all sorts of indignities,' he says. 'But we got there in the end and did the story.' Kenny sent the young reporter overseas, too: first, to cover the South African troubles in 1984. Kenny recalls the young reporter's 'complete commitment' to the South African story. It was a mind-blowing experience, and a dream-come-true because of his lifelong fascination for the Continent and its people. He witnessed the cruel injustices of the apartheid system under white minority rule before the subsequent transition to democracy. The striking images of social apartheid in action hit him immediately. On the highway from the airport in Johannesburg he saw a flat back pick-up truck carrying passengers: a white man sat in the front on his own with two seats empty beside him, and a group of black men sat in the back huddled together against the cold of the morning wind. He went to the railway station next day and saw separate platforms, separate seats and even separate lavatories. It was, he says, like visiting another planet. 'We all thought at that time that a bloodbath was inevitable. It was very hard to see that peace would come.'

Keane returned to South Africa two years later. During that visit he covered a demonstration and found himself on the wrong side of a crowd of 5,000. Shots were fired. Nobody knew where the bullets were coming from. The crowd panicked. Keane says he had to use the gift that Cork had bestowed on him. 'I talked and talked and talked before eventually getting out unscathed.' Kenny said he later compiled 'a superb report for the *This Week* programme.'

Keane was sent to Ethiopia in 1984, where he met little Ande Mikhail. The Eritreans were fighting for independence. Keane linked up with the guerrillas and travelled with them through the war zone. They took him to a makeshift field hospital in the mountains where he met the 10-year-old boy whose body had been badly burned in a napalm attack. Ande had been with his sister at a market when Ethiopian jets struck. He was the sole survivor. Keane saw the boy lying on a bed inside a tent, his shattered body covered only by a thin blanket. Every time the wind blew it aggravated his wounds and Ande screamed out in pain. Keane went outside the tent and cried. The boy died later.

At home, Keane worked on RTÉ's new radio current affairs show, *Morning Ireland*, from the first broadcast in November 1984. Kenny says that Keane, Ronayne and Good were central to the success of this new show. RTÉ posted him to Belfast to cover the troubles where his abilities impressed the BBC. As all good reporters should do, Keane refused to be chained to a desk and got out and about to meet nationalists and unionists and also republican and loyalist paramilitaries. He went further than other reporters, and took greater risks, to get the best stories. The most persistent image from his time in Belfast is of death, and the seemingly endless funerals. He recalls those days: 'There was an overpowering sense of lives being wasted unnecessarily. Nothing justified what happened. It was a vicious little neighbourly war. What made it vicious was that everyone knew each other. Each killing spread like a ripple into the community. Throughout Ireland, north and south, the extended family is very strong. You kill one person and the ripples that follow are extraordinary.'

Keane loathed the bigotry and hatred on all sides, and also the naked tribalism of some people south of the border. He explains: 'Generally, you'll find that the person who beats the republican drum loudest is usually living a long way from the north; most of these people are talking from cloud cuckoo land and it makes me sick. I despise tribalism. I just can't understand how intelligent people that I've met at polite society dinner parties in Dublin could, on the one hand, deplore the Bosnian Serbs and all their works and, in the same breath, rant against Ulster Protestants as if they were creatures from another planet; in other words, people who themselves behaved in an ethnically tribal way. If you scratch some people deep enough in Ireland – and you must be careful about generalisations – you'll find part of the republican mentality which says that the only good Prod is a dead Prod or one that isn't in our country. But there is also a hell of a lot of that on the other side too. I covered militant loyalism in some depth: I know a lot of them and there's a lot of viciousness, prejudice and blind sectarian bigotry. The problem is that one justifies the other and at some point you've got to say stop. But there are positive signs. There are people on the nationalist and loyalist sides who have seen the writing on the wall and realise that there is no future in this nonsense and that an accommodation of some sort must be found. I think the Downing Street Declaration will be seen in the long term as the most pivotal moment in modern Irish history since 1922. I think there are people in loyalism and unionism who realise that the British have definitely given a signal in saying that they have no strategic interest in holding on. That is something that people have heard and heard very clearly. Intelligent people realise that you've got to make an accommodation that takes into account the diverse nature of people's aspirations on this island.'

Keane watched with interest from Hong Kong as the Irish and British governments worked hard to get the IRA ceasefire restored in the summer of 1997 and inject fresh impetus into the peace process. Speaking from his experience of conflicts around the world, he believes that lasting peace won't be easy to achieve. 'It will take us generations to get over the animosity and bitterness,' he says. 'I really wonder whether people realise how difficult it is to achieve peace and reconciliation. Do they have any idea of the pain that so many families are living with as a result of what's happened? They are living with it now and they will live with it for years to come. You can't ignore that legacy of violence; you can't just wipe it away with a few handshakes, with the signing of a few treaties, with platitudes, with appearances on television. Peace is more than the absence of violence. We must get to the point of recognising each other's identities. We must recognise that there is a separate British identity in the north of this island. They must recognise that there is a community which sees itself as Irish. Any political solution has got to find a way of managing those identities, of allowing them to live together. You've got to face up to differences. They exist. And people have a right to feel different.'

By 1989, Keane had switched over to the BBC, reporting from Belfast as their Northern Ireland correspondent. Next he landed the high-profile job of South Africa correspondent in 1990. However, prior to his departure on 5 January, 1990, the day before his 29th birthday, his father died after being taken to hospital in Tralee. It was devastating: Keane later wrote about how he was too far away to hear his last words, his final breath, and all the things they might have wished to say to one another were left unspoken. Keane had tried to help his father before they drifted apart, taking him to doctors and looking after his flat in Dublin. He doesn't claim any special credit for that. He once took his mother to meet him at a clinic during his illness. He says the death of his father was gut-wrenching, and he has since tried to deal with it in his own way.

Keane feels privileged to have witnessed the course of history change in South Africa: the dismantling of the apartheid system and build-up to the country's first democratic election in April 1994. He witnessed the blood, sweat and tears ever since President F. W. de Klerk made his momentous decisions in February 1990 to unban the African National Congress (ANC), release its imprisoned leader, Nelson Mandela, and seek a negotiated settlement. Being Irish was a distinct advantage in trying to understand the dilemmas faced by the Afrikaaners and blacks in sharing a power base. Keane followed the story wherever it went, in spite of the obvious risks. When his mother once visited South Africa, she accompanied him to film the funerals in one of the townships. Trouble broke out and she had to be whisked away in a hurry. There was constant danger: his windscreen was cracked as he tried to drive through Soweto. There were always risks entering townships during times of unrest. He frequently wore a flak jacket to work, often drove an armoured car and lived in a house with steel doors and numerous alarms.

Keane's reports from South Africa were passionate and always full of insight. On the day that Mandela swept to power, he reflected the sense of destiny felt by black Africans after the long years of apartheid and, typically, was just as excited himself. 'Looking back,' he says, 'I often ask myself, "did I really live through all of that?" It was wonderful to have been there through it all. The idea that somebody else pays you to go to foreign countries and witness history is marvellous.'

Keane was honoured as Amnesty International's Human Rights Reporter of the Year in 1993 and also Reporter of the Year in the 1994 Sony Awards. He wrote his first book, *The Bondage of Fear*, a critically-acclaimed account of his experiences in South Africa during the course of a year while also working full-time for the BBC.

Keane was drawn back to the frontline in 1994, this time to bear witness to the mass genocide in Rwanda, a land 'where the dead have no dignity'. He conveyed the images of carnage all around him, bodies chopped and hacked: seeing so many dead people, day after day, left emotional scars. And he was inspired to tell the world what he'd seen. He made an award-winning documentary for the BBC *Panorama* programme. He was named British television reporter of the year by the Royal Television Society. His next book, *Season of Blood*, a personal and moving account of the Rwandan genocide, won the George Orwell Prize. It was a difficult and painful book to write. Of course it's great to win awards, but he doesn't live for them. 'You've got to be careful not to gear your journalism towards the winning of awards,' he says. 'Everybody knows what kind of stuff wins awards and what judges like to see. The minute you start gearing what you do towards the appetites of particular judges in awards systems, then your journalism becomes distorted. You've got to be wary of that.'

Keane likes writing books, mainly due to the freedom to expand his thoughts in a way that's impossible within the confines of a short news report or 40-minute documentary. When he starts a new book, he shuts out the world and becomes absorbed. He writes mostly late at night, when the creative juices are flowing, although 'that knackers me in the morning'.

Forget the clichéd image of foreign correspondents as cold-hearted trouble-shooters who divorce their emotions from the story. It certainly doesn't apply to Keane, as his work testifies. 'Look, foreign correspondents are human beings,' he says. 'If you stop being a human being in the face of the kind of things one sees in Angola, Afghanistan, Rwanda and Bosnia then you should get out of it. What you do is bear witness, and bearing witness involves emotion. The key is to try and calibrate it so that you don't lose it and become over-emotional. I don't set out to be anything: I just try and tell it as I see it. But the idea that I'm the first person to do this is nonsense. There's a long tradition of journalists going out and telling it like it is. I would feel honoured if I thought I was part of that tradition.'

Keane was again standing at an historical crossroads when posted to Hong Kong as the BBC's South East Asia correspondent at the end of 1994 to cover the transition of the colony from imperial to Communist rule in 1997. South Africa had been an uplifting, although dangerous, assignment. Hong Kong was a safer place. In South Africa he had reported on a movement towards democracy; whereas in Hong Kong it was a shift away from democracy. It was a plum assignment in one of the world's greatest cities. 'That mixture of Chinese endeavour and the British gift for order and organising society was definitely a powerful combination,' he says. 'I'm no imperialist. I've seen a hell of a lot of damage that it has done. Yet in Hong Kong there was a sense that something decent had been left behind, that the British presence had a profoundly positive impact in the long term. I had a lot of time for Chris Patten. He's a decent man. I think he did what he did for the right reasons, because he believed in people's right to dignity, their right to choice, and their right to have a say in how their lives are run. He upset a lot of people doing that, but frequently when you're doing the right thing you will upset people.'

The Keanes lived in a three-bedroomed apartment with a commanding view of the busy harbour below. He was away from home a great deal, covering stories anywhere in Asia from Afghanistan to the South Pacific. It seemed like an eternity of airports, hotels and vastly different cultures and people. There were 'so many voices, stories and images'.

Keane has a sentimental attachment to Hong Kong for personal reasons: his son, Daniel, was born there in February 1996. He wrote an open letter to his new-born son, a mixture of experiences and emotions that included personal references to the circumstances of his own birth and his relationship with his father. The letter was broadcast on BBC Radio 4 and RTÉ and captivated listeners. It inspired him back into print with a third book, the best selling *Letter To Daniel*. The arrival of a son was 'a great experience that gets better every day'.

Keane captured the emotionally-charged atmosphere of that farewell ceremony in Hong Kong on 30 June when the Union Jack was lowered under a tropical rain storm and the band struck up *Auld Lang Syne*. BBC television viewers were treated to a typical Keane report on the nine o clock news that painted pictures with well-chosen words. The report stands as one of the pieces he's most proud of: 'They left to the call of trumpets, echoing across the pearl river.'

He recalls the historic event: 'My memories of that night, unfortunately, are largely of being locked into an edit suite with mounds of tapes all around me and myself and a producer and a tape editor just going hell for leather to get the piece done on time. But I do remember climbing up onto the roof of the BBC office: hearing the faint sound of music from *Britannia* and then watching the ship leave the harbour. It was a very striking image.' Keane feels that 'in spite of their initial apprehensions about the takeover, the Hong Kong people will thrive in the future.'

On Tuesday, 18 March, 1997, the former Pres boy went to Buckingham Palace to be conferred with an OBE by Queen Elizabeth for his services to television journalism. The Queen congratulated him on his broadcasts from the world's war zones. 'She was very gracious and said how nice it was to put a face to a voice she knew well,' he says of their meeting. 'She asked me about Hong Kong and what it was like to live there and also asked about the upcoming handover. She seemed to be a decent person. Of course it was nice to get the OBE and receive that kind of recognition.'

At the end of the day, what's so special about Fergal Keane is that in spite of all the awards and accolades he hasn't changed fundamentally or lost the run of himself. That hasn't been easy because top-flight journalists are constantly battling with their own egos.

He says: 'I'll be very frank. I haven't spoken about this in public before. The more success you have, the more you tend to want. We're fundamentally insecure people, those of us who work as foreign correspondents. You want to keep excelling and do better than you did the last time. That's the kind of thing you really need to keep a handle on. There's a great deal of competition. To survive at this level in journalism requires a degree of toughness. It requires a degree of paranoia. It requires a degree of ruthlessness. Keeping a lid on all those three things can be difficult. It's important to do that because otherwise you turn into an absolute ego monster. One has to be very careful about not going down that road. It's an everyday battle. You've got to say to yourself, "hey, get things in perspective here". You've got to keep reminding yourself about what's important in life. It's not a battle I always win. There are parts of myself which, in terms of having to be tough and ruthless, that I don't like and against which I struggle. I guess that struggle will go on as long as I'm in this business. All that said, there is no way that I will ever compromise on my fundamental beliefs and principles for the sake of honours or awards or the story. When you're reporting on peoples' lives and peoples' tragedies you've got to have compassion and decency.'

For the moment, there is always another story to write; another plane to catch to bear witness to something momentous happening somewhere in the world. He has recently been appointed Special Correspondent to the BBC. One day, when he unpacks his suitcase for the last time, he'd like to return to Ireland and write novels. A secret ambition is to sail around the world with Daniel. It's not a pipe dream 'because I've generally done everything I set out to do'. So what drives Keane? 'A mixture of insecurity, idealism and curiosity about the world.' How would he like to be remembered? 'That I did my best and lived my life the way I wanted to live it, beholden to no one.'

FIONA SHAW

ALL THE WORLD'S A STAGE

THERE are, of course, two Fiona Shaws. One is the daredevil who had a go in the movies. She is known to American moviegoers from her roles as Dr Eileen Cole in *My Left Foot* (1989), as the unconventional wife of explorer Sir Richard Burton in *Mountains of the Moon* (1989) and as the frustrated school mistress, Miss Lomax, in *Three Men and a Little Lady* (1990). Shaw was also associated with such Tinseltown tosh as *Super Mario Brothers* (1993) when she played Lena, queen of the dinosaurs and Dennis Hopper's mistress. *Undercover Blues* (1993) was a disaster because the preview audience didn't understand it; the money men were too nervous to leave it alone, so the funniest bits were taken out to leave a mediocre love story between Kathleen Turner and Dennis Quaid. The only good thing about the entire experience was the presence of a wonderful director, Herbert Ross. 'He was one of the old style directors', she says. 'He was paternalistic and nice to me. He was making this dreadful film that was a catastrophe. It wasn't his fault.' During the making of *Super Mario Brothers*, she organised Shakespeare readings for the cast at her rented beach house where one of the brothers, Bob Hoskins, played *Macbeth* in gothic candlelight. She enjoyed Hollywood except for the tedious hours of waiting around the set.

The other Fiona Shaw – and by far the best known – is the doyenne of the international stage, hailed by some as the greatest classical actress on either side of the Atlantic. She has been honoured with Olivier awards for best actress. A critic once paid her the ultimate compliment when he said she embodied the qualities of Gielgud and Olivier: mind and heart, spiritual and animal. Shaw's talent is prodigious; her onstage presence powerful enough to set off a theatrical firestorm. Her trademark is the remarkable and extreme energy channelled into each part: from self-mutilation antics in *Electra*, convulsing death by electric chair in *Machinal* to become the first woman playing the King of England in *Richard II*. Those remarkable performances in *Electra*, *Richard II* and also in *Hedda*

Gabler were daring, playful and fierce. 'She burns before the audience,' remarked one critic, 'radiating not just the heat of her imagination but the glare of her critical intelligence.'

Her interpretation of Gabler was acclaimed as the greatest in living memory. This lady is not afraid to take risks or tempt derision. Shaw is an amalgam of contrasts. To define her essence as an actress is no easy task. When she speaks the passion in her remarkable voice is real; the eyes are piercing and she has a palpable air of authority around her. There's a sense of fun and mischief, too, behind the outer layer of intensity.

When her gender-bending *Richard II* was the talk of London in 1995, most audiences would not have known her real name or origin. The top classical actress is Fiona Mary Wilson, known by her pet name Fifi, the doctor's daughter from Montenotte, Cork. Her home city has basked in her reflected theatrical glory and given her an honorary degree to acknowledge those achievements. Her story began in a tall narrow house by the sea, at 10 Westbourne Place in Cobh. She is the only daughter of Denis and Mary Wilson. Her mother's family, the O'Flynns, were from Cobh. Her dad was the local GP who subsequently became an eye surgeon. Fifi had three brothers, one of whom, Peter, the youngest, died tragically at the age of 18 in a road accident on the way to a rugby match. The other two brothers, John and Mark, now live in the South of France. She was the second child, born at the Bons Secours maternity hospital in Cork on 10 July, 1958.

Fifi's early schooling was at the convent in Cobh where she remembers one of the old nuns, Mother Patrick, cutting toffees in half as a reward for the children. Her first friend was a little Dutch girl, Chanel Stappers. Although neither spoke the other's language, they played together anyway. There was a wonderful sweet shop near the Wilson's home: it was run by a woman called Olive who had a special low counter for children. Fifi remembers her Holy Communion in Cobh because she fell three days beforehand and cut her leg. On the big day, Fifi and another girl, Ann McCarthy, held candles in their hands and led the procession from the convent at the top of the hill to Cobh Cathedral. Although Fifi was seven when the family moved to Montenotte in Cork, they kept their links with Cobh, particularly the tennis club at Rushbrooke which became an important part of her teenage years. The Wilsons had a summer home at nearby East Ferry where they spent three months of the year. Fifi spent summer days playing tennis, boating, going for long walks and picking periwinkles along the sea shore. Her great friends were the Ronan and the Cook children.

Dr Wilson, who had specialised in ophthalmic surgery and worked in hospitals in Cork, moved his young family to the city. Their home at Montenotte had a commanding view of the city. Fifi made friends easily, especially with the children of families who lived along Lower Montenotte. 'We had big apple fights and did all the usual things that kids do,' she says. 'We all joined *The Man From Uncle Club* taken from the TV show and got our own kits and badges.' Fiona's parents placed a strong emphasis on a good education. 'They were very keen on exams and, of course, homework was a big thing,' she says.

The seeds of her acting career were sown during her secondary school years at Scoil Mhuire on Wellington Road, which was within walking distance of her home down the hill through St Luke's Cross. It was a small lay Catholic school, founded in 1951 by the late Miss Kathleen Cahill and by Miss Mary O'Donovan who still manages today. It was small enough to maintain core values and guiding principles. Expression was encouraged. Fifi 'adored' her time at Scoil Mhuire from 1970 to 1976.

'It was more like a tutoring college rather than a school with domestic rooms and small classes. I felt very much at home there. We were, apparently, a noisy class and a very imaginative group. The teachers were very stimulating. I was taught History by Gloria O'Flynn. Her classes were exciting.

'Emelie FitzGibbon taught us English: she was a stunning teacher, really provocative. Emelie, now artistic director of the Graffiti theatre company, let us read Shakespeare aloud. This was my awakening. Subsequently, a rather magnificent woman, Madeline O'Rourke, taught us English, and first introduced me to Richard II. I was certainly very excited by those teachers. I wasn't particularly good at school. I suppose I wasn't so bad at English, History and French.'

Drama was encouraged at Scoil Mhuire under the guidance of Emelie FitzGibbon. 'We did *Trial By Jury* once, which was terrific,' she recalls. 'I played the judge, and all my class were the jury. It was one of my first total theatrical experiences because I was playing a piece right through.' Miss O'Donovan remembers her convincing performance as the judge, 'and I can still see her looking out over the glasses'. The teachers recall her wit: she entertained the other students with her imitations during breaks in the Long Room. 'Fifi was bright, responsive and very amusing,' says Miss O'Donovan. Fifi's former History teacher, Gloria O'Flynn, says she frequently had the class in stitches. 'She was extremely witty, hilariously funny, and had a colourful personality.' Emelie FitzGibbon recalls her charisma and intense performances.

Fifi had wanted to be an actress since the age of 10: her artistic leanings were encouraged by her parents, but schoolwork always had to come first. She studied speech and drama under the careful direction of Abbey Scott at the Cork School of Music. 'A lot of what we do is about energy,' she says. 'Abbey's energy was inspirational; she was such an exciting person to be with.' Fifi entered the Feis in Cork every year, and won medals and cups for speech and drama.

Tennis was a big obsession during her teenage years. Fifi and her friends played mostly at the Rushbrooke Lawn Tennis Club but also occasionally cycled out to the Douglas club. 'Rushbrooke was the whole focus,' she explains. 'We'd nip down on a Saturday, spend the whole day there and come back again on Sunday. The junior tournaments were an enormous social occasion. I remember endless hops during the summer. There was always an influx of people from outside; boys down from Dublin or Limerick for the tournaments.' Fifi played tennis in Mallow where her great friend, Sue Furney, lived. She also spent summer holidays in France, in the hope of learning to speak the language properly.

By now well and truly bitten by the acting bug, Fifi had her sights set on drama school after doing the Matriculation and completing the Leaving Certificate in 1976. However, her parents were adamant that she should get a university degree first. So, she took an arts degree at University College Cork, studying Philosophy with English as a subsidiary subject. She opted for Philosophy because she wanted to do something that was mind expanding and non-functional! The study of Philosophy has since helped her, indirectly, in reading difficult texts: nothing intimidates her once she knows the logic somewhere between the beginning and the end of a sentence. Then other things come into play, like imagination and instinct. Inevitably, she became a leading light in DRAMAT, the student drama society. She devoted as much, if not more, time to drama than philosophy, and took part in student performances at the Granary Theatre.

It was a disorganised society. She remembers the students 'smoking fags in the dressing rooms at the Granary and wondering what to do next'. She says: 'The rehearsals were always full of interruptions. I'm somebody who has to work very hard, consistently. It was only when I went to drama school later that I learned not only how hard one must work but that one must work in an organised structure. The students stopped for coffee breaks and a smoke and we could never really get anywhere. Everything was done on a wing and a prayer. By contrast, Trinity always had a great structure. We envied the students at Trinity, possibly because they lived on campus and were all nearby, whereas, we were all scattered.' But Fifi's final year was exciting because UCC hosted the Irish Student Drama Festival when students came to Cork from third level institutions all over the country. She remembers going to endless planning meetings and 'managing to avoid study yet again.' A pivotal memory is of performing Paul Zindal's *The Effect of Gamma Rays on Man in the Moon, Marigolds*, which took her to Coleraine.

There was no sense of student revolt in Cork in the late '70s. The students were wrapped in a numbing blanket of conformity, unlike the more militant student unions in Dublin or Belfast.

Fifi had to finish her degree before turning seriously to an acting career. 'I have endless memories of walking in and out of that college from town with Kieran Ahern and John Montague. I was actually yearning to be elsewhere, because at the time the atmosphere felt like the last years of the Soviet Republic. I wasn't doing what I wanted to do. Don't get me wrong, I had a great time, but my main memory is of champing at the bit and being with others who were champing as well.' The students had their own haunts off campus: a favourite was The Long Valley bar on Winthrop Street where the proprietor, the late Humphrey Moynihan, played German marching music and made famous sandwiches. When it came to musical taste, she was more classically oriented. She liked to nip over to London to catch the latest plays, and socialise with friends. She also had a boyfriend at Oxford at one point.

After graduating with an arts degree from UCC in 1979, she had made up her mind she wanted to go to drama school. It was her way of testing whether she had what it takes. 'I think you have to be trained properly because otherwise I feared I'd be carrying a shadow of amateurism behind me,' she says. 'There's something vital about taking three years to allow yourself to find the connection between what it is you're doing, how you do it, why you do it and where it comes from.'

For nearly a decade, since her early schooldays at Scoil Mhuire, she had been trained by Abbey Scott at the Cork School of Music. She had won scholarships and prizes there and pursued her studies to the point where she had a shelf full of prizes and got her Licentiate of Trinity College London (LTCL) in speech and drama. Abbey prepared her for an audition at the prestigious Royal Academy of Dramatic Art (RADA) in London, of which Queen Elizabeth and the Queen Mother are patrons. Competition for places is fierce. 'Her success shows that there is no substitute for training and application,' says Abbey. 'Looking back, I would describe her as mercurial. She had a terrific sense of comedy; very quick. Her personality was always bubbling. She was easily my most famous pupil.' Fifi went for an audition at RADA in the spring of 1980.

She was accepted into a class of 22 students who began their first term in the summer. It was a noteworthy achievement considering there were over 1,000 applications. Abbey, who is also a graduate of RADA, wasn't surprised that she made such a strong impression.

The opportunity to study at RADA also forced the biggest change in her life, opening up new horizons. 'Somebody told me recently you only emigrate once in your lifetime,' she says. 'On top of that, getting into RADA was the biggest quantum leap of my life. I'm sure I found it traumatic at the time. But all my friends were leaving home. So, I met up again in London with my friends from UCC and Trinity. For the first years I lived in Camden and then Brixton. Eventually, though, I was torn away from my Irish friends because I had gone back into a new college environment. I had entered a whole new world while they were still part of a group. I still had my friends; it's just that there was this other world I lived in too. I never really gave myself entirely to those friends at RADA. I already had my friends and a world that I used to play in.' Nothing would ever be the same again, once her talents were nurtured and given full expression at RADA. It was a hard classical training, but immensely rewarding.

'I worked terribly hard there. The teachers' input was incredible: you were being shifted, challenged, changed, looked after, studied, encouraged, oriented, helped and stimulated. There were only about 22 students and 18 teachers. You were being dealt with privately an awful lot of the time: private singing, private voice, private movement, and private tutor. Progress was monitored all the time. You were there from 10 a.m. until 10 p.m. so you became completely a creature of it; you knew no other reality. I think from then on it became difficult coming home to Cork because I was schizophrenic in a way. I was so immersed in this world of hard work at RADA that it seemed so strange to come back to the lackadaisical life here.'

Fifi is fondly remembered at RADA for her open personality and an outstanding talent easily recognisable to others. After completing seven terms, she graduated with an honours diploma in August, 1982. She won the prized Bancroft Gold Medal, the highest award, which had been won the previous year by Kenneth Branagh and which would be won a year later by Janet McTeer. She won several other prizes: notably the Ronson Award, given to the best all round actor most likely to succeed, and the Tree Prize, awarded to the best student in the opinion of an invited audience of casting agents and agents. She won other awards including the Sherek, Fabia Drake's comedy prize and the Edmund Grey High Comedy Prize. The most prestigious awards yielded valuable publicity, particularly in *The Evening Standard*, and the industry sat up and took notice of the promising Irish actress. She was 'snapped up' by a good agent and 'away it went from there'. She changed her name to the more serious sounding Fiona Shaw. Apparently, someone else in the actor's union, Equity, had the same name. It wasn't unusual since several of her classmates at RADA also changed their names on the advice of agents.

Within months, she landed her first part in a TV film, *Fireworks for Elspeth*, and was also busy with other television work. Her first big break came in 1983 when she joined the National Theatre to play Julia in *The Rivals*. It was hailed as a notable debut, described as fresh and funny. 'My career really jumped at that stage,' she recalls. 'Looking back, I think early success is both a blessing and an albatross.' She goes on: 'I was in *The Rivals* with great actors who were all stars as far as I was concerned. It felt terrifying at the time. I just couldn't believe I had a start like that and never looked back.' This was soon followed by the part of Mary Shelley in *Bloody Poetry*, and her introduction to the theatre at the highest level. She joined the Royal Shakespeare Company (RSC) in 1985 'and my life began all over again'. She made two lifelong friends, Alan Rickman and Juliet Stevenson, both of whom had also been Bancroft medal winners. 'They taught me an awful lot,' she says.

Shaw established herself as a talented comedienne at the RSC in the company of Stevenson, Rickman, Harriet Walter, Lindsay Duncan and Brian Cox, who were very much the new classical vanguard. She played in Gorky's *The Philistines*, taking on Celia in *As You Like It*, Beatrice in *Much Ado About Nothing* and Mistress Carol in James Shirley's *Hyde Park*. She had the title role in *Mary Stuart*, and also success in Christopher Hampton's *Les Liaison Dangereuses*. 'I was crammed with work and experience,' she says of that frenetic period in her life.

'Suddenly, within two years I'd done eight or nine plays and most of these were leading parts. I was getting a lot of publicity. We were becoming stars not only because we were leading actresses but also because Juliet and I were very political. I spent four years at the RSC, a long time, but I adored it. We worked very hard but it was great fun. We'd perform on a Friday night, stay up all night, perform a matinee on Saturday and then do another play that evening. I couldn't do it now; I'd have to sleep for the day.'

She spent most of her days and nights rehearsing and performing plays. The work was obsessive, and emotionally draining. She seemed to be 'locked in the seventeenth century' and yearned to do something modern. After spending three years at the RSC she said it felt like ten. 'Shakespearean characters live at a level where there is a mixture of thought and passion – a level where all of us should live,' she remarks. 'When Shakespeare's characters say something like "I love you" they really say it and they really feel it.' The actors were happy then if they managed to send a member of the audience home with some line from the play 'rattling around in their head'. She liked to make people laugh too. It was a charmed lifestyle in Stratford, taking long country walks and picnics by the river during gorgeous, heady summers. 'It was just a whole way of life,' she says. 'We lived in the cottages. It was very cosy, like being at Oxford.'

By the end of the '80s, Fiona Shaw had played a lot of the classical heroines. Such was the early volume of work that she said at the time she'd measured out her life 'not in coffee spoons but in plays'. Shaw first teamed up with Deborah Warner, her director and close friend, on the RSC's *Electra* by Sophocles in 1988. Warner was the leader of a new generation of British female directors whose work, no less than Shaw's, galvanized the British theatre over the past 10 years. 'I had played a lot of comedy and wanted to do a tragedy,' she recalls. 'Deborah asked me to do *Electra*. That changed my entire life because suddenly I discovered this play had people queuing and sleeping on the benches outside the theatre in January.' Although her forte had been comedy, she had now fallen in love with tragedy. Warner and Shaw worked 12-hour days rehearsing *Electra*, staged at the Barbican. The Irish actress delivered an electrifying performance in the *Electra*, her 'princess of grief', crop-haired and dressed only in a tattered black robe. Her performance was striking because of its total unsentimentality. One reviewer described how Shaw used the clean lines of her physique and features as a 'magnificently expressive tool' and 'the result is a performance of ferocity and pain I have not seen equalled in a quarter century's voracious play-going'. It was an uninhibited portrait of a woman – unsexed, unhinged and uncompromising – 'clawing at her flesh and at the walls as she mourns her father's death and determines to seek his revenge.' Critics also said it was directed with lucidity and intensity that marked Warner out and had taken her from the fringe to the major theatre companies. Later, their production was revived in London in 1991 and caused a sensation in Paris before moving on to Glasgow and Derry.

The year 1989 marked one of the busiest years of her career when she says she was 'commuting all over the place'. There were diversions into the movie business with the Jim Sheridan-directed *My Left Foot*, the life story of writer and painter Christy Brown which won Oscars for Daniel Day Lewis and Brenda Fricker; and also with the Bob Rafelson-directed *Mountains of the Moon* which also starred another Irish actor, Patrick Bergin, who played the nineteenth-century English adventurer, Richard Francis Burton. Shaw played his wife, Isabel Arundel, who accompanied her husband around the world. She recalls her punishing acting schedule: 'I was also playing Katherina in *The Taming of the Shrew* at the Barbican. I'd finish *The Shrew* at night at the Barbican, get into a car and drive up to Liverpool for *Mountains of the Moon*, film all day and then take a private plane to London, go in and do *The Shrew*, then back into a car and up again to film all day and then fly back again. That went on for weeks. It was very funny really, because there was just me and a pilot. I was both passenger and air hostess, so I poured tea for the pilot.' She regarded her real work as the theatre. 'It's just that when you get invited to do movies they make a great break from long months of working in the theatre.'

After *My Left Foot* and *Mountains of the Moon*, Shaw could have moved to Hollywood. Rather, she preferred the emotional charge of the theatre, although continued to make 'the odd gesture' to her American agent.

Shaw liked the working relationship with Warner in *Electra*, so came back for more. She played Rosalind in *As You Like It* at the Old Vic. Warner sent her a card and asked her, 'rather beautifully', to play Brecht's *The Good Person of Sichuan* at the National Theatre's Olivier stage. Warner's production – her first for the National – of the comic parable about the possibility of doing good in a capitalist society had her customary clarity. Shaw says she worked well with Warner because she directed intuitively, channelled actor's ideas and allowed actors greater freedom in rehearsal. 'I can be wilder with her than I've ever been with anybody in my life,' she said at the time. 'The basis of her approach is correct. It is not a question of superiority of actor over director, but the action itself is the performance, after all.' For this formidably talented duo, it was just the start of a theatrical explosion.

Shaw won the prestigious Laurence Olivier Award on 8 April, 1990, for her scorching performances in *Electra*, *As You Like It* and *The Good Person of Sichuan*. She was crowned Best Actress at a ceremony beamed live to millions of TV viewers from the Dominion Theatre, London. In her speech she described her performances as 'an experiment in mental mud wrestling'. It was a double victory for Cork because Bob Crowley won an Olivier as Best Designer. In the same year, Warner's production of *King*

Lear for the Royal National Theatre played the Cork Opera House, with Brian Cox in the lead role. By now, Shaw, who had also received The Critics Award in London, was being hailed as the new Vanessa Redgrave, a salute that used to drive her bananas.

Shaw took a break from changing the face of British theatre to return to a comic role on the big screen, somewhat to her embarrassment, in *Three Men and a Little Lady*, the sequel to *Three Men and a Baby* (1987). Her flair as a comedienne hadn't diminished in her role as the school mistress who fell in love with the architect played by Tom Selleck. After the US premiere, she was offered a TV comedy series in Los Angeles but turned it down. She shared the same views as Juliet Stevenson who once said that Hollywood was only interested in youth and perfection and not particularly interested in talent.

Warner and Shaw set off another theatrical firestorm with Ibsen's *Hedda Gabler*. Warner's production first surfaced on the stage of the Abbey in Dublin in July 1991, transferred a couple of months later to the Playhouse Theatre in London and also became a BBC TV film. The duo succeeded in bringing extraordinary freshness to one of the most frequently performed of all Ibsen's plays. The title role had become the female equivalent of *Hamlet*, but Shaw's Hedda was a mind-blowing suicide note. Like Electra, her Hedda was relentless.

One writer compared the actress to a professional runaway bus, purpose-built to career down the street and flatten pedestrians. *The Sunday Times* said Shaw's performance had the terror of an earthquake and the hopelessness of a torture chamber. Typically, she wasn't afraid to go over the top: violently shifting and kicking furniture around the stage and beating her fists against the up-stage double doors. *The Daily Telegraph* said her extraordinary display of destructive desperation would haunt the memory for a long time. *Time Out* said Ibsen's bourgeois tragedy would never be the same again. By February 1992, Shaw won her second London Critics Award for her performance in *Hedda Gabler* and returned to Cork to receive a UCC/AIB Hall of Fame Award. In fact, she became the second actor to join UCC's Hall of Fame; Donall Farmer had won the award in 1990.

Shaw strapped herself into an electric chair and died screaming as the 'young woman' in Sophie Treadwell's *Machinal* at the Royal National's Lyttleton Theatre in 1993. It was another heart-wrenching performance. She played an American stenographer who married the boss, refused a maternal role, took a lover, killed her husband and ended up being slowly grilled in the electric chair. *The Observer* described Shaw's performance as staggering, conceived triumphantly in competition with an all-action hydraulic set. She regarded the play as experimental and, as always, went with the flow. She found the part incredibly tiring and physically depressing. That was hardly surprising. To make it all look convincing she used to bang her head against the chair and almost knock herself unconscious. 'Sometimes I actually went out,' she reflects. 'It was a tremendous event because the entire machinery of the theatre was being utilised. You see, it was the last of this poor woman's endless tortures. You just imagine her dying and go for it; the ritual of being strapped into the electric chair was dangerously like the real thing. It wasn't at all pleasant acting it. In a way, though, it was a novel experience because *Hedda Gabler* had been such an enormous thing with Deborah in 1992.'

The critics were impressed: one reviewer noted that his main memories of what he regarded as the outstanding performance of 1993 were not groans, not cries, but Shaw's 'big stricken smiles'. *Machinal* was directed by the daring Stephen Daldry, to whom bringing off major theatrical facelifts seemed to come easy. 'I loved working with him,' she says. 'I found him brave and bold.' For the remarkable *Machinal*, Shaw won the Olivier and Evening Standard Best Actress awards in 1993.

After *Machinal*, Deborah Warner asked her to do Samuel Beckett's *Footfalls* in the balcony of the Garrick Theatre in 1994 and immediately ran into a storm of controversy. Warner's reallocation of some of the lines and her deviation from Beckett's precise stage directions angered the late author's estate. The estate had them closed down after only a week of performances.

Shaw, the classical heavy-hitter, felt that audiences were hungry for something different and brand new. So she became the first woman to play the deposed king in Shakespeare's *Richard II* in Warner's production at the National. The role made her the talk of London in 1995, even before the play opened. *Newsweek* reported that the Irish actress had stirred up a 'tornado' in London's teapots. Shaw was upsetting the British press again, who didn't like their monarchs being tampered with. It wasn't just an exercise in gender-bending. 'It's not a feminist or feminine gesture,' she insisted. 'I'm not playing a man; I'm playing a king. I play Richard not from my gender centre but from my imaginative centre. Different aspects of Shakespeare will be revealed in each new generation. There is an enormous taboo about women playing male roles. I underestimated it. I thought the world was more advanced.' Warner's production was universally praised, although Shaw's performance got distinctly mixed reviews in Britain. The reactions ranged from 'audacious' and 'imaginative' to 'recklessly animated' and 'a stereotypical girlie'. The actress succeeded in making waves which, in a way, made a refreshing change for someone so unaccustomed to receiving brickbats. Her portrayal of the irresponsible man-boy inevitably drew some analogies with the present generation of royals. One critic fumed that no king would behave like Shaw's thumb-sucking Richard. 'Have one look at the royal family now,' she replied.

Shaw spent one morning in the company of the late Princess Diana at an awards ceremony in The National Theatre and found her inspiring. She recalls their meeting: 'I was introduced to her by Lady Soames. Diana was delightful and very natural. We talked about Patrick Jephson, a mutual Irish friend who was her Private Secretary at the time. I particularly remember how protective Diana was of me when the press photographers began to move in on us.'

It was, of course, a reflection of Fiona Shaw's high status within the ranks of British classical theatre that her performance of *Richard II* provoked such extreme reactions. In a way, she was delighted that what she'd set out to do had come out differently than expected. She liked doing experiments and getting into trouble. In her own words, she didn't do *Richard II* as a crowd pleaser. It was an attempt at a new style of theatre. 'It was saying goodbye to awards,' she reflects. 'It was saying, "right, let's play something that we really don't know how to do".'

Shaw recalls the first entrance as being 'absolutely terrifying'. What the audience did not realise was the extent of her mental preparation before making that transformation to become the boy king. 'I remember just willing the audience to believe it as I walked on. I said to myself, "they either believe it, or I'm doomed to three hours of hell. If they do believe it, I'm away." I just would stand there and will it and the concentration used to kill me. Looking back, it was wonderful because it's not everyday you get the chance to play a King of England. I wouldn't want to play one again.'

Controversy is commercial. *Richard II* was a box office hit: sold out in London and Austria and acclaimed in Paris where Warner and Shaw made the front page of *Le Monde*. The French had long been in love with Warner's work. The woman-who-played-the-king became an international success story. During a visit to Germany, Shaw was approached by a young woman in the street who asked her, 'aren't you *Richard II*?' That encounter has been repeated many times elsewhere. Others have stared at her with a puzzled look and asked, 'are you who I think you are?' Shaw laughs: 'I think I've got a lifetime of that ahead of me.' She often wishes that Cork audiences could see exciting productions of Shakespeare, and would have loved to have taken *Richard II* to her home town.

Typically, Shaw was rushing around in a hyperactive world, and seemed to be eternally between shows. At the same time as playing *Richard*, she delivered a high-styled comic performance in Congreve's Restoration classic, *The Way of the World*, also at the National.

Warner and Shaw – nicknamed the terrible twins by the critics – dived into unchartered waters with their staging of T. S. Eliot's 1922 epic poem of modern civilisation, *The Waste Land*. In 37 minutes alone on stage Shaw took her audiences through Eliot's haunting poem of terrible despair in one swift, electrifying burst, moving with intense power from character to character, voice to voice. Shaw's appearance – cropped hair and tall, lithe figure – helped to convey the poem's sexual ambiguities. The text wasn't written as a theatre piece, of course. Shaw's reading brought it roaring to life, mostly done in non-theatrical sites chosen by Warner for their atmospheric reaction.

In Brussels, where the piece originated in 1995, Warner found an abandoned department store in which she considered staging it down a lift shaft; in the end it was performed in an old discotheque building. *The Waste Land* was seen in The Magazine Fort in Dublin's Phoenix Park during the 1995 Dublin Theatre Festival. The production was taken to Paris, Montreal, Toronto and New York where it was greeted with standing ovations and rave reviews. Shaw made her US debut performing the poem in a run down abandoned theatre, *The Liberty*, on 42nd Street in New York. Their film version of *The Waste Land* premiered at the 1996 Cannes Film Festival. Away from the stage in New York, Shaw conducted master classes.

Shaw's interpretation of *The Waste Land*, and her previous award-winning performances, owed much to the encouragement of her partner. 'Deborah is the most precise and genius director,' she says. 'She is so brilliant because she doesn't talk about the thing, she only perfects it. In a way, she is the sculptor of imagination: you can come with a morass of ideas and she will sculpt them, whereas a lot of directors come with a conception and they want you to fit into it. She takes what you are and makes it out of that, which is a very wise way of working. She cuts away anything that you don't need and that prevents you from being absolutely near the centre of the thing itself. It's very slow work: she's very patient and very silent. The actors can racket away and she just quietly fixes everything.'

On a sunny day, 3 May, 1996, Fifi Wilson walked back through the gates of UCC – this time to receive an honorary doctorate of laws from the National University of Ireland to mark her outstanding achievements. Predictably, she was the centre of attention amid all the pomp and ceremony. She looked radiant and posed with her family for *The Examiner* photographer. 'I loved every minute of it,' she recalls. 'I felt very honoured because I was only somebody who barely studied philosophy. It was great fun to come back and meet everybody again.' A year later, Warner and Shaw accepted an invitation from the UCC Granary Theatre to stage *The Waste Land* at the Everyman Palace Theatre in Cork. Shaw says she wanted to bring the production to Cork 'as a fitting reply to that lovely degree given to me'.

There is always another project on the horizon, ready to take more risks with her take-no-prisoners approach. In early 1997, she made an insightful documentary for BBC Radio Four chronicling her two weeks in an enclosed nunnery in central London during which time she shared a life of seclusion without any contact with the outside world and observing silence for 22 hours a day. The documentary was compelling stuff. Shaw made further forays in front of the cameras: the film version of Jane Austen's *Persuasion*; *Jane Eyre*; a part in *The Butcher Boy*, Neil Jordan's adaptation of Pat McCabe's macabre novel; and also playing the Head of Intelligence in the film version of *The Avengers*. That's just for starters. 'I don't think I'm a workaholic,' she concludes, 'but I do think you have to work terribly hard to achieve anything worthwhile.' That's partly the secret of her success.

Looking to the future, she says: 'I am more interested in film. I look forward to being part of the new film industry, where we are telling our stories to ourselves. I would like to write a book about acting. I will return to UCC to lecture occasionally.'

She enjoys an independent lifestyle in London, and wouldn't have it any other way. Her diverse range of interests include travelling, cinema, gardening and archery.

As an actress, Fifi Wilson would like to be remembered for helping to bring younger generations into the theatre. 'I think it essential that the upcoming generations be excited by the theatre and the notion of its infinite possibilities. I will also continue to invent experiments that crack open the theatrical form.'

BEN DUNNE

THE BIG FELLA

BEN Dunne squatted at the bottom of a freshly-dug grave in the dark. Ironically, a hole in the ground prepared for the dead seemed the safest place in the world on the night of Wednesday, 21 October, 1981. The scene was the graveyard at St Patrick's Catholic Church, situated on an elevated site overlooking the tiny South Armagh village of Cullyhanna. Shortly before midnight, a car had stopped outside the church gates at Tullynavall Road, a few hundred yards from the village. Dunne, the 32-year-old supermarket millionaire, was bundled out onto the roadway by his kidnappers. They told him to turn his back as they removed a hood from his head, and not to look at the number plate of their car. He would be collected in about 20 minutes. And they were gone.

Dunne, heavily unshaven after six days in captivity and still clothed in the now tattered blue suit he was wearing at the time of his abduction, stood on the road paralysed with a mixture of fear and uncertainty. The sound of the car engine faded in the distance. It was a peaceful late autumn night in border country. He felt the cold hillside breeze against his face. He looked up at the bright starry sky, and then below saw the twinking lights of the scattered houses of Cullyhanna. Families settled into their beds, unaware that the young businessman at the centre of a massive police hunt on both sides of the border had been released unharmed outside their local church.

Dunne's first reaction was to thank the Lord he was free. Then panic set in. He felt like a caged animal, suddenly freed to the wild. He froze momentarily, and then bolted into the graveyard. His instinct was to hide, fearing the kidnappers or their accomplices might return to kill him. He took shelter first behind the headstones, and recalls in particular a large Celtic stone cross. He discovered a freshly dug grave and thought it would be a good hiding place. 'I wedged myself down into the ground,' he says, 'where I couldn't be seen.' His mind was a blur of 'crazy' thoughts as he squatted in the dirt. What if they came back and found him there? He could be shot dead and buried on the spot. 'Jaysus,' he said to himself, 'get out of here.' He climbed out of the grave. The sound of another car engine about half-an-hour later heightened his sense of foreboding. He heard a man shouting his name in a northern accent. He was bewildered, though slightly calmer after a short time on his own. If he heard someone calling his name earlier when first left on the road he'd have 'run a million miles'. It was Eamonn Mallie, a Belfast radio reporter who'd been tipped off by an anonymous telephone caller about Dunne's whereabouts. Mallie found him standing in the dark, dazed and nervous; dishevelled with his shirt open to his waist. Mallie confirmed his identity to Dunne who, in a confused state, asked him: 'Are you sure?' The reporter recalls the meeting: 'He reminded me of a young calf out for the first time. He was unsure of his ground, disoriented.' They knocked on the door of the nearby parochial house and were shown inside by the then parish priest, Fr Hugh O'Neill. The freed man made a phone call to a friend in Dublin and drank a bottle of Macardles ale at the fireside before being driven home by the reporter through the back roads of South Armagh and across the border to his family at Castleknock, Dublin. Once safely south of the border, he phoned his wife, Mary, from a kiosk about half an hour's journey from home.

Ireland's most controversial businessman spoke reluctantly of the kidnapping afterwards and then only to close friends. There was no professional counselling later. Amid all the well-publicised business and personal crises since, nobody knew that he had returned many times over the years to the graveyard at St Patrick's to retrace his steps and come to terms with the kidnapping in his own way. 'It doesn't feel weird or anything when I go back,' he says. 'It's just part of my history.' The experience on that fateful night left its mark: for one thing, it banished his fear of graveyards forever. 'Up to then I would have been afraid, but I wouldn't worry about the dead ones any more. I'd walk any graveyard now,' he says. What's more, he often does. Graveyards fascinate him. 'No matter where I am around the world I love calling into graveyards,' he explains. 'I was in Washington some time ago and spent a day in Arlington Cemetery. My father's people are buried in Rostrevor, Co. Down, and I've been there many times, not just to look at their graves. It's one of my interests.'

Looking back, the kidnapping was 'like something out of the movies'. It was business as usual for the joint managing director of the rich and powerful family firm on Thursday, 15 October, 1981. He chartered a small single-engine aircraft to return from the west of Ireland and touched down at Dublin Airport in the evening. He drove to head office at Henry

Street where he met his parents. They talked business and about their next retail project: opening a new supermarket in Portadown, Co. Armagh. Dunnes Stores, at the time ranked seventh of the top 500 Irish businesses, had over 40 branches in the Republic and had been expanding in Northern Ireland since the '70s. The chain already had outlets in Belfast, Lisburn, Larne, Antrim, Bangor, Warrenpoint, Newry and Coleraine with an annual turnover of £15 million in the north. He told his father, Ben Senior, company founder and chairman, that evening about his plans to drive north to Portadown early next morning to open the doors of the new store at 10 a.m. He was looking forward to the trip in his new black 500 SEL Mercedes. Before leaving Henry Street, his mother, Nora, said: 'Don't forget to wear the safety belt. Goodbye.' He chided her for using the word goodbye. 'Mum, don't say goodbye. I'll see you soon.'

Given the advance publicity about the new shop, it was relatively easy for the kidnap gang to map out the businessman's itinerary on the morning of Friday, 16 October. They were suspected to have been a gang of maverick Provisional IRA men known in the border area as 'The Edentubber Brigade' who planned a spectacular fundraising operation. The trap was laid south of the Killeen border customs post on the main road to Newry. Dunne was travelling at around 70-80 mph when a green Opel car, heading south on the other side, overtook a lorry and then pulled diagonally across the road in front of him. The lorry driver, who witnessed the set up, was forced to stop. Dunne saw the car blocking the road and took evasive action: he 'stood on the brakes', swerved over to the side of the road to avoid the car and continued for another 100 yards before coming to a halt. He hit the brakes so hard he could see smoke coming from his tyres. He got a jolt but was okay, saying to himself: 'Thanks be to God, mum told me to wear the safety belt.' He recalls the roadside scene in a sequence of slow-motion images: 'I was unclicking the belt and opening the door to let some air in. I could see in the mirror they were coming back towards me. I thought they were coming to apologise for making such a stupid move.'

Four masked men, armed with rifles, ordered him out of the car. He thought something or somebody would intervene to stop them. One of the men dragged him by the arm and pushed him inside the back seat of the green car. Two of the men sat on either side of him. They handed him a hood and told him to pull it over his head. The car spun around and drove in the direction of the south. 'Are you going to shoot me,' asked Dunne. 'For fuck's sake,' said one of them, 'if we wanted to shoot you we'd have shot you on the side of the road.' He asked them to let him say some prayers before anything else happened. 'Look,' snapped the gunman, 'I'm telling you, we're not fuckin' shooting you.' Dunne decided 'to give this thing a chance because your natural instinct to survive takes over'.

After a 20-minute car journey, he was taken out and brought to a kind of shed with stone walls and a mud floor. All the time the hood was over his head. He was left there for a few hours. He guessed they were after a ransom. Later, as the British security forces approached the area, he was pulled out and dragged through the fields, running with two of them on either side and still wearing the hood. He asked them to slow down. They shouted the Brits were too close and kept running until they reached a ditch where they stopped for a while. They moved beside a road. When traffic passed they told him to get his head down, poking him in the ribs with the muzzle of a gun. Then he was bundled into another vehicle and driven for about 15 minutes to the house that would be his prison for six days.

Nothing in his privileged Cork upbringing could have prepared him for the psychological torment of being a hostage, with a death sentence hanging over him for six days. Those long hours were spent in a bedroom, in darkness, with the hood only taken off at night. First, they laid down the rules: nothing would happen as long as he did what he was told; he couldn't make even the slightest physical move without asking permission. He was forced to lie on a hard floor throughout the day, and helped on to a bed at night. 'I was wedged between the bed and the wall during the day,' he recalls. 'There was a window. I'd be underneath the window lying down on the floor.' He tried to avoid stiffness by moving his body into different positions: from his back to his side, from his side to his stomach. He was guarded by at least two men all the time. Every time he shifted into a new position he had to tell them beforehand. 'I'm moving now, okay?' It demanded mental strength to cope with being treated like a trapped animal, dumped on the floor. 'I've often wondered since how I was able to do it, but I did it,' he says. 'It's amazing what you can do when there are guns pointed at you.' He was given food and had to partially lift up the hood to eat or drink. He was 'scared stiff' so food didn't bother him at all. If he saw anything he would be shot. He says he didn't look at anything, even if he had the opportunity.

The kidnappers kept in touch with the nationwide police and army search by listening to news bulletins. Upon arrival at the house on the Friday evening, the captured man heard the first bulletin coming from another room. The gravel voice of RTÉ newsreader Maurice O'Doherty told the nation at six o'clock that 30-year-old businessman Ben Dunne had been kidnapped on his way to work in Northern Ireland; at seven o'clock he said that 32-year-old Ben Dunne had been kidnapped; and then at eight o'clock that 34-year-old Dunne had been kidnapped. O'Doherty managed to age him by four years in two hours. 'I remember thinking that's the only thing they've got right because I'm certainly ageing quickly with the fear I was under.'

There was little communication between Dunne and his kidnappers, apart from the gang's demands for contact names and telephone numbers. He thinks those guarding him were under instructions to keep conversations to a minimum. One of them was referred to by the others as 'boss'. They told him at first they weren't going to hold him for long, and daily promises that he'd be out each night evaporated. As he lay for hours on the floor, hooded, Dunne experienced extreme mood swings, from elation at the thought of freedom to depression at the fear of not seeing his family again. 'I'd say there were huge swings that played on my mind,' he says. 'For the first day or two, I was convinced I was getting out. Then, no, I wasn't getting out. I was going through highs and lows every couple of hours. Sometimes you felt confident about things. Other times, you'd ask yourself, "what am I doing here?".' During the low moments he convinced himself he wouldn't get out alive. There were regrets: if only he had more time with his wife and children to say a proper farewell. He prayed and talked to God, too. At some point, he came to the conclusion that these periods of 'highs and lows' were counter-productive. It's how his father would have reacted in the same situation: tough and determined to brazen it through. Tough guys don't crack under pressure. He told himself to 'cut this out, hang in, hold on, you're going to survive this'. Anyway, if they decided to shoot him, there was nothing he could do to stop them.

The high-profile kidnapping put everybody under pressure. The Irish and British governments were under pressure not to give in to the kidnappers and yet secure Dunne's safe release. The Taoiseach, Dr Garret FitzGerald, called in the British ambassador on the day after Dunne was kidnapped. The Gardaí and RUC were under political pressure to get a result. But he was being held in the 'no-go' area of South Armagh where there had been no real policing, where the border was criss-crossed by minor roads and where the rough terrain provided perfect cover. A British Army SAS squad was ordered into South Armagh. The Dunne family, the richest in the land, were under pressure to pay up: indeed, they were willing to strike a deal and made a number of attempts to pay a ransom. It was a battle of wills between police on both sides of the border, the Dunne family, kidnappers and the IRA leadership especially around Crossmaglen. IRA leaders were embarrassed at the large number of police and army raids: the kidnapping was badly timed for them as they planned to step up their campaign in Britain and launch a fresh border offensive. They made it clear to the Edentubber Group – so called after a village in Co. Armagh – that the time had come to end the kidnapping.

The release was carried out in great secrecy on the night of Wednesday, 21 October. Fr Dermod McCarthy, a close family friend who married the couple, had met three masked and armed men at Hackballs Cross in Co. Louth on the previous Sunday night and managed to give them a note for Dunne before the meeting was intercepted by an Irish security patrol. On Wednesday, Fr McCarthy broadcast a nationwide appeal to the kidnappers. 'Cut your losses now,' he pleaded. 'Release Ben and get out fast while you still have time.' The businessman said the priest's radio appeal, heard by the kidnappers, came 'like Manna from Heaven'. Afterwards, they told him he would be freed. Later, on Wednesday evening, gardaí along the border were alerted to a possible fourth bid to pay a ransom. There were reports that a car had left the northside of Dublin carrying a large amount of cash and heading for the north. Hundreds of cars were stopped and searched in the Dundalk area. But the search was hampered by thousands of football fans pouring into Dundalk for the Dundalk-Spurs European Cup match.

Dunne recalls 'rumblings' on Wednesday night that he might be let go. He disregarded them 'because I heard that so many times before and, anyway, I was in the frame of mind that I wasn't about to go through any more highs and lows. I didn't let it affect me.' Then it happened. 'Come on, you're going,' a voice shouted to him. He was taken from the house and put into the back seat of a car, still hooded. The kidnappers gave him a souvenir: three bullets, two from Armalite rifles and a third from a revolver used to guard him in the house. It all ended outside the churchyard in Cullyhanna. Dunne had no idea whether he was in the north or in the republic. The border was two miles west as the crow flies, and Dundalk about 10 miles away. To this day, Dunne won't comment publicly about whether a £500,000 ransom was paid. Freedom was an 'unbelievable' feeling. 'To put it simply, it's no different than if your finger is caught in a door,' he says. 'The moment it's released, even though the pain might still be there, you know it's over and you're out of it. That's the kind of feeling I had.'

Mallie, the reporter who collected Dunne at the churchyard, now sums up: 'He was a very lucky man because a lot of people didn't come out of South Armagh alive.' Ben Dunne Senior, the Rostrevor-born self-made millionaire and a man of few, if any, words for the media, stated: 'We thank God for this happy outcome.' He soon realised that his son was destined to be a national figure. A few days later, he told young Ben: 'You know, you've really made it. I was walking down the street today. I saw two people pointing at me and heard one saying to the other, "look, there's Ben Dunne's father".'

The kidnapping had psychological after-effects, which he accepts he should have handled through professional help. But he won't use the abduction as a convenient excuse for his cocaine and call-girl escapade in Florida that hit the headlines in 1992. 'I'm not blaming the kidnapping for anything I've done afterwards,' he insists. 'I suppose there were a certain amount of psychological hang-ups that I should have dealt with. The kidnapping was done to me by somebody else. What happened in Florida I did to myself. In the case of the kidnapping, I suppose I should have learned to be thankful that I survived it.' He has long since come to terms with the events of October 1981 and says he doesn't harbour any grudges against the kidnappers; 'none whatsoever'. Hypothetically speaking, if they said sorry now, 'I'd accept their apologies. I'd have no difficulty with that!'

By any yardstick, the drama-filled life and times of Ben Dunne have been extraordinary. He is one of Ireland's richest men, with a fortune loosely estimated between £80-100 million. He once swept the floors of his father's shops and ended up running a £1 billion pound retail empire with his brother and sisters. He worked hard, and played even harder. A big, affable man, full of bonhomie, who likes a good laugh and good company. He's happiest on the golf course or sipping a quiet pint with locals in a country pub. The landmark events of his life would have stretched the wildest imagination of Hollywood scriptwriters: kidnapped by terrorists in 1981; busted for cocaine after frolicking with an escort girl in a Florida hotel and later sent on a drug treatment programme to London in 1992; ousted as executive chairman of the family firm with a reported £125 million settlement in 1994; startling revelations of his stewardship and highly unorthodox payments to suppliers including a Dunnes-funded extension to the Co. Tipperary home of former Transport, Energy and Communications Minister Michael Lowry; next, his sensational disclosures at the 1997 Tribunal of Inquiry into Dunnes payments to politicians that he had paid £1.3 million to then Taoiseach Charles Haughey. Looking back, he says he's amazed at everything that happened to him from 1974-97. It all happened so fast: it seemed more like a 10-year period than 23 years. 'Lord God, I've never seen time to go so quickly,' he says. 'It flew. It was just one thing after another.'

Ben Dunne is a Corkman, though the family's roots can be traced to Northern Ireland. His grandfather, Barney Dunn, was known as a colourful character in Rostrevor, Co. Down, where he made a good living as an auctioneer and also had a café on the quay that attracted tourists. He delighted in being the life and soul of the pub, but drank far too much and was really a sad figure behind the alcoholic's mask. He married Margaret Byrne from Co. Kilkenny who started a drapery business and a shipping agency for people in the locality taking the emigrant ships. She was well liked, and fluent in a couple of foreign languages. They had three children: Annie (1906), Bernard (1908) and Denis John (1909).

The first Bernard wanted to go places. As a schoolboy, he made money by fixing punctures and mending bicycles for his pals in Rostrevor. He left school at the age of 14, drawn to business where he knew money could be made. His first job was shortlived, at Quinn's of the Milestone in Newry, which was part of a chain of stores across Down and Antrim. Mr Quinn spotted the youngster one morning and asked him his age. 'You're too young to be working here,' he snapped, handing him a 10-shilling note before showing him the door. Ben's pride was wounded, and he decided he would buy out Quinn's one day. And he did.

Around this time Ben, who was better known as Benny, thought of emigrating to America. His mother got him a job as a draper's apprentice in Anderson's, Drogheda. The rule was that all apprentices had to live over the shop. In time, while serving as a union official, he did a deal with the firm to make his own living arrangements. The union was incensed that he should get special treatment. So he broke ranks with the union, and moved on. The union had lost a potential leader. He added an 'e' to his surname in the south. After serving his time at Cameron's department store in Longford, he moved south to Roches Stores in Cork during the mid-1930s. His father's alcoholism had caused a lot of friction in the family. Within a decade, the rest of his family, including his mother, joined him in Cork. Barney Dunne was buried in Rostrevor in February 1949, after spending the last years of his life in a workhouse.

Ben didn't have to look far for a wife in the late 1930s. Nora Moloney, one of four sisters working in Roches Stores on Patrick Street, caught his eye. The Moloneys had settled in Midleton. Their father, Pat, was a butcher who came originally from Abbeyfeale. Nora, a tall and striking woman, was ambitious and like Ben wanted to make something of her life. She was a sales assistant and he had a buyer's job. He was a 'good catch' for the butcher's daughter. They were married in Midleton on 5 September, 1939.

Ben thrived in the retail business. He was so good that he earned more than his salary in bonuses at Roches during the early '40s. The boss, Mr Fitzgerald, called him into the office one day, paid him his bonus and told him: 'You're now earning more than some of the directors.' Ben retorted: 'But, Mr Fitzgerald, I'm worth more than the directors.' The boss said they couldn't afford to keep paying him. Again, it was time to move on to bigger things. He went into partnership with a friend, Des Darrer, also from the North, and they leased a vacant premises, Luke Burke's drapery store, opposite Roches at 105 Patrick Street, in 1944. That's how it all began.

The business landscape of Cork was dominated by the merchant prince families who resented an outsider opening his doors on Patrick Street. While they were on the golf course or sailing their yachts he was on the shopfloor, selling 'Blarney socks at sixpence a pair'. He put everything into building up the business, including his young family. The key to his success was low profit margins based on high turnover. He was even willing to sell below cost just to get people to cross the street and come in his door.

Ben and Nora Dunne made their first home in the middle-class Cork suburb of Douglas, at Browningstown Park. They had six children: Margaret, Frank, Anne, Elizabeth, Bernard and Therese. Ben Junior, the second youngest, was born on 11 March, 1949. His earliest memory is of their next home at Barnstead, a splendid detached house on a few acres facing St Michael's Church at Church Road, Blackrock. As a small child he had some close shaves. At the age of two he nearly died after suffering severe burns and electric shock. He had been put to bed at home in Barnstead. Their parents heard screams coming from the bedroom. Ben had chewed the electric wires from a bedside lamp. He took them from his mouth and they stuck to his hands. The scars are still visible on his hands to this day. At the age of 10, he was nearly killed in a riding accident on their land at Church Road. Their father had knocked a wall between two fields and the rubble lay in a heap. Ben was on the back of a pony, Planet, belonging to his older brother, Frank. The animal bolted and threw him from the saddle. His foot got caught in the stirrup and he was dragged along the ground. Luckily, the leather strap broke and released him before the pony jumped over the remains of the wall. Otherwise he would have been smashed against the stones. He broke his leg.

Ben Junior was concocting schemes from an early stage. He got fed up spending all his pocket money on chewing gum at Miss Cotter's sweetshop in the hope of getting a free 'squeezie mouse'. To win the prize you had to find a black piece of gum in the pack. He bought gum for weeks, but to no avail. So he used his water colours at home to paint the gum black. He returned to the shop next day, bought another pack of gum and made the switch outside. He walked back in and said, excitedly: 'Look, Miss Cotter, I've got the black one.' He won the 'squeezie' at long last.

Nora and Ben Dunne were good parents: they provided well for their young family but did not spoil them. They worked tirelessly to expand the shops in the '50s, first to North Main Street in Cork and on to Waterford. The firm's founder preferred to do things his way, so the partnership with Darrer ended and he struck out on his own. Thus the Dunnes empire was born. He was unstoppable. By the time the business had expanded to Henry Street, and then Georges Street, in Dublin at the end of the '50s, he spent the working week in the capital, returning to Cork by train on Saturday nights.

As a father and businessman, Ben Senior was 'firm but fair'. Ben Junior became particularly close to his father in later life. He feels the communication is better between today's generation of parents and their teenage children. 'My kids find it a lot easier to talk to me,' he says. 'I'll go out with my sons and have a pint with them. They bring their pals home. Everything is more open. I loved my parents but when I had a problem I wouldn't necessarily go and talk to them about it.'

Of his brother and sisters, Ben Junior was closest to Therese, the youngest of the family. Ben and Therese were known as 'the two young ones'. They usually stayed at home when the four others went on holiday to the South of France. By Ben Junior's teens, the Dunnes had sold Barnstead and bought Ringmahon House, a mansion complete with a 100-acre farm on land that later became the suburb of Mahon beside Blackrock.

Ben Junior's youth was divided between school and the shop floor. He went to school at the Presentation Brothers College on the Western Road, one of the city's premier schools with a big rugby reputation. He was a quiet, gentle type who wasn't academically inclined. Former Lord Mayor of Cork, Jim Corr, who taught him History and Maths in fourth year, says he was an unremarkable student, always cooperative and respectful towards the teachers. His old classmates say he gave up a lot of free time to work in his father's shops. And he always seemed to have plenty of pocket money. Ben Junior was also known as Benny to his pals, just like his father before him. He didn't like school and preferred to be packing shelves in Dunnes Stores than doing homework. The students were separated according to their ability into groups of As, A1s and Bs. He never got further than the Bs. 'I didn't like school and couldn't get out of the place quick enough,' he recalls. 'You see, I was working from the age of twelve, wheeling and dealing and packing shelves. I'd come out of school at four o'clock and while other lads went playing rugby or going home to study I'd go down to Patrick Street and start packing shelves. I was getting a shilling an hour. I used to say to myself, "what in the name of God is all this study for when I could be earning 10 shillings a week?" I did the Inter Cert and scraped through it.' A close schoolfriend, Barry Twomey, son of the late Bill Twomey who managed the Cork Opera House, recalls that while he and other lads hung around the Savoy Cinema after school, chatting up the girls from St Aloysius and Scoil Mhuire, Ben Junior was working in his father's shop. Flying model airplanes was a big hobby, especially out at the Lee Fields on fine days.

During his last two years at school, he spent the summer holidays and all his days off working in the shops at Patrick Street or North Main Street. The boss's son was treated no differently than anybody else and got a bollocking if he messed up. He met some great characters who regarded his father as a tough task master but who knew that he rewarded loyalty and hard work. Joe Holt, who ran the grocery business, had once been their gardener at Barnstead and farm manager at Ringmahon.

At the age of 16, it seemed perfectly logical to quit school and follow the rest of the family into the shops. His oldest sister, Margaret, had been involved in the business since the age of 14 when her father stuck a sweeping brush in her hand and told her to sweep the floor of the Patrick Street store. Dan Barrett, one of the senior men at Dunnes, could see that Ben Junior was 'fierce keen' so he asked the chairman to 'let him go on'. Ben would never have gone to college anyway, although in hindsight he feels he may not have done certain things in his life if he had had more education.

He started off in the hardware department in 1965, and remembers going every Tuesday morning to buy pots and pans from Dwyers, the big wholesalers in Cork. Then he won promotion to the fruit and veg counter, where he learned some early lessons about buying and selling perishable goods. The first was that if bananas over-ripened before he sold them, he had no option but to dump them. He was stung many times but soon wised up. A local supplier had bought a load of bananas in the Canaries and offered them to him. The young Dunnes buyer knew the bananas were being ripened in a warehouse while he negotiated on price over a few days. He told the supplier: 'If we don't do a decent deal then you're going to get nothing for your bananas.' He got his price. He struck another deal with a supplier of tomatoes. The produce was delivered in 'lovely timber boxes' which, at the end of every day, were always collected by the supplier. Dunne stopped the practice, 'knowing right well that the guy would come forward looking for the boxes'. It turned out that the boxes were being re-used by the supplier to grow plants. 'I told him I'd another use for them,' he says. 'So we negotiated a deal and I sold him the boxes from then on.' Meanwhile, as a hardy youngster he was also put to work on the farm at Ringmahon. He bought and sold animals, and spent Mondays in the cattle mart. He tended the sheep, too. 'I lambed so many sheep as a young fellow,' he says, 'that I can't stand lamb today. I don't eat lamb at all. Even the smell is offputting. I decided that whatever happened I'd never become a farmer.'

Saturday nights were spent on the dancefloor where the mating game was played in the '60s. The girls followed young showband idols and the boys chased the girls who chased them. Dunne danced to the showband beat at the Majorca Ballroom in Crosshaven. He particularly liked The Freshmen from Ballymena and was a fan of the late Rory Gallagher, who played guitar with the Impact showband around Cork. He went to dances at Highfield and Dolphin rugby clubs as well as the Lee rowing club. He says he wasn't a good dancer. Another favourite haunt on a Saturday night was Bunnyconnellan bar, overlooking the sea at Myrtleville. He had an eye for the girls, and did two 'steadies' during his late teens in Cork. He took girlfriends to the rugby club dances or to the pictures at the Savoy Cinema.

His first car was an Anglia and then a Triumph 2000. But he nearly came a cropper in the Triumph while on the way to a party with Barry Twomey at Crosshaven one night. Young Dunne lost control as the car went into a bad bend. It left the road, hit a telegraph pole, went over a ditch and ended upside down in a dyke. 'I froze in the car,' he recalls. 'There was a smell of smoke. I thought it was going to blow up and I'd had it. Barry managed to push out the door on his side, put in his hand and drag me out.'

Twomey, now a travel agent in New York, says Ben Junior was a 'sound guy'. The two pals once competed for the same girl. 'Benny had a car and I had a motorbike, so he won.' Twomey dated his late sister, Therese. Benny was protective of his youngest sister. When Twomey brought her home after dances at Dolphin, his pal always followed behind to make sure there were no unscheduled stops along the way.

Ben Senior flourished in the '60s culture of enterprise. The policies of Taoiseach Seán Lemass and his economics guru, T. K. Whitaker, encouraged initiative. The drapery trade was a perfect feast for Dunne's entrepreneurial appetite, and he started a retailing revolution. The Cork, Patrick Street flagship had become part of a chain of 10 by 1964. Outlets at Georges Street and Henry Street in Dublin were followed by expansion in the south of the city and the Cornelscourt development. Their slogan was aggressive: 'Dunnes Stores Better Value Beats Them All'. Dunne Senior pushed himself hard as the business grew in the '60s and '70s, and never saw any limits to his business. 'He always felt that things could only go forward or backwards and should never be static,' explains Ben Junior. 'If you put him on a football team, and they were two or three goals up, he'd want to score more goals and keep playing until the final whistle.' American businessmen once voted Ben Senior 'The Most Outstanding Retailer in the World'. At home, *Checkout* Magazine named him 'Man of the Year' in 1980, an honour that also went to his son subsequently. When he died in 1983, the empire comprised 64 retail branches, including the Quinn chain in Northern Ireland, had 3,500 employees and a turnover of £350 million.

The founder had always kept one step ahead of the competition, predicting business trends before the rest. He went on regular trips to America where he got ideas for the supermarket business. He promoted the *St Bernard* trademark at Irish trade fairs in the States, much to the displeasure of the then Finance Minister, Charles Haughey, who made his feelings known to the draper. Ben Senior had the reputation as being a tough businessman, who once boasted: 'I don't get ulcers, I give them.' Buying in huge bulk quantities gave him the power to dictate long credit terms with suppliers. The suppliers could take it or leave it. Some of them even had to stack his shelves as part of the agreement. The key to making money in the retail game, particularly in the lower margin grocery area, was through cash control. If a supermarket chain got long credit terms from suppliers and expanded sales at the same time, then this generated a huge cash flow which could be invested profitably for short periods with the banks. The company founder once remarked that he felt more like a banker than a retailer. He despised publicity, and disliked the way other businessmen boasted. 'The two people I don't like are the people who talk about what they've done and the people who talk about what they're going to do,' he said. Asked to do a radio interview, he said he would only say one thing: 'Dunnes Stores, better value, beats them all.'

The Dunnes chairman brought his children into the business. Dunnes Stores was family owned and family controlled: Dunne Senior passed on to his children a code of conduct and philosophy of life and they were expected to live up to his high standards. He promoted an ethic of hard work and religious belief for his family and workforce. He was a religious man, too, who went to Mass every day and recited the Rosary at night with his wife, Nora.

Ben Junior idolised and feared his father. 'I was frightened of him in those days,' he says. 'No question about it. He'd give you a right good snarl; maybe not the first time, but you wouldn't want to make the same mistake a second time. He'd never sit you down in the office for a chat. He gave it to you straight and what you saw was what you got. He was extremely firm but extremely fair. If there had been a ferocious row and he bumped into you 20 minutes later on a different issue it had all been forgotten. He didn't hold grudges.'

Ben Junior was toughened up in business by his father. He learned how to cut a deal and make a profit. The philosophy was blissfully simple: give the customers what they want at the right price and they'll come back for more. So he built up the *St Bernard* label and dressed and fed generations at a price they could afford. Ben Junior says his father's greatest asset was common sense. 'If someone wanted to sell him something and told him it was selling in Roches Stores for 40 pounds and he could sell it for 10 pounds, the first question he asked was not about the cost price but how much was the customer prepared to pay for it. His approach was: what did the customer want and how much would they pay for it? He often told me that in his early days he'd go into a showroom. The guy would show him his whole range. But all my father wanted to know was what they were sold out of. Whatever was sold out and he couldn't have, then these were the best selling lines. And they were the only lines he wanted. He used to say, too, that you couldn't teach people to be great businessmen. Otherwise, the world would be full of Ben Dunnes.'

Ben Junior moved to Dublin in 1969. He'd actually been commuting between the cities for two years, leaving Cork on Tuesday mornings and returning on Friday evenings. His father told him to make up his mind and decide whether he wanted to work in Cork or Dublin. After moving to head office, he took responsibility for footwear and menswear and, later, the food side of the business. Ben Senior made Junior a director of the firm while in his early twenties. And he got married in the early '70s to Mary Godwin, an air hostess from Kilkenny.

Ben Junior moved to the heart of what was already the biggest private company in the State. He was at his father's side, now the apparent heir to the chairmanship during the firm's expansion in the late '70s. His parents lived in the Shelbourne Hotel. Ben Senior maintained strong religious commitment, doing the Stations of the Cross every morning before going to work. Ben drew particularly close to his father during this period. 'We got on really well,' he says. 'That's when I really saw the way he operated, the angles he saw on things and the fairness of the man.' He also saw another side of his father: someone who suffered at least some anxieties. After doing the Stations of the Cross one morning, Ben Senior told his son he felt that people in the church were staring at him and talking behind his back. Young Ben told him to take no notice. 'It might have been his own imagination', he says, 'but I think he suffered from some low self-esteem'.

On his father's death in 1983, Ben Junior and his older brother, Frank, became joint managing directors, with three of their four sisters also involved in the business.

Ben Junior, the proverbial chip off the old block, was very much the driving force. He continued his father's policy of expansion, first in Northern Ireland and then in the North of England. Dunnes expanded on the home market with a huge store in Tallaght and the St Stephen's Green Centre in Dublin. The empire dropped anchor in new shopping centres around the country, among them Merchants Quay, Douglas and Bishopstown in Cork. Their turnover in the grocery trade alone in the Republic was around £400 million, holding over 20% of the market. The chain had over 50 outlets in the Republic. Dunnes was the fourth biggest business in the country, with annual turnover estimated at over £900 million and profits over £50 million. The company was managed very tightly, with a constant flow of information from all branches to the Dublin HQ and the other family members installed in top management positions.

But the public perception was that it was Ben's company. It was a private company, too, which meant he could go to war at a moment's notice with the opposition. Sitting on a money mountain of millions, he could sustain the cost of undercutting the competition. Dunne engaged in milk and bread price wars with the other chains, particularly Quinnsworth. He kept intense pressure on his suppliers for extra credit. There were battles with the Confederation of Irish Industry over credit periods for suppliers, and also with the Director of Consumer Affairs over Dunnes' free £5 vouchers scheme at Tallaght. He had little time for the unions and refused to back down during the bitter strike over the handling of South African fruit from 1984-1987 at the Dunnes' Henry Street branch. Those closest to Dunne during his years at the helm describe him as tough, but impossible to dislike.

Like his father, he personally shunned publicity. Unlike his father, however, he was a much more social animal: he played hard and enjoyed the company of close friends. There was certainly a ruthless streak in business, but also astounding generosity. A picture emerges of a genuinely good-natured person who thought nothing of writing cheques for charitable organisations, doing a good turn for friends in trouble or even picking up the tab for pals who accompanied him on golfing trips. His largesse towards politicians only surfaced after he had departed the family firm. He has always been a good family man, devoting a lot of time to his four children: three sons and a daughter. He could be counted on to attend their school events, family celebrations and even took them to pop concerts. Typically, he took them to the Michael Jackson concert at Páirc Uí Chaoimh in Cork in 1988 when during the show, to his delight, the younger ones were asked to join other children on stage with their pop idol.

On Thursday morning, 20 February, 1992, police in Orlando, Florida, were alerted by the Hyatt Regency-owned Grand Cypress Hotel to an incident involving one of their guests on the seventeenth floor. Police officers found a man standing near a railing on a balcony overlooking the interior atrium of the hotel. He was shouting for the police and saying he was being surrounded. They spent 65 minutes convincing him to go back into his room. They handcuffed him and, during a search, found cocaine in his pocket and inside his luggage as well as nearly $10,000 in the room safe. After being taken to a local hospital, the chairman of Dunnes Stores was charged with trafficking in cocaine because the amount found, 32.5 grammes, was above the limit deemed by the Florida State to be for personal use. To make matters worse, the drug-induced paranoia on the seventeenth floor had been witnessed by a substantial number of guests. Dunne was taken to Orange County Jail, released on bail of $25,000 and flew home to Ireland in disgrace. He had brought shame on the Dunnes' empire; he knew if his father were alive he'd have blown a fuse.

It was an escapade too far for the extravagant Dunnes' boss who had gone to Florida on a golfing expedition with a group of friends. In hindsight, he's sure the panic attack was caused by a flashback, in his drugged state, to the 1981 kidnapping and a fear of being taken again. After snorting a large quantity of cocaine and worried about his stash of money, he summoned hotel security to his room, number 1708. In a moment of paranoia, he didn't think the security staff who turned up were bona fide, and he panicked. He recalls: 'Normally I'd expect security men in a hotel in America to be in uniform. Instead, along comes this fellow in a pair of black trousers, with one of those narrow little leather ties and a pony tail. I said to myself, "this fellow isn't security, what's going wrong here?" So I made a run out. I just went into a spin and flipped. I was actually shouting out the names of fellows staying in the hotel with me. The breakfast room was down below. I didn't realise that your voice doesn't carry 17 floors. Then the police came and said, "stand back". I said to myself, 'Jaysus, what's going on here?' Now there were guys with guns. Some of the papers wrote that I was threatening suicide but that's not what happened. There was never any intention of jumping or suicide. That's a bit of folklore. Then I had to come home and face my wife and face the music. I'm not a fellow who believes in running away.'

Luckily, Dunne escaped a jail sentence. The serious trafficking charge was dropped after the police search of his hotel room had been found to be illegal. The penalty of his Florida escapade was a $5,000 fine, legal fees and a month at a drug abuse clinic in London. 'I wouldn't have anything to do with drugs today because, first, I know it would be bad for me and, second, I'm really happy with what I have in life today. There was a period in my life when I lost respect for myself. I went down a path for a particular period – short, thanks be to God – but I've learned by it. The bottom line is that once you lose respect for yourself, you're liable to do anything. You'll squander money. You're quite capable of using drugs. For example, it's only when people get a heart attack that they say, "I'm going off the smokes now". Well, my heart attack in relation to using drugs was what happened in Florida. That was my crossroads.'

In a sense, getting caught in Florida was the best thing to happen to Big Ben. It put him on the road to self-discovery, and that wasn't an easy journey. In characteristic blunt language, he says his brain was like a computer without a programme. That programming started in therapy at the London clinic.

The ripples caused by Dunne's drug conviction went wider than he imagined: triggering a chain of events that led to his removal as executive chairman of Dunnes Stores, the Price Waterhouse report on his stewardship, the revelations of payments to top politicians, the tribunal chaired by Mr Justice Brian McCracken and, ultimately and indirectly, to the public humiliation of Charles J. Haughey.

Dunne knew his stewardship of the family firm was on the line: like any manager of Dunnes Stores, he put had his job at risk by taking drugs. The scandal of his cocaine-and-escort girl adventure was the talk of the nation. The fallout caused a bitter dispute over the future control of the retail chain. Ben Dunne was dismissed by the board as executive chairman in 1993. After nearly two years of feuding, Ben settled with his family for a reported £125 million in November 1994 to give up his shares in the company. It was a 'kick in the pants' to be removed from the chairmanship. 'I've had those kicks all my life and I'm sure I'll get a lot more of them,' he says, philosophically of his dismissal. 'That's life. You don't go through this world without getting plenty of kicks in the pants. You have to cope. Looking back, I would now say it was a great thing to happen to me because I've gotten on with my life. I've new interests. I've a fantastic relationship with my wife and kids. My priorities have changed for the better, no question about it. I'm family oriented and I'm not chasing my tail.'

However, he concedes it was hard to walk away from the family firm. 'It's like when somebody dies you're full of hurt. But everything passes and moves on. Time is a fantastic healer. I've no grudges against anybody in the family. It's like when you get separated or divorced the weak one will always hold a grudge against the other partner. Although I have weaknesses I'm not a weak man. I got a very good deal from my family. I'm very happy with my life.'

In spite of the much-publicised disputes between Ben and his sister Margaret Heffernan – the new head of the store – he says that blood is thicker than water. Of course he would shake hands with her and the rest of the family. 'Anytime I see her we say hello and have a chat. Her kids hang around with my kids. All the normal things. The media says things to sell newspapers but I'm not going to ring them up and say, "you're wrong". Any rows I've had with my family have been about business. I've been in business all my life and, by Jaysus, I've had some rows with people, but that doesn't go on after hours. I don't say, "there's that so-and-so and I won't talk to them." Look at politics. You'll see fellows in politics going at each other's throats during the day. After hours they don't go on that way. It's the same in business. There's none of that bitterness whatsoever.' Another personal loss came with the deaths of his sisters, Therese and Elizabeth, after he had departed from Dunnes Stores. 'It was a huge blow,' he says. 'That's life. It was no different for me than for anyone else who loses members of their families.'

Big Ben set sail on new business adventures, his bank balance boosted by millions. He set his sights on property investment and the leisure industry and built a massive £7 million health, fitness and leisure centre, called Westpoint, at Blanchardstown in Co. Dublin. He swapped a business suit for a track suit. He injected the same philosophy as before: providing customers with the best service possible at the best price. He likes the business and even uses the exercise bikes himself. 'I've no big ambitions at Westpoint,' he says. 'I'll see how this goes, and if it goes well, I'll look at building another one. I'm heading towards 50 years of age and I'm very happy with what I have out of life.'

Then came the Dunnes Payments Tribunal that made Ben Dunne Newsmaker of the Year in 1997. He took a starring role in the best show in town. His evidence was like Russian Roulette for top politicians: skeletons locked away for years came tumbling out of the cupboards. The nation was given a rare insight into his unorthodox business practices at Dunnes: the way he paid his suppliers and rewarded his friends. High-flying Fine Gael Minister Michael Lowry, who had a business relationship with Dunnes, paid a heavy price for doing things Ben's way. Ben's generosity to politicians went all the way to the top: he'd even given £1.3 million to the former Taoiseach, Charles Haughey, between 1987–1991. Charlie was in financial trouble and Ben felt sorry for him. On his way home from a round of golf, he personally handed the then Taoiseach three bank drafts to fictitious names in November, 1991, totalling £210,000. This handout was given to Haughey at Abbeville, his mansion in north County Dublin. 'There's something for yourself,' Ben told Charlie. 'Thanks, big fella,' he replied. Haughey led the tribunal on a merry dance before he eventually came to Dublin Castle with his hands up. It was the day a legend died.

Haughey had consistently denied receiving any money from Dunne until very late in the seven-month operation of the tribunal. Now he accepted he received £1.3 million, including the three drafts for £210,000. He said all his financial affairs in the relevant period had been dealt with by his adviser, the late Des Traynor. He apologised for his failure to co-operate with the tribunal. The tribunal report –published on 25 August, 1997 – delivered a blunt verdict on Haughey: it could not accept or believe much of his evidence. Lowry was criticised for tax evasion, assisted by Dunne. The report found no evidence of any favours sought of Haughey by Dunne. And it found no evidence of any political impropriety by Lowry for the benefit of Dunnes Stores. The report concluded that Ben Dunne appeared to be trying to 'buy the friendship' of a powerful politician when he made the payments to Haughey. The tribunal summed up Dunne as 'an impetuously generous person' – he escaped the more serious criticism meted out to the other two main players in the drama. After considering the implications of the McCracken Report, the Fianna Fáil/Progressive Democrats government decided to hold a second tribunal of inquiry.

Does he still respect Haughey? 'Of course I do. I'd respect anybody who ran this country. You have to respect a man who did a lot of good things. A lot of people still respect me and I've done some extraordinary things. People in glass houses just can't throw stones: show me anybody who hasn't always behaved the way they should have behaved. You've got to look at the good and the bad. If you look at me in isolation and take all my faults and all the bad things I've done you'd reach a very bad opinion about me very quickly. But to view somebody you've got to look at them in total and take a balanced view of good and bad. That would apply to Charlie Haughey as well. Charlie will be remembered. There's no doubt about that. And if he's remembered you can't just remember all the bad things.'

Ben Dunne would like to be remembered as more than just a chip off the old block: perhaps for his courage in overcoming adversity. 'I'd like to be remembered as someone who didn't walk away when I had plenty of opportunities to walk away; that I faced up to whatever situations I got myself into; that I stood my ground and took the hard medicine when I had to.' On the day when Charlie Haughey made history at Dublin Castle for reasons he never expected, Dunne was elsewhere, talking frankly about his life and times.

Finally he spilled another secret kept hidden for years. If his fairy godmother granted him a wish, he would like to launch a second career on the stage. That's his fantasy. To be a stand-up comic: cracking jokes and making the audience laugh. The Big Fella could count on a full house.

INDEX

BIBLIOGRAPHY

Ryan, Tim. (1994) *Albert Reynolds, The Longford Leader*, Dublin: Blackwater Press.

Tóibín, Niall. (1995) *Smile and be a Villain*, Dublin: Town House.

Cramer, Tim. (1992) *The Life of Other Days*, Cork: The Collins Press.

Power, Vincent. (1990) *Send 'em Home Sweatin'*, Dublin: Kildanore Press.

Kenny, Shane. (1990) *Go Dance on Somebody Else's Grave*, Dublin: Kildanore Press.

Cyriax, Oliver. (1996) *The Penguin Encyclopedia of Crime*, London: Penguin Books.

Doherty, J. E. Hickey, D. J. (1989) *A Chronology of Irish History Since 1500*, Dublin: Gill and Macmillan.